A War Too Far

Based on True Events

DAVID LEE CORLEY

TABLE OF CONTENTS

DEDICATION

To those that fought, died, and survived in the Vietnam Wars. Your sacrifices will not be forgotten.

PROLOGUE

On May 7, 1945, Germany surrendered to the Allies. However, World War II continued to rage in Asia and the Pacific. With hopes of eliminating China from the war, the Japanese launched Operation Ichigo – the largest Japanese offensive of all time. Over one million Japanese soldiers were committed to action in China. Troops and supplies from Vietnam supported the massive operation.

The Deer Team – an elite American OSS unit was secretly sent into Vietnam to shut down the Japanese supply routes and prevent the Japanese from venturing further into China. It was the beginning of America's involvement in Vietnam.

This story is based on true events.

"There is no deceit in death. It delivers precisely what it has promised. Betrayal, though ... betrayal is the willful slaughter of hope."
Steven Deitz

ONE

Southern China – May 23, 1945

Two Japanese soldiers chatted in a truck cab; one driving, the other watching the passing countryside for potential ambushes. It was the usual banter between comrades-in-arms about the size of an old girlfriend's breasts and the wild times they had drinking too much sake with their friends before the war. The news of the German surrender hadn't dampened their spirits. Like most Japanese soldiers, they didn't think much of their German allies, if at all. That wasn't their reality. They were fighting the Americans in the Pacific and the Chinese in China. Everything else was a sideshow. Their commanders kept the bad news from the troops as much as possible. As far as the average Japanese soldier knew, they were winning the war and would soon be going home to their sweethearts and families victorious.

The truck engine groaned as it climbed a long incline. The Japanese were transporting troops to the front line, which was just outside of Chihkiang, China. It wasn't a particularly heavy load for the six-wheeled Type 94 truck, but the roads were in bad shape, forcing them to keep all the truck's wheels engaged, which slowed them down.

As the lead truck in the convoy, it was following the commander's vehicle – a four-wheel-drive Type 95 Korugane – Japan's early version of a jeep. The truck driver's eyes went wide when he saw two Curtiss P-40 Warhawks with shark teeth nose art appear over the crest of the hill. It was the damned Americans.

Each Warhawk carried a 500lb bomb on the center hardpoint under its fuselage. It was a general-purpose bomb that exploded on impact. It wasn't anything fancy. It didn't need to be. The aircraft was also armed with six Browning .50 Caliber machine guns with 235 rounds per gun. It wasn't a lot of ammunition for a gun that shot 750 rounds per minute, but it packed a powerful punch.

The nose art identified the fighters as part of General Chennault's Air Group, nicknamed "The Flying Tigers." The shark mouth artwork struck fear into the Japanese who respected the American pilots and their aircraft far more than the Chinese Air Force, which they saw as inferior.

The lead pilot was James "Earthquake McGoon" McGovern, a mountain of a man with the confidence to match. His nickname "McGoon" came from the Li'l Abner comic strip printed daily in most American newspapers. At six feet tall and weighing in at two hundred and sixty pounds, McGoon was unusually large for a pilot and had his seat modified so he could fit comfortably in the cockpit of his fighter.

His wingman was Casey "Smitty" Smith, shy, wiry, and one hell of a shot with his aircraft's machine guns. He had saved McGoon from certain death more than once during a dogfight. While McGoon was good at getting them into trouble, Smitty was good at getting them out.

They had been searching all morning for targets. They could have just flown to the front lines where there were plenty of targets, but those areas were well protected by Japanese anti-aircraft guns and squadrons of Zeros providing overwatch. It was safer to hunt down enemy supply convoys. They were running low on fuel and headed back to their airbase when McGoon spotted the convoy heading up a hill. It was a juicy target – transportation trucks filled with troops.

McGoon and Smitty had chosen to approach the

convoy flying on the deck just three hundred feet from the ground in hopes of surprising it before it could defend itself with its mobile anti-aircraft battery. It worked. The Japanese were caught completely off guard as witnessed when the lead truck accidentally slammed into the back of the commander's vehicle when the driver slowed on seeing the aircraft.

McGoon pickled the weapon button and released his Warhawk's only bomb.

The bomb landed ten feet in front of the command vehicle. That was close enough to rip it apart, killing everyone inside. The lead truck's engine was peppered with shrapnel, disabling it. The truck's windshield imploded into the faces of the driver and passenger, but it was the bomb's shockwave that killed them, turning their insides to mush.

McGoon did not waste his machine gun ammunition on the first pass. Instead, he studied the disposition of the Japanese troops abandoning the vehicles and diving for cover along the roadside. He also got a good look at the anti-aircraft battery mounted on the back of a truck. It was a twin-barrel Type 96 based on the French 25mm Hotchkiss gun. Very effective. Very deadly. "Block 'em in good, Smitty," said McGoon over the radio. "They got a Type 96, and we're low on fuel. We're only gonna get one more run at 'em."

"Got it, Boss," said Smitty.

As the two aircraft approached the end of the convoy, McGoon peeled off, giving Smitty a clear shot at the last vehicle. Smitty released his bomb.

It was a direct hit and annihilated the truck. Only one of the three axles remained with the left tire still attached and burning. If it weren't for the huge crater in the road, the truck's debris would not have been enough to keep the convoy from escaping.

The remaining trucks were sandwiched between two bomb craters and burning wreckage. There wasn't enough room on the road to turn around, and the heavy vegetation prevented them from driving off-road. They were trapped and at the mercy of the Americans. Their only hope was the anti-aircraft battery in the middle of the convoy. The gun crew scrambled to get the battery operational and return fire.

McGoon banked his aircraft and lined up his strafing run. It was a bit like sewing – once he started, he didn't want to stop. He would only have a fifteen-second burst. He needed to leave a small amount of ammunition in his guns in case they encountered enemy aircraft on their way back to the base. As he approached the last vehicle in the convoy, he opened fire down the left side of the road where half of the troops were hiding. Troops were more important than trucks, especially when they were lined up nicely like these were. All six of the Warhawk's machine guns fired in unison; seventy-five-bullets per second. They laid out a ribbon of death, twenty feet wide and moving at three hundred miles per hour.

There was no time for the Japanese troops to avoid the fusillade. They just closed their eyes and hoped for the best.

As the barrage of bullets approached the middle of the convoy, McGoon nudged his plane over toward the center of the road and strafed the anti-aircraft battery on the back of the truck, killing the gunner, two loaders and damaging the weapon. It never got a shot off. Satisfied with the result, McGoon jogged his plane back to the troops hiding along the left side of the road and finished his run.

Smitty was next. He lined up his aircraft down the right side of the road and unleashed hell on the surviving Japanese troops. The results were similar to McGoon's, but Smitty skipped the anti-aircraft battery, which already looked disabled. Instead, he saved the last of his run for the lead truck where he saw someone trying to climb out of the back. He zigged over and strafed the truck, tearing holes in the canvas used to shade the troops from the hot sun. The burning phosphate from the tracer rounds set the vehicle ablaze.

"Sorry, boys. We're outta bullets. But don't worry... We'll catch up with ya real soon. You can count on it," said McGoon over the radio for Smitty's enjoyment.

In all, twenty-two Japanese soldiers were killed or critically wounded in less than a minute. Most of the vehicles in the convoy were badly damaged, and several were on fire. It would take two extra days for the rest of the troops to reach the front lines. It was a good day's work for McGoon and Smitty. They formed up, banked south and headed for home.

The air was muggy and smelled of gasoline mixed with decaying vegetation around the airfield. The sun hung low on the horizon, and the shadows were long. Almost all the planes out on patrol had landed for the day. But the Allied airbase was still abuzz. The mechanics were hard at work performing maintenance on the aircraft engines and patching Japanese bullet holes in the wings and fuselages. The fighters had to be patched up, rearmed, and refueled for takeoff by sunup. That meant a long night for the ground crews under the work lights.

McGoon frowned as he watched a Chinese artist carefully paint a red circle on the side of the Douglas DC-3 transport plane. "Now that's a crying shame," said McGoon. "Perfectly good aircraft being defaced like that."

"You think the japs will buy it?" said Smitty standing beside him, watching.

"Why wouldn't they? It's the same airframe as the Showa. 'Sides, I don't plan on getting close enough for them to get a good look at it."

"The best-laid plans of mice and men..."

"Smitty, you been reading again?"

"Yeah. Steinbeck."

"You really gotta knock that off. A brain can only remember so much. You're filling yours up with literature."

"Is that so bad?"

"What's the fuel consumption rate of a DC-3?"

"I don't know… eighty… maybe a hundred gallons per hour?"

"Now, ya see… that's my point. You can't remember cuz you replaced that knowledge with useless fiction."

"I suppose."

"Good. No more reading till the war's over."

McGoon was in an unusually foul mood. After their successful assault on the Japanese convoy, he and Smitty had been taken off the flight roster. "Don't make no sense grounding your two best pilots," said McGoon.

"The commandant didn't ground us. We're still gonna fly," said Smitty.

"I don't know about you, but I ain't no taxi service."

"Come on, McGoon. It's a cakewalk. We should be thankful we're not gonna be shot at."

"Damn it, Smitty. We're fighter pilots. They pay us to get shot at."

"Pay's the same, McGoon. It's a couple of missions. And they must be pretty important if they want guys like us to fly 'em."

"I guess. I do know the area pretty well. I flew over it a buncha times when I was stationed in Burma."

"There you go. Your expertise is needed."

"You think these guys we're gonna drop are pretty important, huh?"

"Must be. Donovan called Chennault directly and asked for his two best pilots."

"Really?"

"Would I lie to you, McGoon?"

"You might just to shut me up."

"Fair enough," said Smitty with a shrug. "I'll see ya later. I got a letter to write to my wife."

Smitty headed for his tent while McGoon stayed to supervise the artist as the sun set.

McGoon and Smitty flew for the 14th Air Force's 118th Tactical Reconnaissance Squadron, 23rd Fighter Group. The pilots of the 118th were supposed to be flying the newer P-51 Mustangs, but their shipment of the aircraft was diverted after the Japanese Navy bombed Pearl Harbor. The P-51s were faster, turned tighter, and were better armed than the P-40s, but it didn't seem to bother McGoon too much as long as he got to kill japs. The Warhawks could out dive the Japanese Zeros, and that was all the advantage McGoon needed. He had been credited with downing four Zeros in dogfights and destroying an additional five on the ground. That made him an ace, which he mentioned as often as possible when meeting young ladies.

The airfield at Laohwangping was shared with 35th Reconnaissance Squadron. The 35th flew P-38s because of their range. McGoon liked the P-38. It was fast, plus it looked real slick with its twin engines and tail booms. He had trained on them before the war but was politely asked to train on the cheaper Mustang after he crashed a P-38 during a dive bomb exercise. It wasn't his fault. The plane had stalled. But it didn't matter to the brass. Besides, McGoon wanted to fly for the Chinese, and they were going to use the Mustang anyway. The Chinese were already in the war with Japan, and the pay was three times that of a US Air Force pilot. And to top it off, he already liked eggrolls. The three hundred Americans in the Chinese Air Force were under the command of Major General Claire Lee Chennault, nicknamed "Old Leatherface."

The entire Laohwangping airfield compound wasn't more than a compressed earth runway with a line of aircraft on the edge. There were a couple of dozen tents used by the pilots and ground crews, plus a few small wooden buildings used as support facilities. The smallest building had been converted into an officers' club at the insistence of McGoon. "It ain't American if there ain't a bar," he said to his squadron commander. "We don't mind getting our asses shot off as long as we can come back to a cold beer at the end of the day."

"And where do you plan on getting the ice?" said his commander.

"Let me worry about that. You just give us the building. I'll take care of the rest."

It took some doing, but McGoon got his officers club and the ice that kept the beer cold. He trained a local man to be the bartender and only made him pay half his tips for the privilege. He liked the Chinese, at least the ones that weren't communists. He could see that they were really smart. They picked up the things that they were taught quickly, and they remembered them. He didn't think they would make good fighter pilots. He had seen a lot of Chinese paintings. They were two-dimensional. Flying in combat took a certain amount of creativity, and you had to think in three dimensions. In his opinion, that was not the strong suit of the Chinese.

When the Chinese artist finished painting the transport plane's insignia, McGoon headed for the bar. His bar. That's the way he saw it. The officers club had a Polynesian décor with tiki torches, native masks and tasteful posters of topless native women from a Frenchie artist named 'Paul Gauguin.' The bartender was Tian Xinyou, but McGoon couldn't remember it, so he just started calling him Kwon.

Kwon opened a cold beer the moment he saw McGoon walk through the door. Being the boss man, McGoon drank for free. Everyone else paid, even the squadron commanders. McGoon kept up appearances by always saying, "Thanks, Kwon. Put it on my tab." Kwon would make an X on whatever piece of paper was lying around at the time, then throw it away when the officer's club closed for the night.

There were six men already seated at one of the bamboo tables when McGoon arrived. They wore jungle fatigues but without insignia so nobody could tell their rank or country. McGoon walked over and said, "You guys must be the package I'm delivering tomorrow."

The six men went quiet like some sort of etiquette had been broken. "You might not want to say that too loud," said Peter Dewey, the commander of the group.

"Why is that? We're all on the same side here."

"Discretion is the better part of valor in our line of work."

"And what line of work would that be?"

"Like I said… discretion."

"Must be spooks then."

One of the men rose from his chair and moved toward McGoon. He was tall like McGoon, but his body was tight and fit. His name was René Granier, but the men in his unit called him "Buck" because he liked deer hunting. His dead eyes locked with McGoon's. He said nothing but McGoon could tell he was a serious man and meant to do him harm. "Buck," said Dewey. "…order another round, will you? And one for the good captain."

"Much obliged, but I already got one," said McGoon keeping his eyes on Granier.

"Then you'll have two, and we'll be happier for it."

"Alright. If you insist."

"We do. Please sit with us."

Granier moved off to the bar and McGoon pulled up a chair at the table. "You're familiar with where we are going tomorrow?" said Dewey in a hushed voice.

"I've been in the area a few times. Chased a Zero across the border last month. Japs got plenty of flak."

"Which you will avoid?"

"Best I can. That's why they picked me. I don't usually fly transport. I'm a fighter pilot. But we all do what we gotta do for the cause, right?"

"We appreciate the sacrifice."

"Ain't no sacrifice. Those Vietnamese have saved a lot of downed American pilots. Prevented them from being captured by the Japs. If we can help 'em, we should."

"Good to know. Now, about the drop…?"

"We'll have a fighter escort up to the border. After that, we'll be on our own. We're going to fly low and fast through the mountains. Any of your boys ain't used to rough flying might wanna bring a barf bag just in case. I'd hate to see your boots get wet."

"I assure you, my men are quite used to… rough flying."

"Suit yourselves."

Granier walked back over and set seven open bottles of beer down on the table. He pushed one toward McGoon like it was special. "You won't mind switching, would ya?" said McGoon. "I ain't fond of spit."

Granier switched bottles with McGoon and took a sip. McGoon took a big swig from his bottle. Granier kept a straight face as he glanced over at McGoon. "Ah, shit," said McGoon taking a second look at his bottle then setting it on the table like it had cooties. Granier offered a faint smile while everyone else laughed, including McGoon. McGoon could dish it out, but he could also take it. The package, as McGoon had called them, was the OSS Deer Team.

It was early morning. Patches of fog hung over the emerald valleys of the northern highlands of Vietnam. The long shadow of an aircraft swept across a thick canopy of trees. The American DC-3 disguised as a Japanese L2D Showa hugged the ridgelines.

It was a rollercoaster ride for the Deer Team members

riding in back. Their faces and hands were painted with black and green greasepaint that promised to stay on even when wet. Everyone but Granier looked queasy. Granier thought about the first time he took part in a battle. It was on Guadalcanal...

It rained. Granier moved through a grove of coconut trees at the head of his Marine recon platoon. He was on point. Heavy clouds and a storm had masked the Marine's arrival on the island and caught the Japanese army off guard. The Marines landed on the beach with little resistance, then pushed inland. No Japanese in sight. Only hastily abandoned camps. The Japanese had gone to ground, and it was the job of Marine Recon to find them. The probability of ambush and boobytraps was high. Granier was careful where he stepped. His eyes darted around, taking everything in, searching for danger.

At night, the Japanese and American navies slugged it out offshore as the Marines watched. Big guns were firing. Explosions that lit up the night sky. It was hard to tell who won, until the next morning when the American fleet was gone. The Marines were on their own with most of their ammunition and supplies at the bottom of the ocean. "Too little. Too Late. Too bad. Welcome to the war, Pups," said the platoon's staff sergeant. "Time to nut up and show the Japs who we really are. Can't stop a Marine. Can't stop the Corp."

The sergeant was a relic from World War I. He fought in the trenches during the Battle of Belleau Wood. It was nasty and gut-wrenching warfare even for a Marine. Lessons learned the hard way. Lessons that would keep Granier and the other 'pups' alive.

That's what Granier was... a pup. A virgin to war. Just about everyone in the platoon was a pup. Veterans like the sergeant were few and far between. The sergeant's job was to keep Granier and the others alive long enough to learn how to survive. It was the way of the Corp — the old teaching the young.

Granier would never admit it, but he liked the sergeant. He was tough, and tough was something Granier understood. The only way to stay on the sergeant's good side was always to pay attention and not fuck up. The sergeant expected his men to make mistakes, but he didn't coddle them when they happened. Any mistake got a marine the sergeant's boot up his ass accompanied by soul-crushing criticism. This was war. There were no second chances on the battlefield.

From the beginning, the sergeant could see that Granier didn't like authority and was a loner. Granier had been a hardship case. As a teenager, he had joined a street gang and got caught stealing a car. The judge gave him a choice – jail or the Corp. The sergeant didn't like anybody that didn't come to the Marines by their own free will. But Granier had been a good marine and paid attention, unlike some of the others. Still, the sergeant kept an eye on him and waited for him to mess up so he could bust him out. The sergeant knew that the Corp required marines to work as one unit. It wasn't for loners. The way he saw it, he'd be doing Granier a favor.

When the platoon made camp on the third night, the sergeant had assigned Granier to share a foxhole with Taylor – the platoon screw up. Every platoon had one – a guy that was clumsy, stupid, or unlucky. Taylor was all three. Granier could see that Taylor was not long for this world and tried to keep his distance whenever possible. But the sergeant, in his wisdom, had made that impossible. They took shifts sleeping while the other one kept watch. Even though he was tired, Granier slept lightly. He didn't trust Taylor to stay awake during his watch. Their foxhole was on the left flank of the platoon's position. It was vulnerable. The only good news was that they hadn't seen any Japanese troops since they arrived, and Granier was hopeful that it might stay that way.

Granier was asleep when he heard his name whispered. It was Taylor trying to wake him up. "What?" said Granier, pissed.

"I think I see something," said Taylor.

"Like what?"

"Something in the trees."

Granier was going to tell him it was probably the wind when he thought for a moment... He didn't trust Taylor to know what he saw. Granier climbed over to the edge of the foxhole and looked out. The clouds covered the moon, and it was pitch black. Everything was still. The wind, he thought. Then something moved. He wasn't sure what it was. Then he saw something else move. "Did you see it?"

said Taylor.

"Shut the fuck up," said Granier, squinting, trying to get a better look. He watched as an entire company of Japanese soldiers emerged from the jungle and trotted towards the platoon's position. Granier reacted, picking up his rifle and firing. He didn't care if he hit anything. He just wanted to make enough noise to wake up the other members of the platoon and alert them to the oncoming danger. It worked. The platoon joined the battle, first a few shots, then a cacophony of rifles and machine guns. The Japanese yelled a battle cry and broke into a run. Japanese mortar shells added to the chaos as they dropped on the American positions with blinding flashes of light, torrents of dirt and deadly shrapnel.

The sergeant ran over and dove into the foxhole. Taylor and Granier were firing and reloading as fast as they could. "Granier, you keep a good eye on that flank. They'll be coming that way sure as shit," said the sergeant.

"Got it," said Granier.

A clump of Japanese emerged from the trees on the flank just as the sergeant had said they would. "Here they come," said Granier firing at them.

Taylor looked over and panicked. He grabbed a grenade from a pouch on his belt and pulled the pin. He started to throw it when it slipped from his hand and landed in the foxhole next to Granier. Granier froze for no more than a second, but it was enough for the sergeant to realize that there wasn't time to pick the grenade and throw it clear. "Taylor, you sorry sack of shit," said the sergeant as he dove on top of the grenade.

The explosion pushed the sergeant three feet into the air as his body absorbed the concussion. He landed face down with a heavy thud. He had saved both Granier and Taylor. Granier fired the rest of his ammunition at the Japanese, killing two and driving the rest to the ground. "Keep firing," said Granier to Taylor. "I'm gonna check on the sergeant."

Taylor obeyed. Granier carefully turned the sergeant over. His stomach was gone, a smoking cavity of charred flesh. To Granier's surprise, the sergeant was still alive. "I knew that dumb bastard was gonna kill someone. Just didn't think it'd be me," said the sergeant *as he went limp and died.*

The sergeant's sacrifice wasn't lost on Granier. He had died saving the members of his pack — the Marine Corp. Granier picked up his rifle, reloaded and fired. There was no time to grieve, only time to fight and survive. His sergeant would have been proud if he had lived.

When the battle was over, Granier thought about killing Taylor. He didn't need a judge or jury to know that Taylor was a danger to the platoon. Granier would protect the others in his unit even if it meant killing one of their own. He decided that he didn't need to do anything. Taylor would be killed sooner rather than later. He was too much of a screw up to survive. He just needed to stay out of Taylor's way and let him self-destruct at a safe distance. He was right. A few days later, Taylor got run over by a Sherman tank. The pack was safe again.

Granier snapped back to reality. They would be jumping soon, and he needed to be ready to move with his gear when the command came. Granier's rifle, a Springfield M1C Garand with scope mount and muzzle flash suppressor, was tucked carefully away in a padded carrying case leaning against his leg. The weapon was a semi-automatic sniper rifle that carried eight .30-06 rounds in an internal magazine. The wooden stock had a leather cheekpiece to help the shooter's eye align properly with the side-mounted scope. Granier's M81 scope was wrapped in a towel and placed in the very center of his leg bag to keep it from being damaged on landing. His life and the lives of the other team members would depend on that rifle and scope more than once in the months that followed. Once he was in the field, Granier never let it out of his sight.

Dewey had handpicked his team. Each member was an expert in his assigned combat role and had previously distinguished himself in battle. Although they had trained together, this was their first mission as a team. Dewey was confident they were the best men available for the job at hand. The success of their mission depended on it.

Dewey, his face and hands also camouflaged, stood by McGoon, seated in the pilot's seat. Smitty was in the co-pilot's seat and flying the aircraft while McGoon talked with Dewey. "The supply drop zone is just over the next ridge. The drop is one week from today at oh nine hundred. Don't forget to pop smoke when you hear our engines or we won't know where you are," said McGoon.

"What if the enemy sees the smoke?" said Dewey.

"You can do what you want, but you're gonna have a helluva time finding your supplies in that jungle."

"Alright. We'll take the risk and pop smoke if the area looks clear. Otherwise, just drop it, and we'll do our best to find it."

"Okay. There's the supply drop zone," said McGoon pointing out the windshield. "We're five minutes out from your team's drop zone. You'd better get your guys up and ready. Good luck. Beer's on me when you make it out."

"Thanks," said Dewey heading out the cockpit door.

The Deer Team jumped from the DC-3 as it passed over the drop zone. Granier, the most experienced woodsman, was the first out the side door. He kicked out his leg bag and jumped. The static line snapped tight and opened his parachute. He disliked using static lines. He preferred to open his chute. A static line was just one more thing that could go wrong. He could get tangled in it and dragged behind the aircraft. It could get snagged and fail to open his chute. The team was jumping low at eight hundred feet. There was no room for error. He liked simplicity.

Dewey had insisted on static lines to keep the team close together as they descended. Granier didn't think much of Dewey, but he obeyed his commander. There was little question that Granier was the real alpha dog of the team – the one nobody wanted to mess with – but Dewey had the rank. Granier had learned to respect rank. He had learned to obey. Unlike the other team members, Granier's concept of loyalty and patriotism did not go much beyond the squad level. He believed in the men that fought by his side and protected him. They were his pack. He would sacrifice for them, not for some obscure concept of country or honor.

The rest of the team jumped and followed Granier down into the forest. It was going to be a rough landing. There wasn't much choice. There were no meadows in this part of the forest — just trees.

Granier crashed through the top of the canopy. His legs, crotch, and arms broke twigs and small branches as he continued his downward plunge. His chute snarled in the foliage and brought him to an abrupt stop. Still twenty-five feet from the ground, he dangled like a puppet without a master. The other team members crashed through the trees with yelps and grunts, but he couldn't see them. He released the leg strap holding his pack and rifle. They landed with a thud. Releasing the snap hooks around his legs put his full weight on his chest harness. He pulled the chest straps together, but the hook wouldn't release; there was too much pressure. He pulled his knife. Once he cut the chest strap, if either arm snarled in the straps, he could dislocate a shoulder. And then there was the knife. It was razor-sharp and could also get hung up as he slipped out of the harness. He decided to toss the knife clear once he cut the harness and hope he could find it on the ground. Once the plan was clear in his mind, there was nothing to be gained by thinking any more about the situation. It was a long drop, and the landing was going to hurt. He executed. A swift stroke of the knife cut the chest strap. He was free. He tossed the knife away as he slipped out of the harness and fell clean.

He bent his legs at the knees and relaxed. He hit the ground and tumbled with a grunt. He rose to his feet and searched for his knife. It was sticking hilt up a few yards away, the blade embedded in the soft soil. *Stuck it,* he thought. He was relieved. It was a good knife, and he would need it. He retrieved it and gave both sides of the blade a quick swipe on his pants to clean off the soil before sliding it back in its sheath.

He could hear the other team members struggling to free themselves. Helping them was not his problem at the moment. *They can take care of themselves,* he thought. He squatted next to his leg bag, released the strap from his rifle bag, and inspected his rifle. He slid the bolt open and released it to ensure the slide was functioning properly. It was. He checked the trigger and the hard sights. Everything looked okay. He pulled a clip from the ammunition belt on his waist and inspected the bullets to ensure they were still properly aligned in the clip and gave them two taps on his helmet. He opened the bolt again, locking it back. He pushed the bolt lever back with the side of his hand as he pushed the clip through the open bolt and into the internal magazine. Releasing the bolt chambered the first round. He was armed and ready.

He leveled his rifle at the surrounding trees. As the first team member on the ground, it was his responsibility to provide security for the others still attempting to free themselves from their harnesses stuck in the canopy. His eyes searched the horizon surrounding the drop zone. No movement except for the leaves and twigs that fell from above. It was clear. He made another sweep looking in the surrounding trees for possible snipers. Again, clear. The tropical forest smelled like rotting vegetation, a bit sweet with a lot of sour.

He wanted to check his rifle scope to make sure it wasn't damaged. It bothered him not knowing if all his gear was working properly, but he knew there would be time for that later, once the team was safe. He didn't need his scope in the forest. His sightline was only fifty to a hundred feet out. He could shoot that distance accurately with his weapon's fixed sights. The scope was for distance.

He counted the thuds and grunts of the team members falling to the ground. "Buck, you okay?" said Dewey in a hushed voice.

"Yes," said Granier. It was the shortest answer he could think of. His eyes never left the tree line. He kept searching for the enemy. Granier didn't waste any effort in communicating. He knew his part of the mission. He didn't need to discuss it or be reminded. He just executed. Consistently. Constantly.

His lack of comradery pissed off the others in the team who thought him an overzealous perfectionist and a loner. He didn't care. It wasn't his job to make them happy. He protected them from the enemy. He kept the pack safe. That was all that matter.

Granier was born in France in an academic community just outside of Paris where his mother was a professor of history at a well-known university. As a child, his grandfather had taught him survival skills while hunting boar and deer in the woods. At the age of twelve, he and his family moved to Willington, Delaware, when his father, a chemical engineer, was recruited by DuPont to develop advanced polymers. Even though he and his family became American citizens, Granier never quite fit in as a teenager and spent most of his free time hunting deer and turkey alone in the nearby forests and hills. French was his first language, but he also was fluent in English, and Spanish.

"Buck, check our perimeter," said Dewey.

"On it," said Granier rising, disappearing into the trees, eyes searching.

There was little sunlight beneath the canopy. Shafts of light alternating with the darkness of the forest. The eyes played tricks. Saw things that weren't there. He had learned to distinguish the real from the imagined. He stopped fifty yards out and made a large counter-clockwise circle around the team members. His eyes flicked to the ground to check for tripwires and signs of an enemy, then back to the horizon, then up into the trees and back to the horizon. Always moving. Avoiding dry leaves and twigs in his path. Deadly quiet. His rifle leveled, swinging smoothly from side to side. Hunting. His mind drifted, and he remembered…

The same flickering of sunlight as a boy walked through the trees with his grandfather. It was his first boar hunt. He was ten. He carried a Lebel Model 1886 rifle that his grandfather had given him to use. It fired 8mm bullets which were not particularly large compared to more modern rifles. The gun still kicked like a mule. He had been allowed three practice shots so he could get used to the weight and using the bolt action. It was too big for a boy that had not yet had his teenage growth spurt, but his grandfather had insisted, saying, "When hunting boar, it is better to go in heavy rather than light. Light can get you gored by a tusk, and your mother would never let me hear the end of it."

His grandfather did not carry a rifle. It was the boy's task to kill the beast, not his. Instead, he carried a pair of flintlock dueling pistols loaded with .56 caliber lead balls. "A good hunter only needs one shot to kill his prey," explained the old man.

"Then why do you carry two pistols?" asked the boy.

"I could be wrong," said the old man with a shrug.

As they approached a knoll, the grandfather saw a line of footprints in the loose soil. He motioned for the boy to come closer. "What do you see?" said the old man.

The boy took a few moments to examine the footprints and then said, "Wolf?"

"Are you asking or telling?"

"Wolf."

"Yes. Several. They're close."

The boy looked worried. He knew his grandfather saw this as a moment of instruction rather than danger. "Keep low and stay downwind," said the grandfather moving off.

The boy followed.

The boy and his grandfather belly crawled over a large boulder and looked down. Below, a pack of grey wolves mulled around their lair, their bellies full from a recent kill. Females tended their young. Males kept watch for danger. "They're beautiful," whispered the boy.

"Yes," said the grandfather. "Alone, they are dangerous. Together, they are invincible. They hunt as a pack and share their kills. If ever attacked, they will defend each other to the death. They desire no honor or even thanks. They are not selfish, like men. That's what gives them great power."

The lesson was not lost on the boy.

Granier snapped out of his daydream. He knew he needed to keep his focus. The forest was clear for the moment. He returned to the group. The other team members were gathered around Dewey in defensive positions.

Herbert Green was the team's automatic rifle specialist and the largest man in the unit at six-three, all muscle. He carried a BAR automatic rifle with a belt holding six of the 20-round box magazines and two bandoleers with three magazines each slung across his chest. His pack was loaded with far more spare ammunition than the others. It weighed almost a hundred pounds, but Green could handle the pack and the weapon because of his size. He spoke English, Chinese, and a bit of Spanish.

Victor Santana was the team's communications specialist and a rifleman. He carried the heavy field radio Dewey required to communicate with command headquarters in China. Santana knew the radio inside and out. He carried an M1 with a folding stock and spoke English, Spanish and Lao. He was short and stocky. His skin was dark, and his hair coal black. He loved to tell jokes about Mexicans and Central Americans walking into a bar. He was Puerto Rican and feisty as hell in a firefight.

Willard Davis was the team's grenadier and tunnel rat. He was lanky but surprisingly strong. He had started his career in the Army as an engineer before being selected as a commando. He knew explosives and could build just about anything from tree branches and 50-feet of rope. He carried a half dozen hand grenades plus two smoke grenades on bandoleers around his chest. In his pack were a dozen more grenades and TNT high-explosive blocks that could be used to breach a steel door or remove an obstacle. He looked like a pack mule when fully loaded with gear. His rifle was an M1 with a folding stock. He spoke English, Japanese, and a bit of Khmer.

Paul Hoagland rounded out the group as the team medic and a rifleman. He was in his second year of medical school when the war broke out and immediately volunteered. He was forced to renounce his Hippocratic oath when he joined the commandos. All commandos, even the medics, were expected to fight. He carried an M1 and was an excellent shot. Good eyes and steady fingers. He spoke English, Vietnamese and a few of the highlands' tribal dialects.

Granier knew them as good soldiers. Reliable. Brave. A strong pack. The team members broke off pieces of foliage and stuck them in the netting on their helmets and in the buckles on their packs to create natural camouflage. The area around the drop zone was already littered with debris. The few additional broken twigs wouldn't give the team's position away to the enemy more than the broken tree branches and scattering of leaves. They would repeat this process each time they moved into new terrain with different foliage. Good camouflage could be the difference between life and death.

Hoagland tended to a nasty cut on Dewey's shin. A broken branch had caught him on the way down. It could have been worse. Much worse. "Buck, are we good?" said Dewey, wincing as Hoagland pulled a shard of wood from the wound.

"Clear," said Granier. There was nothing else to report. Granier rarely made eye contact with anyone even while talking, which was unnerving and annoying to those around him. He was always looking someplace else. Searching for threats. He kept his eyes on the surrounding trees; his weapon cradled in his arms. "I need to build my scope," said Granier.

"Of course. We'll keep watch," said Dewey studying his compass and map as Hoagland finished dressing the wound.

Granier knew that even if every team member kept watch, they would not see the things that he could see. He didn't like that the team was all in the same place. They should have spread out more, but that wasn't his call. It was Dewey's. Granier kept his mouth shut and focused on the task at hand. He needed to check his gear and build his scope.

He pulled the metal mount and the bundled scope from his pack. The scope was undamaged. He pulled out and opened a small tool kit with a flat blade screwdriver, a small wrench, and a nylon hammer. He laid the towel wrapped around the scope on the ground to keep the rifle's parts from getting dirty and took a quick look around to ensure they were safe. His weapon would be useless while being assembled with the mount and scope. He needed to work quickly. He was ready.

He opened the rifle's bolt, removed the chambered round and the clip. The rifle was empty. Safe. First, he removed the rifle stock from the bolt and barrel and placed it on the towel. Then he attached the mount to the barrel and tightened the screws. He set the scope, closed the mount, and tightened the locking screw. After he'd reattached the stock to the bolt and barrel, he reloaded the weapon and chambered a round. The entire process took less than two minutes. He could have done it with his eyes closed if needed. He had done it before. He was operational.

The Garand was a well-designed, reliable weapon. It did not jam easily, even in the harshest conditions. The rifle's scope was side-mounted to keep the bolt opening clear for ejecting shells and inserting clips. This allowed the operator to use either the scope or the hard sights on the barrel. There were more high-powered scopes available, but he chose not to use them because they blocked the hard sight. His was a dual role in the squad – sniper and scout. When there was a firefight, options were important, especially in a thick forest or jungle. "Ready," said Granier.

"Let's move out," said Dewey pointing the direction.

Granier took the lead and advanced through the forest. He felt more comfortable moving within the trees — lots of cover. His senses were focused – ears, eyes, and nose. None more important than the other. All were working together. He knew it was highly likely that he would hear or see the enemy before the enemy heard or saw him. That was good. That kept the pack safe.

He kept a good distance in front of the others. They were loud, even though they thought they were quiet. It wasn't their fault. They didn't know what quiet was. Not like he knew quiet. They moved through the trees in a wedge formation, not a column, but stayed close together. Their weapons were always at the ready, never slung over their shoulders. Safety on, finger off the trigger, a round chambered. They would not take a path through the forest even if they found one. It was too dangerous. There were boobytraps and ambushes on trails. It was safer to stay off-trail even if it made traveling more difficult.

If there were contact, Granier would move off to the side and let the enemy focus on the approaching team with their heavy footfalls. That would give him the advantage he needed. If they were few, he would kill the enemy before they fired on his team. That was the hope. If they were many, he would be in a good position to flank them. Either way, his opening shots would warn his team members and draw the enemy away. His team would have time to disperse into defensive positions. Attacking from two angles was far better than attacking from one. Some might see his using his team as bait as cowardly, but he knew better. He didn't care what others thought… as long as the pack was safe.

The first day passed without incident. Even with Dewey's wounded shin, the team made good time and traveled fifteen miles through the forest before night fell.

There was no fire to warm their food or make coffee. They spoke only when necessary. Mostly they listened. Sound traveled slower in the cooler night air. There would be less warning if a Japanese patrol stumbled upon them. Two team members kept watch at all times. They slept in shifts. Sleep was important. They needed to stay sharp.

Hoagland checked Dewey's shin. It was swollen as he expected, but there were no signs of infection. The sulfanilamide powder he had poured on the wound had done the trick. It would hurt to walk, but Dewey was tough like all the team members. Even though it looked good, Hoagland would keep an eye on it. An infection in a tropical forest could kill a man just as sure as a bullet if left unattended. Once he redressed the wound, Hoagland moved to check on each of the team members. They were fit and healthy, but even a healthy man could become dehydrated easily in humid conditions. Hoagland checked each canteen to ensure the men were drinking enough and reminded them to eat their salt tablets. If Granier was their seldom seen protector, Hoagland was surely their doting mother. Both did their jobs well.

The Deer Team had only been walking an hour when Granier came to a stop, raise his fist to signal the others, and crouched down to make himself less visible. Dewey, his nose in his map, didn't notice. Hoagland, right behind Dewey, saw Granier and tapped Dewey on the shoulder to get his attention. Hoagland pointed in Granier's direction. Dewey, seeing Granier crouching, signaled the rest of the team to take up defensive positions. The team members spread out, crouched down and kept watch in their assigned direction.

Granier had seen nothing. It was a new smell that had

got his attention. New was not good. It was faint. A hint of fish sauce. He scanned the horizon and the surrounding trees. Nothing. That didn't mean that nothing was out there. It just meant he couldn't see it. But he could smell it, and that was enough to make the hairs on his neck stand tall. He waited. Silent. Listened. Watched. Nothing. He still didn't trust the smell. It could have been a farmer passing nearby. But if it was, he was sure he would have heard his footsteps. Farmers were not trained to be quiet. In fact, they liked to be noisy in the forest to frighten away jungle creatures like tigers, panthers, and snakes that might be on the path ahead. Granier still heard and saw nothing. But there was that smell – fish sauce. He was sure of it. He waited a full three minutes before motioning the team to continue. Their senses were heightened like Granier's and kept a close watch for any motion as they advanced… cautiously, slowing their pace.

The team moved out of the trees and into a narrow meadow covered with large ferns with more trees on the far side. Granier moved forward fifty yards into the meadow and stopped again. Same sign to the team – fist in the air. They stopped and again took up defensive positions. "What now?" whispered Hoagland.

Dewey, not knowing, shook his head. He trusted Granier's instincts and would wait to proceed until Granier gave him the go-ahead. Dewey had carefully picked his team, but Granier was a prize. Granier's commanding officer was pissed when Dewey chose Granier and spirited him away from his Marine battalion. Granier didn't like going either. Change was difficult for him, especially if it involved getting to know new people. Granier was not a fan of humans. He preferred the company of dogs who were very loyal and didn't whine unless it was important.

Granier smelled something new – charcoal mixed with freshly cooked rice and shit. Human shit. Cooked rice and human shit meant there was a village or camp up ahead. He looked around for signs of a footpath. There was none.

A village would have footpaths leading from it. It was a military camp. The big question was who was in it. It didn't take long to find the answer...

One hundred yards ahead, Granier saw movement. It was just a glimpse through the trees, but something or someone was moving toward him. He gave the hand signal for contact to Dewey.

Dewey relayed the signal to the other team members. Everyone moved deeper into the surrounding foliage in hopes of not being seen. Dewey worried about the footprints the team might have left behind them. If it were the enemy, footprints would lead them right to the team. It wasn't that Dewey or the others were afraid to fight. They were OSS commandos. They loved to fight. The adrenaline. The contest. But it was not their mission. Not yet.

Granier watched as a Japanese soldier carrying a rifle appeared through the trees. The way he held himself, his head turning from side to side, his weapon at the ready, Granier could tell he was a scout like himself. There would be more following him. *How many?* he thought.

Thirty feet behind the scout, more soldiers emerged. Fifty in all – a Japanese-sized platoon. They were spread out in a vee formation as if they were hunting for something. A lieutenant led them near the base of the vee. Next to the lieutenant was his radioman. Granier would keep a close eye on the radioman and kill him first if a firefight broke out. Hopefully, his shots would damage the radio so they could not call for reinforcements. The American team was already outnumbered more than eight to one. They didn't need more soldiers to shoot at or chase them if things went to shit – the most likely scenario. The officer would be his second target. Take out the head of the snake.

Granier stayed low and out of sight as the scout approached. He could feel his heart rate increasing. The scout was close. Very close. For a moment, he thought the unknowing soldier would step right on him. Granier didn't move, not even his eyes. Nothing to draw attention. The scout passed. Granier shifted his gaze to locate the radioman and the lieutenant. They were less than thirty-five feet from his position. An easy distance. He wouldn't miss. *Two shots each,* he thought. *That still leaves me four in the magazine before I need to reload. That's a good number. I can live with that.* Two shots each was overkill for a marksman like Granier, but the targets were important, and he didn't want to leave anything to chance.

Granier always knew exactly which pouches on his ammo belt had clips and which were empty. He never wasted any movement while reloading. Additional ammunition was stored in the exterior pockets on his pack. Pack ammo would take more time to retrieve, but he knew exactly where each clip was stored. He didn't need to take his eyes off the enemy or take off his pack to find the right pocket. It was a discipline. Practiced. As the scout, he would be separated from the team in a firefight and forced to fight alone. Ammo kept him alive.

His fire plan was simple – fire four rounds then duck for three seconds so the enemy would lose track of him, fire another four rounds, duck and reload. With that plan and a little luck, he could kill ten to twelve enemy per minute. Granier didn't like depending on luck, but he knew it was a factor in a brawl – an up close and personal firefight. He kept a gold 20-franc coin that his grandfather had given him in his front pants pocket. It was his luck.

He could not see Dewey from his hidden position and was unable to receive orders on when to open fire. But he knew what Dewey would want – to avoid contact if possible. Mission was first – to make contact with the Viet Minh and help them to fight the Japanese army that had invaded their country. Granier would wait until his team or the Japanese platoon opened fire before revealing his position and engaging the enemy.

·Sweat beaded on Granier's greasepaint-covered brow

as the Japanese formation approached. The Japanese soldiers walked past Granier, then past the team. The camouflage had worked. Granier breathed a quiet sign of relief. Then all hell broke loose…

Fifty yards past the American team was the close group of trees the American team had walked through. As the Japanese scout was about to enter the grove, he was blasted backward by a single rifle shot and landed on his back on the ground. A small Asian-looking man wearing a conical hat covered with camouflage sprang from the ground and plunged the bayonet on the end of his rifle into the scout, killing him. A light machine gun hidden in the grove opened fire, killing several more Japanese soldiers. Dozens of gun flares among the trees revealed a line of hidden riflemen firing their weapons. On the orders of their commander, the Japanese lieutenant, the platoon pulled back, moving toward the unseen Americans.

For a moment, Granier was confused and angry. It seemed two Japanese forces were killing each other. What bothered him was that he hadn't seen them when he walked by their positions. *Damn fish sauce,* he thought remembering the smell. *It don't matter. Japanese are dying. That's good.* He popped up from his hidden position and fired – two rounds into the radioman and two into the lieutenant, who had their backs to him. Both went down. He was pretty sure at least one of his rounds had hit the radio. Granier ducked, waited three seconds, popped up and shot four more Japanese soldiers, one bullet for each. His aim was deadly this close to the enemy. It was like shooting fish in a barrel – except that the fish fired back.

Dewey and the rest of the American team also opened fire on the Japanese as they moved back past their position. The Americans were hesitant to fire on the grove of trees even though the bullets aimed at the Japanese soldiers were flying past them. The hidden machine gunner and riflemen were killing the enemy. A Japanese rifleman pulled out a grenade, pulled the pin and tossed it. It landed next to Santana and Davis. "Oh, shit!", said Davis grabbing Santana's radio and placing it between them and the grenade like a shield. "No," said Santana, knowing what would happen. It worked. The grenade exploded, sending shrapnel into the radio set, destroying it, but protecting them.

Granier reloaded, popped up, four more shots, ducked down, three seconds, popped up again, fired four more shots emptying his rifle. The empty clip sprang from the magazine and tumbled through the air. It was a dead giveaway that his weapon was empty. The Japanese platoon had been decimated. Most of the survivors were running for their lives. He was running out of targets. Granier didn't notice the lone Japanese soldier, a bayonet on the end of his rifle, closing on his position from behind.

Granier reloaded. He was fast, but the Japanese soldier sprang into a dead run leveling his bayonet. Granier saw the soldier's shadow and reacted pitching to one side, falling onto the butt of his weapon. The bayonet plunged into the ground between Granier's arm and side. The Japanese soldier withdrew and prepared to stab again. Granier tried to bring his rifle around. It was awkward. He was laying on his rifle. The Japanese soldier lunged with his rifle but then fell sideways before he could complete the attack. A bullet had hit him in the shoulder and spun him around. The soldier landed on the ground. He wasn't dead. He struggled to bring his weapon around. Granier pulled out his knife and thrust it into the soldier's upper leg. The soldier screamed in pain.

Granier saw another soldier running toward him from a different angle, a bayonet on the end of his rifle. Granier again reached for his rifle. The soldier on the ground swung his rifle barrel around. Granier saw it and lunged backward to avoid the wounded soldier's bayonet. Again, Granier stumbled awkwardly. His weapon out of position to fend off the new threat, the old threat still alive and trying to kill him.

The new soldier yelled like a samurai and plunged the bayonet into the chest of the wounded soldier, killing him. Granier, confused, swung his rifle barrel around ready to fire at the new soldier. And then he saw something that confused him even more… a slight shadow below the new soldier's chest. *Breasts,* he thought. He looked up and saw a woman's face below the camouflaged conical hat. Her eyes weren't Japanese. They were Vietnamese. She pulled her bayonet from the dead soldier and swung her rifle barrel around toward Granier, hitting his rifle with her bayonet. His finger jerked against the trigger and his gun fired. It missed her, but just barely. She scowled in anger and swung the butt of her rifle into the side of Granier's head, knocking him out. Everything went black.

TWO

Granier woke a few minutes later and saw Hoagland's face above him. Smelling salts stung his nostrils, and he jerked his head trying to move away. Pain bolted through his head. He winced. "Shit," said Granier.

"Relax, Buck," said Hoagland. "You've got a mean bump on the side of your head."

"The girl that hit me…?"

"You mean the woman that saved your life?" said Hoagland pointing to the woman collecting weapons, ammunition and ransacking the pockets and packs of the dead Japanese soldiers.

"Viet Minh?"

"Yeah. About a hundred of 'em. They had set an ambush for the Japanese. We walked right through it and almost spoiled the whole game. They wanted the radio you shot. They're not too happy about that."

"Are they the right group?"

"Yeah. They were sent to find us when they stumbled upon the Japanese patrol. Their camp is a good day's march. We'll leave as soon as you feel fit."

"I'm alright," said Granier climbing to his feet, taking a few steps then almost falling over like he was dizzy.

"Give it rest. You've got a concussion. She whacked you pretty hard," said Hoagland grabbing Granier, helping him to sit on the ground again. "We'll leave soon enough. There's not enough time to make it back before nightfall anyway."

"Alright. Maybe a minute or two," said Granier as

31

lightning flashed behind his eyeballs with head-splitting pain.

He lay down in the long grass. "That-a-boy," said Hoagland. "I've got to tend to their wounded. I'll be back to check on you."

Hoagland moved off. Granier closed his eyes. It didn't help much. The lightning kept flashing in time with the beat of his heart. After a few moments, he sensed something and opened his eyes. The woman that had hit him was standing over him, three Japanese rifles cradled in her arms and a half dozen ammunition belts slung over her shoulder. He already knew she was strong, judging by the lump on his head. She looked down at him. He looked up at her. Their eyes met. She spat on him. "Hey," said Granier wanting to jump up and smack her but knowing he would fall down and make a further fool of himself.

She let loose a string of angry words that made no sense to Granier and shook her fist at him. She made the motion of a rifle with her hands, and he understood. She was mad that he had pointed his weapon at her after she had saved his life. She turned in a huff, and he watched her move off. Her skin was dark and beautiful. He figured she was from the Northern hill tribes, maybe the H'mong, Dzao or even Black Thai. Probably spoke some dialect, maybe a little Vietnamese. It didn't matter. He didn't know any Vietnamese beyond a couple of phrases, and he sure didn't know any of the tribal dialects. *A barbarian,* he thought. *More savage than civilized, more animal than human.* Lightning struck. His head whirled. He collapsed and fell unconscious.

It was late in the afternoon. The air was cooling. Granier could smell the sweet, trampled grass. The lightning strikes behind his eyes had dissipated into a dull throbbing throughout his head. It was painful, but he'd survive. A good night's sleep probably wouldn't hurt. Not an easy thing in the field. He and the other members of the Deer Team were sandwiched between the Viet Minh troops following a trail. The company was divided into three sections, each taking a different path in the same direction, each within supporting distance of the others in case they encountered the enemy.

Granier wasn't worried about boobytraps or mines. If there were any, the Viet Minh would trigger them long before he or the team members reached them. But the Viet Minh seemed to know what they were doing. They certainly fought better than he had imagined. He wondered who taught them or whether they just learned by experience. They were brave too. They moved forward when they heard gunfire, not back.

The Spitting Woman was not with his section. She was a scout, like him. She traveled far ahead, sometimes a mile or two, then came back to report to the Viet Minh commander. Granier wondered why his mood lightened when he saw her. Not the usual reaction of a man that had been spat on by a woman, but Granier was no ordinary man. He imagined she knew these hills like the back of her hand, that she knew the signs of a nearby enemy and the safest place to make camp. It was comforting and a little irritating. He wasn't in control. She was. That was unusual for him and ground on him like sand in a boot.

The company made camp just before sunset. Sentries were posted, and scouts roamed the surrounding terrain. Spitting Woman came back thirty minutes later. Granier could tell she was tired by the way she plopped down on the ground, not caring much where she sat. She pulled out a hand-carved pipe, filled it with something that looked like a dried weed, and lit it with a match. The smoke was thick and brown. Even at a distance, Granier could smell it. It wasn't pleasant but did make his headache recede a bit, or at least he didn't seem to mind the throbbing as much. Either way, it was welcome.

There were other women in the company, but they seemed more subservient – fetching water, making the evening fire, cooking. Spitting Woman was treated as an equal among the Viet Minh men. He even saw her smack a fellow soldier in the balls when he made what seemed to be a crude remark about her. She didn't hurt him. Not really. But from that point on, the fellow soldier avoided her when possible. *Not the sociable type,* Granier thought.

Granier waited until dinner was finished before approaching Spitting Woman. He felt like they had gotten off on the wrong foot, and he wanted to make things right. Normally, he didn't care what others thought, but Spitting Woman was different for some reason. He wasn't sure why, but her opinion of him mattered as he walked over to her. She watched him, seeming a bit wary like he might attack her. He knew she wouldn't understand his words, but he hoped she could recognize his intent by the tone of his voice. "Hi," said Granier. She said nothing. "I just came over to apologize. I didn't know who you were when I shot at you. You probably saved my life, and I'm grateful. Anyway, thanks, and have a good night." She still said nothing. Granier shrugged, turned, and walked away.

With his back turned to her, she climbed to her feet, ran over and kicked his back foot mid-stride. He tripped and fell to the ground. He turned over, angry as hellfire. "God damn it, woman," he said, climbing to his feet.

Her eyes went wide as he marched toward her. He outweighed her by double and towered over her small frame. She wasn't afraid. She was angry. She kicked at his crotch. He grabbed her foot mid-air and twisted it. She spun around to keep him from breaking her ankle. He yanked her leg upward, and she lost her balance. She flew up into the air and came back down like a board tossed from a pickup truck landing facedown with a thud. She didn't move. Granier wasn't sure what to do and looked around as if hoping for a suggestion. Everyone had stopped what they were doing and watched like they knew what was going to happen next and that it shouldn't be missed.

Spitting Woman climbed to her feet, turned and pulled out her knife like she was going to gut him. "Seriously?" said Granier a bit surprised. He considered pulling out his knife but then thought better of it. Things had gone far enough. He had been in enough knife fights to know that they never ended well. *It was only an apology,* he thought. She moved in the opposite direction of her hand holding the knife. He countered, moving in the same direction, keeping his distance. "I'm done with your shit. If you don't put that down, I'm going to shove it up your ass," he said.

She replied with a barrage of words in her dialect. He didn't understand the words, but the tone was clear. She wasn't backing down.

They danced for a few moments more, then she lunged. He pivoted, grabbed her wrist, and pulled her forward. She almost lost her balance but recovered. She used her nails on her free hand to scrap his forearm. He bled. He accepted the pain. He brought his knee up and smacked her wrist holding the knife. She released the knife, letting it fall to the ground. She put her foot between his legs to tangle them. He put his boot behind her leg. They both fell. She on top of him. He rolled her over. Him on top of her, their faces inches apart. He looked into her eyes. She seemed to be beckoning him. He lowered his head closer to her. She raised hers ... then she bit him on the upper lip. He jerked away, tearing flesh. Blood flowed. "Ah, shit!" he said, raising his fist, ready to pummel her.

"Buck!" said Dewey. "Enough."

Another voice barked out orders in Vietnamese. They came from the Viet Minh commander standing beside Dewey.

The two belligerents stopped fighting. Granier rolled off Spitting Woman. They both climbed to their feet. "This is not our mission," said Dewey and Granier understood.

More Vietnamese shouting came from the Viet Minh commander. Spitting Woman hung her head in shame, then stomped off. Strangely, Granier wanted to go after her and explain that he just got carried away, that he didn't mean it. He was confused. He never really cared what anyone thought, let alone a Southeast Asian aboriginal. *Why was she different?*

The next morning, the column of soldiers snaked its way through the hills and valleys of the highlands. They picked up the pace when crossing an open hilltop or a treeless meadow. They did not want to be spotted by the Japanese reconnaissance planes that often patrolled the area. They were more relaxed when in the morning fog or when the sky was heavily overcast. The rain was always a welcome relief, offering respite from the heat, refreshment, and cover. It made the long grass and fallen leaves slippery, but the Viet Minh were surefooted and enjoyed the break in the monotony of walking. They took pleasure in simple things like raindrops and cool running streams. Their bellies were full from the supplies pilfered from the Japanese. They asked for little more.

They formed human chains by holding hands as they crossed rivers. Some did not know how to swim and were fearful of the fast-moving water even when shallow. The strong helped the weak. Loads were shifted and shared when one person tired, no questions asked. They carried everything. There were no animals to carry the burden of weapons and supplies. All of their animals had been slaughtered for food long ago. Waterfalls offered a quick shower and freshwater. They would soak their neck scarfs to cool their shoulders and heads while walking. Reeds growing in the water along the shore were cut and used to clean the rice and bits of fish from their teeth as they walked.

The Viet Minh would not drink from the American canteens when offered. The stupid Americans put tablets in their canteens that made the water sour. The Americans also wasted perfectly good food, rejecting fish heads and chicken feet. Americans were strange. Many Viet Minh blamed it on their strange god, others on their wealth. Their skin was strange too. It was pink and sometimes red when in the sun for too long. Some of the Americans had light-colored hair which the women found interesting and would save after a haircut in little wooden boxes hung around their necks for luck.

When the sun hung low across the verdant mountain tops, the column of soldiers descended a steep trail into a narrow valley. Limestone cliffs cast long shadows that cooled the air. A stream divided the valley and formed turquoise pools like liquid steps in a descending staircase. Vines grew in every direction like a giant web across the forest canopy, some reaching down for a sip from the slow-flowing water.

According to Dewey's map and compass, they were only a few miles from the Sino-Vietnamese border. The Chinese had been providing some logistical support to the Viet Minh before the Japanese invasion of their mainland. Now, the weapons and supplies had slowed to a trickle. The path they traveled on was covered with freshly cut grass to mask the tan dirt from Japanese reconnaissance aircraft.

The Chinese had finally fought the Japanese to a standstill. The Chinese were deeply concerned with Japanese troops crossing the border from Vietnam to reinforce their troops in Southern China. On the other hand, the Japanese were worried about Chinese troops invading Vietnam. The Viet Minh were caught in the middle. Their numbers were growing, making it more and more difficult to stay hidden from the Japanese.

The valley of Pac Bo in Cao Bang Province was the

home of the Viet Minh. On first look, the entire valley seemed void of civilization. No smoke from fires was visible during daylight hours. Cooking fires were only allowed at night and only in an area where the flames could be completely hidden from view.

The Deer Team passed a half-dozen women using knives to cut grass and gathering it in baskets that they had woven. Young boys were using hand nets to catch fish in the stream. Women used knives tied to the ends of bamboo poles to cut fruit from trees. There were light machine gun positions set up and manned by the Viet Minh on both sides of the trail and shielded overhead by grass-covered mats. Everyone wore dark pajamas with conical hats made of straw and camouflaged with local leaves and grass. Concealment from the Japanese seemed the highest priority.

The Americans smelled the village far before they could see it. It was sour and rank. Slit trenches had been dug and surrounded with grass mats for privacy in an attempt to control the sewage produced by the two thousand inhabitants, but most of the villagers just relieved themselves behind the closest tree or bush. The young children had a bad habit of urinating and even defecating in the stream – the village's only freshwater supply. This primitive method worked alright in the hill villages which were usually occupied by less than a dozen families, but it was a major health problem in a village this size.

Hoagland was deeply concerned as he saw more of the villagers. Many had dark circles under their eyes and looked tired. Their skin was drawn and jaundice. "Amoebic Dysentery," he whispered to Dewey.

"I see. Make sure you warn the men to stick to their canteens and use their Halazone tablets for purification," said Dewey.

The majority of the Viet Minh lived and slept in dozens of caves carved in the sides of the limestone cliffs. The few community huts that had been permitted by the commander were used for a school, meeting house, and hospital. They were well camouflaged with newly cut grass on their thatched roofs to blend with the surrounding trees and foliage. Secrecy was the ally of the Viet Minh. What the Japanese couldn't spot from the air, couldn't be hunted on the ground. The Americans were impressed by the Viet Minh's ingenuity at keeping so many people hidden for such a long period of time.

The majority of the villagers were the families of the rebel fighters. There were no crops being grown or animal pens like most Vietnamese villages. Nothing that could be spotted from the air. The village produced no commodities or crafts to sell or trade. They were warriors. Violence is what they offered.

The majority of the men were assigned to forage for food. They could not scavenge from nearby villages. That would be a dead giveaway to the Japanese and invited betrayal. They were forced to travel long distances, sometimes fifty miles or more. While the Viet Minh claimed to have over 600,000 followers scattered around Indochina, the group with the Americans were the only rebels actually fighting the Japanese. They were the bravest and had the most experience in warfare. They were given the best arms available – stolen weapons from the Japanese. But even the warriors would scavenge for food when available. Daily survival was a constant struggle for the Viet Minh.

The Americans watched the Viet Minh as they walked through the village and the Viet Minh watched the Americans. Many of the villagers had never seen a foreigner, not even a Frenchman. They were suspicious and wondered what omens the Americans might bring with them. Hoagland was particularly disturbed by what he saw and moved up next to Dewey. "They're starving," he said.

"What's that?" said Dewey.

"The children's bellies are swollen, and their skin is

translucent and drawn. They're starving to death, and they don't even know it."

"How's that?"

"When the stomach is empty, it recedes in size. They stop feeling hunger and grow weak. Do you see any children playing?"

"No. No, I don't."

"That's not normal."

"I suppose not."

"They've been reduced to a primitive society. All their efforts go into foraging for food. It's no wonder they've shown so little progress in fighting the Japanese."

"So, what do we do?"

"I would suggest feeding them. Slowly at first. Too much, too fast could overwhelm their systems."

"Will they recover?"

"Yes, in time."

"How much time? We have a war to fight."

"I don't know. A week or two for some, others longer."

"Well, we'll do what we can."

"We could share our rations. They won't make a dent in the entire village, but they might save some of the extreme cases."

"Alright. But we must leave enough for ourselves until the first supply drop. We cannot afford to get sick or be unable to defend ourselves if attacked."

"Okay. Half rations should be enough for us to stay healthy."

"You must only distribute food to those that you are sure will survive. I know it's cruel, but you must triage."

"Of course, Commander. I understand."

The Americans were led to an open structure with a thatched roof in the center of the village. This was the Viet Minh headquarters. French military maps were spread across a rough-hewn wooden table. Several rebel commanders were listening to Vo Nguyen Giap, the Viet Minh military leader, as he reviewed a battle plan for their next raid. He was only thirty-four years old and already considered a respected rebel leader. He saw the Americans approaching and stopped the meeting. Hoagland, the only Deer Team member to speak Vietnamese, greeted Giap. Giap responded in English, "Welcome. We have been looking forward to your arrival. My name is Mister Van."

Dewey stepped forward when Hoagland introduced him as the team leader and shook Giap's hand. He introduced the other members of the Deer Team and Giap, in turn, introduced his commanders. "If I may inquire, do you have medical supplies?" said Giap.

"Some," said Hoagland. "More will come with the supply drop."

"I am afraid we cannot wait that long. Commander Dewey, may I borrow your doctor?"

"Of course," said Dewey.

"I'm not a doctor," said Hoagland.

"You are in my country if you have medicine. Please follow me," said Giap and led the way.

Hoagland followed Giap to a nearby cave. The entrance was small, unlike the other caves, the entrance covered with a blanket. They entered. It was dark inside. Only the light from a small fire boiling a pot of water to create steam lit the smoke-filled room. Several Vietnamese women were hovering around an older man, slight of build, lying on a cot in the corner of the cave. He was delirious, moving in and out of consciousness, sweating profusely, his skin drawn and jaundiced. The women took turns tending to him as if it was a privilege, dabbing his forehead, exposed chest, and arms with wet clothes from the nearby stream. The women were tender and loving. "This is Mister Hoo," said Giap. "If you can help him, I will personally be grateful as will all Viet Minh."

"What happened?" said Hoagland.

"As a matter of equality, he will only drink the water and eat the food that his fellow Viet Minh consume. I am afraid his sense of ethics has taken its toll."

"I see. May I examine him?"

"Of course."

Hoagland moved to the side of Mr. Hoo and gently examined him, checking his eyes, listening to his labored breathing, feeling his weak pulse, his muscles and stomach, which were sore when pressed. "Dysentery and malaria, I think. Maybe Dengue Fever. I don't know," said Hoagland to Giap.

"Oh, dear," said Giap. "I feared as much. Can you help him?"

"I will be honest. He's pretty dehydrated. I will do what I can."

"Thank you. You will be in my thoughts, good doctor."

"I'm not a doctor."

"You are all we have."

"Very well then. Let me get to it. I will keep you informed."

Giap moved to Mr. Hoo's side and picked up his hand, "Not yet, my friend. There is still work to be done. Not yet."

Mr. Hoo stirred slightly on hearing Giap's voice. His eyes flickered open for a moment; then he fell unconscious once again. Saddened, Giap left, leaving Hoagland to try to save the life of Mr. Hoo, also known as Ho Chi Minh.

Late in the evening, Hoagland emerged from the cave and stretched. He walked back to where the Americans were gathered. "What were you doing in there?" said Dewey.

"There is a man. Mr. Hoo they call him. He's very sick. Maybe dying," said Hoagland making himself a plate of food and drinking from his canteen.

"You don't have to go into a cave to find the sick and dying."

"No. But this man... he's special. They revere him. I believe he's their leader."

"Is he the one that sent the letter to Donovan?"

"I don't know. He's been in and out of consciousness. I haven't been able to talk to him."

"I see. I suppose we would fare better if you keep him alive."

"Yes. But I am not sure that is possible. He's pretty far gone. Dysentery and malaria for sure. Maybe other conditions, too. I can't be sure without blood tests."

"So what do you do?"

"Quinine for the malaria. Sulfa for the dysentery. Keep trying to get him to eat and drink. It's not easy. He's on the verge of a coma. Once that happens, I believe he will be lost."

"Then what?"

"I don't know. But Mr. Van realizes he's very sick. I doubt there will be repercussions if he dies."

"Let's hope not. You should get some sleep. It's been a long day."

"Yes."

"Perhaps you should stay in the cave. You must appear to be doing everything you can."

"I am. But you're probably right. I will."

"We'll bed down nearby... just in case things take a turn for the worse."

"How's the rest of the village?"

"It's as you said. The people are weak from lack of food and dysentery. The entire place smells like an open sewer. I don't imagine you have enough sulfa to treat everyone."

"No. I don't. We need to rethink what we are doing here."

"In what way?"

"Our training mission has turned into a rescue mission. These people can't fight in this condition."

"I realize that. The good news is that some of them are

very good fighters. They're brave and aggressive, and they know how to use the terrain to their advantage."

"Their weapons?"

"Lacking, but surprisingly well maintained. They've made good use of what they have. Their intelligence is excellent. They know where the Japanese are based, how many troops they have, and their supply routes. If we can get them back on their feet, I think we can make a real difference."

"We're going to need medicine. A lot of it. And food with Vitamin D. I feel the current supply drop will be far from adequate."

"Yes. We've already discussed it. Without the radio, we'll have to send a messenger on foot. I'm sending Buck back over the border to explain the situation in person to Colonel Patti."

"That's risky. The Japanese will be watching the border for Chinese troop incursions."

"It's worth the risk. Mr. Van has agreed to send one of his scouts to avoid the Japanese outposts. Buck thinks he can cover the distance in two days."

"And if Buck doesn't make it?"

"Then we'll just have to make do with what we are given."

"And what about Buck…and the scout?"

"They know the risks better than most. I wouldn't send them if it weren't vitally important."

"Okay, I'll make a list of what we need."

"And Hoagland… I'd like to see Mr. Hoo as soon as he's able. There is much to discuss."

"Of course."

Off by himself in the woods, Granier knelt on a blanket. His rifle laid before him, disassembled. Each part had been meticulously cleaned. He studied the layout of the pieces, each in the position that allowed him to quickly reach for the part when he needed it. He was ready. He glanced at his watch. When the second hand reached four seconds before the hour, he closed his eyes and took a breath. He didn't need to see the second hand click to twelve. He could feel the length of four seconds. He began reassembling the rifle, with his eyes firmly closed. Working from memory and touch, he picked up the parts and slid them together, some big, like the barrel assembly, others small, like the gas cylinder lock. His motions were well-rehearsed, smooth but certain.

When he'd finished, he cycled the action twice to ensure it was working properly then locked it in place. He glanced at his watch – one minute, twelve seconds had passed. It wasn't his best time, but it wasn't bad either. He would practice later when he was out of the field. He knew that a well-cleaned rifle did not require a lot of gun oil. There was no dirt or even dust to cause friction and wear down the metal. He oiled the parts that needed it sparingly, using a small can from his tool kit.

Once he was satisfied his rifle was ready, he went to work on the ammunition. He had selected seventeen bullets to replace the rounds he had expended during the firefight with the Japanese. He inspected each round, using a small piece of sandpaper to remove any metal burrs and scratches on the shell. Then he wiped each bullet down with a clean piece of cloth to eliminate any grit left behind from the sandpaper, before carefully loading the bullets into two clips and placing them in his ammunition belt. It was a ritual. It gave him confidence.

From a distance, Spitting Woman, unseen and silent, watched the American.

It was early morning. A heavy fog rested over the village, protecting it from prying eyes. Granier lightened his pack to the bare essentials and checked his weapon. Dewey and

Giap approached with Spitting Woman. "You can't be serious," said Granier. "I'd be better off alone with a compass and a map."

"Apparently she's the best scout they have," said Dewey.

"I'll be lucky if she doesn't cut my throat in the middle of the night."

"She's been ordered not to do that."

Granier grunted. "You would be wise to trust her," said Giap. "She knows the border area well and will get you through the Japanese lines."

"I guess I don't have any say in the matter," said Granier, resigned, turning to Spitting Woman. "Try to keep up."

Giap said something to her that Granier didn't understand. She frowned but nodded affirmatively. Granier slipped on his pack, picked up his weapon, and headed off up the trail. Spitting Woman clucked her tongue twice like she was trying to get the attention of an animal. Granier stopped and turned back, annoyed, "What?"

She turned and walked in the opposite direction. "Shit," said Granier, and he followed her.

Granier and Spitting Woman hiked through the jungle at a brisk pace, legs pumping, climbing, never slowing, never resting. They stayed off trails and wound their way through the trees and foliage. When the vines and undergrowth got too thick, Spitting Woman used her aranyik – a traditional machete of the highland tribes – to cut a path. Her frame was small, but she was strong and sturdy. Granier followed, impressed, but giving her no indication.

They came to a fast-flowing mountain stream, the water clear and clean. She knelt on the muddy bank, drank with her hand, and refilled her water bag. Granier filled his canteen, slipped in a purification tablet, swooshed it around and drank the bitter water. She watched and shook her head in disgust. Granier considered, spat out the canteen water and drank with his hand from the stream. She was right. It tasted much better, fresh.

A mosquito landed on Granier. She slapped his neck without warning. Granier jerked around, angry. She opened her hand and showed him the dead mosquito. He nodded a disgruntled thanks. She scooped up a handful of mud and smeared a thick layer on her arms, hands, and face, showing him. She made a hand motion and shook her head to communicate that mosquitos can't bite through the mud. She looked hideous. Granier held back a laugh to a just a smirk. She pointed to the mud along the stream. He followed her example and smeared a thick layer on his exposed skin. She tried to smear mud on a spot he missed. He batted her hand away like he could do it himself. She frowned. He shrugged and relented. She covered the exposed patch with mud. Satisfied they were both protected, they rose and continued to trek through the forest. Granier had been hoping for a longer break, but he was surprised by her endurance. Not willing to show his weakness, he rose and followed her.

After a half-mile hike through the forest, Spitting Woman slowed and motioned to Granier to stop. Granier moved up beside her. "What?" he whispered.

She motioned for him to be silent. She climbed slowly, quietly, up a small rise with thick undergrowth. As she reached the top, she dropped silently to her hands and crawled, then dropped further and belly-crawled slowly, quietly, careful not to move the foliage to attract attention. Granier followed her example. She stopped. He slowly moved up beside her.

She scanned the surrounding forest until she found what she was looking for. Then she pointed slowly, deliberately. Granier followed the direction of her finger. At first, he didn't see it. He squinted and glared harder.

There was a slight movement in the distance – one hundred yards, in a tree, barely visible. It took a moment for him to recognize it – a Japanese soldier, his rifle cradled in his arm, sat on a lookout platform high in the tree, completely camouflaged. He was facing in the opposite direction, toward the Chinese border and didn't spot them. *I would have walked right by him and never noticed until a bullet hit the back of my head,* Granier thought, a bit embarrassed.

They studied the sniper for a few moments, then surveyed the opposite side of the forest and saw nothing. That was the way they would go. They belly-crawled backward down the hill, disappearing into the safety of the undergrowth.

Hoagland entered the cave. He was surprised to see Mr. Hoo awake and lucid. "You are awake. That's good," said Hoagland in Vietnamese.

"You're American," said Mr. Hoo, weakly in English.

"Yes. My name is Hoagland. I'm with the OSS. There are six of us. I'm the medic. Do you mind if I examine you?"

"Of course not. I think you may have saved my life. I'm grateful."

"You're welcome," said Hoagland feeling Mr. Hoo's pulse, checking his pupils, listening to his chest with a stethoscope. "You're breathing is much better. I had the women move the fire outside. The steam was a good idea, but the smoke wasn't helping."

"You're Vietnamese is good, better than my English."

"I still have trouble placing the accents in the right places."

"It's not an easy language."

"How are you feeling?"

"I'm alive. That's what is important. There is still much to do."

"I'd like to keep you that way, but you need to eat."

"I'm afraid I don't have much of an appetite."

"Regardless. You need to eat… and drink. You're dehydrated."

"I will do my best."

"Good. I like cooperative patients."

"My head hurts."

"It's the malaria. The quinine will help, but it takes time to build up in your system. You will feel a lot better tomorrow, especially if you take fluids."

"Some tea perhaps."

"I'd like you to have some broth if you think you can keep it down."

"I make no promises."

"But you will do your best?"

"Of course."

Hoagland called one of the women over and asked for her to prepare tea and a fish broth. She went to work, happy that Mr. Hoo was going to try and eat. "When you are up to it, I'd like you to try and eat some rice. It will help with the diarrhea."

"Then I shall eat rice. My ass feels like it is on fire."

"It's the dysentery. I have some ointment in my pack that might help soothe the burning."

"It would be welcomed."

"I will get it," said Hoagland rising. "My commander would like to see you when you are able."

"And I, him. But I would like to be more presentable. I feel I smell like an outhouse."

"I'm sure he won't mind."

"But I will. Politics is a delicate game."

"Right. Of course. Tomorrow, perhaps?"

"Yes. Tomorrow."

"I'll get that ointment," said Hoagland moving off.

The forest was pitch black. Night had fallen. Granier and

Spitting Woman sat near a large tree, eating the food they carried in their packs. Their eyes had already adjusted to the darkness, and they could see even without flashlights or fire, both too risky this close to the border.

Granier looked at her while he munched on canned meatloaf using his fingers as a spoon. She was eating a dried fish and rice wrapped in a leaf. She looked back at him like maybe he wanted something. She looked at the fish and offered him some. He didn't want to be rude. He took the piece of fish flesh from her fingers, popped it in his mouth and chewed. He swallowed hard and smiled with a shrug as if he liked it. He didn't. He offered her two fingers full of meatloaf. She took it, popped it in her mouth and chewed. She gagged and spat it out on the ground. "Hey. That's good. Don't waste it," he said.

She rolled her eyes and finished her fish and rice. He finished the last of his meatloaf, took a swig of the water from his canteen. It made him miss the freshwater from the stream. He pulled a thirty-foot coil of cord from his pack, pulled out a mosquito net, and ran the cord through the top. He tied the cord between two trees, making a mosquito net tent. He rubbed his hands all over his clothes and mud-caked skin to ensure that no mosquitos or bugs were lingering, then crawled inside the tent and zipped it up. He grabbed his pack through the netting and placed it under the tent on one end as his pillow. Then he laid down and closed his eyes.

Spitting Woman shook her head like white people were so complicated. She laid down using her pack as a pillow. A mosquito landed on her arm. She swatted it. Then another and another. She kept swatting. Granier looked over and shrugged pity. "You want to come in here with me?" he said motioning with his hands.

She shook her head and gave him a look like he was stupid for even asking. He turned away from her and closed his eyes. "Savage," he said to himself.

More mosquitos and more swatting. There was no

evening fire to generate the smoke that kept the mosquitos away. She would get eaten alive once she fell asleep... if she fell asleep. Granier turned back over and motioned to her. "Stop being stubborn and get in here. You can't fight the Japs if you get malaria."

She didn't understand the words, but she caught the drift of what he was saying. She picked up her pack, slipped it under the netting, and waited for him to unzip the tent. "No. Clean yourself off. One mosquito gets inside, and we will be his snack all night," he said, motioning what to do.

Frustrated, she mimicked his movements and made sure there were no mosquitos on her. He unzipped the tent and let her crawl in. She laid down beside him. There wasn't much room in the tent meant for one. They turned their backs to each other and closed their eyes. Two minutes later, he heard her snore like a very large bear. His eyes opened. He was wide awake. "No way," he said, listening to how incredibly loud she snored.

He gave her a little shove, hoping to wake her. Nothing. He poked her side. She stirred a little, swatted at his hand, and went back to sleep, snoring. He rolled over again and closed his eyes. It was going to be a long night.

Spitting Woman was the first to wake as the sky began to brighten, just after sunrise. Granier has his arm around her and his hand on one of her breasts. She jumped up, unzipped the tent, and tumbled out on to the ground. Granier woke and spoke in a hushed voice, confused, "What's wrong?"

She spat out a string of curse words in her dialect. Granier was lost. "What did I do?"

She motioned where his hands had been. "Oh, come on. I didn't mean anything. I was sleeping."

She pointed to the erect penis in his pants. "That's nothing. It happens to men when they wake up. It's involuntary. It doesn't mean anything."

She spat at him. "With the spitting again. Really? You ever hear of manners?" he said as she stomped off into the forest. "Don't worry. A snake won't bite you. I ain't that lucky."

Hoagland entered the cave, followed by Dewey. Ho was sitting up in bed. Two bamboo chairs were placed nearby as if he had been expecting them. "Welcome, gentlemen," said Ho. "Please come in and have a seat.

"Mr. Hoo, this is our unit commander, Lieutenant Colonel Dewey," said Hoagland.

"I would offer you my hand, Colonel, but I fear I may still be contagious."

"I appreciate the thought, but I think if I was going to get something I probably would have caught it by now," said Dewey, offering his hand.

"Still, just to be safe…" said Hoagland, motioning for Dewey to withdraw his hand.

"Alright. Later. When you're feeling better."

"Which we all hope is soon," said Hoagland.

Hoagland and Dewey sat. Two women brought in tea and biscuits. "I took the liberty of having refreshments prepared," said Ho.

"You're very gracious," said Dewey.

"It is our culture," said Ho. "I appreciate General Donovan accepting my invitation, Colonel Dewey. There was some question as to whether he would."

"Please call me, Mr. Dewey. We don't like to use rank in the field."

"Of course."

"I will be honest, Mr. Hoo, there was some question on our end as well."

"I'm sure. The French are your allies. They will not be pleased if you assist us."

"I think you may underestimate the French. They too

want the Japanese out of Vietnam."

"Yes, but for very different reasons."

"True."

"We see both the French and the Japanese as invaders."

"Perhaps, but I think we would all do better to focus on the Japanese and leave the French problem for a different time... after the war."

"Very well... as long as the issue will be addressed."

"I assure you it will."

"I have your promise then?"

"Yes."

"And your government?"

"They have no interest in seeing colonialism continue in Southeast Asia if that is what you are asking."

"I thought as much. Our interests are aligned."

"Yes. Now for the problem at hand... With the surrender of the Germans and the Italians, America and its allies are now free to focus on the Pacific and Asia. If we want the war to end quickly, we must keep the Japanese in a box. They cannot be allowed to expand further, especially into China. The Japanese use Indochina as their rice bowl. Their army cannot survive long without rice. If we can sever their supply line with Indochina, their army will be forced to withdraw. Once contained, it is just a matter of time before the Allied forces overrun all of Japan and force their surrender. If you are in agreement, it is our job to help you sever the Japanese supply lines."

"We are in agreement."

"Good. How many men can you put in the field against the Japanese?"

"Given time and the right support, an entire division."

"I appreciate your optimism. But we must be more practical. How many men can you put in the field within the next two weeks?"

"Our problem is food, gentlemen. The Japanese take everything we grow to feed their troops. Our people are starving."

"Let's assume for the moment that we can solve your food problem and you are no longer forced to scavenge. How many men?"

"Hmm… I think five hundred within two weeks is a doable number."

"That's good. Would they be the same quality as the troops that accompanied us from our drop zone?"

"No. Those that picked you up are our best soldiers. The increased numbers would need some training and experience in battle before they could fight like our core unit. What I can promise you is that they will be brave and fight hard."

"I appreciate your honesty. If the additional troops support the current unit, I believe they will gain the experience you talk about. Our team can help with the training."

"And the weapons and ammunition we need?"

"Of course. You will be given all that is required."

"Very well. We shall be allies and kill the Japanese," said Ho with a smile.

"With your permission, I would like to coordinate with Mr. Van for an attack on the supply train from Hanoi to Lang Son."

"A worthy target. I will inform him."

Dewey had what he needed and decided not to push his luck. He finished his tea and asked to be excused. Hoagland stayed with Ho. "You look much better today," said Hoagland.

"I feel better. My appetite is coming back slowly. I eat more with each meal."

"Plenty of rice, I hope?"

"Yes with the broth."

"Good. May I examine you?"

"Yes. Please."

Hoagland began his examination. "May I ask you something?" said Ho.

"Of course."

"Do you believe Mr. Dewey was speaking for the Americans when he said 'They have no interest in seeing colonialism continue in Southeast Asia,' or was he speaking from his own perspective?"

Hoagland considered for a moment. He wanted to be honest, but he also had a loyalty to his commander and country. "I don't know. But what I can tell you is that Mr. Dewey is an honorable man and that America is an honorable country. You know our past. We threw off the shackles of colonialism in our war with the British. We haven't forgotten our roots. Our Declaration of Independence reminds us of that."

"Nothing is more precious than independence and liberty."

"I must say that sounds a bit strange coming from a communist."

"It is patriotism, not communism that inspires me," said Ho. "Communism is a means to an end. A way to redistribute wealth the French have stolen from us over the years."

"And you can't do that through capitalism?"

"Capitalism is what the French brought to our land, and it has been proven to be harsh. I feel it is time for our people to find a new path to equality."

"And democracy?"

"Democracy is for the educated. Most of my people do not even read. We can hardly expect them to rule themselves. They can be easily swayed by smooth-talking politicians that seem to have all the answers but in reality, seek only to enrich themselves."

"For a man of vision, you have little confidence in your followers."

"I am a realist and must be honest."

"I appreciate that."

"The Vietnamese are a gentle people with good hearts. If anything, they are naïve and innocent."

"I've seen them fight. They are hardly innocent and definitely not naïve."

"Some, yes. But most are just simple farmers wanting to raise their families. They don't know violence."

"I see."

Ho fell silent for a moment as if deep in thought, then said, "Do you think it would be possible to examine a copy of your Declaration of Independence?"

"It may take a little doing, but I don't see why not."

"My people will be forming a nation one day soon. Such a document could come in useful."

"I hope you do... form your own nation soon. And there are no better words than those of our founding fathers."

"I believe you, Doctor."

"I'm not a doctor," said Hoagland with a shy smile.

"That's why I believe you," said Ho Chi Minh.

Granier and Spitting Woman trudged through the forest at a good clip, their anger at each other pushing them harder. They came to a small clearing. In the lead, Spitting Woman entered the clearing first. She stopped and froze. Granier seeing something was wrong, slowed, and moved up beside her, his rifle at the ready.

An Asiatic Black Bear, splitting a rotting log open with his paws to search for insects, turned and stared at the two creatures in his territory. "Oh, shit," said Granier.

Granier had seen larger bears in the wild, but never this close. The bear's arms were long, as were his claws. He had a white, v-shaped patch on his chest. The bear snorted his displeasure at the interruption. Granier aimed. It was an easy shot, and he was sure that one or two .30-06 bullets would take the animal down. The problem was the noise. They were still close to the border with its Japanese outposts. Spitting Woman placed her hand over the barrel of Granier's rifle and pushed it downward. She slowly motioned for Granier to stay put as she moved to one side of the clearing.

The bear was now facing threats from two different angles. The creature rose up on his hide feet and belched a menacing roar.

Unafraid, Spitting Woman raised her hands over her head and took a step closer to the beast. The bear took a step forward to meet her. Granier had had enough. He raised his rifle, aimed at the bottom of white, v-shaped patch figuring that is where the bear's heart would be and slowly squeezed the trigger. Spitting Woman clapped her hands together twice to create loud snapping sounds. Surprised by the strange noise, he turned and ran into the bushes, disappearing.

Spitting Woman was pleased with herself. Granier was surprised by the bear's sudden retreat. "Pat yourself on the back later. Let's get the hell out of here before he comes back," said Granier moving in the opposite direction from the bear. Spitting Woman followed.

They ran several hundred yards through the forest. It was rough terrain. Granier laughed relieved. Spitting Woman laughed back. It was the first time either of them heard the other happy. Granier didn't think twice when they crossed a trail in the direction they wanted to go. He took it. Spitting Woman followed. "I gotta admit… that was impressive. And don't give me some bullshit about you knew what you were doing the entire time. Nobody knows how a wild animal will react, especially a bear," said Granier, ignoring the fact that she didn't understand a word he was saying.

She blurted something back that Granier didn't understand, but imagined it was some sort of brag. "Yeah, yeah. You scared a black bear. Big deal. Now if it was a grizzly…"

Granier didn't notice the tripwire across the trail. It had been coated with a thin layer of dark grease and dirt, making it almost invisible. He was still moving at a pretty good clip. The wire caught the eyelets of his boot. He lost his balance, tripped, and fell forward. The wire yanked the safety pin from a Chinese grenade attached to a tree next to the trail. Its timer had been set to zero. It exploded instantly. Granier was lucky he had fallen flat and that there was a fallen log paralleling the trail. The grenade's shrapnel hit the log and flew over him. "Jesus Christ!" he said. He rolled over and felt up and down his body for wet spots and looked for holes in his uniform. Nothing. He rose to his feet and said, "It's okay. I'm still in one piece. No damage."

He saw Spitting Woman and smiled. She didn't smile back. There was pain in her eyes. He looked down at her hands, holding her thigh. She groaned in pain. Granier ran to her, panicking. "Oh, God. Oh, God. Show me."

He pulled her hands away. Smoke rose out of a quarter-sized hole in her black pajamas. The red-hot shrapnel inside the wound was burning her. He ripped open the hole in her pants to expose the wound. Smoke poured out of it. It smelled of cordite and burning flesh. He pushed his index finger and his thumb into the wound, trying to reach the shrapnel. She yelped. His fingers were too big. He pulled out his knife and cut the edges of the wound making it bigger. She groaned again. Blood flowed. Again, he reached inside. He felt the burning shrapnel burning the tips of his finger and thumb. It hurt like hell. He pushed further into the wound to get a hold of the metal. He jerked out the shrapnel through the wound's entrance and flung it to the ground, ripping off the skin on the tips of his finger and thumb. "Ah, fuck," he said, looking at his fingers, the tips raw, the flesh torn.

He looked back at her wound. Blood was flowing out. He whipped off his pack and reached into a side pocket to retrieve a bandage and a packet of sulfide. Ripping the packet open with his teeth, he poured the powder into her wound. He placed the bandage over the wound and wrapped the cloth bands around her leg. The pad of the bandage turned red, filled with blood in just a matter of a few seconds. He pressed down on the bandage over the wound, hoping to restrict the flow. Blood seeped through his fingers. She was still bleeding. "Damn it. It must have nicked something," he said, his mind racing for a solution. He reached into the back of his pack and pulled out the cord he used for the mosquito netting. He cut off a five-foot piece and wrapped it around her leg above the wound. He tied it like a constriction bandage so he would not cut off all blood flow but restrict it. "I've got to get you to a doctor. It can't be more than ten or fifteen miles to a Chinese village."

He pulled off her pack and picked up her rifle. She grunted her objection at her weapon being taken. "Relax. I'll come back for it," he said, hoping his tone would reassure her.

He set the rifle and pack next to his pack in the bushes. He removed her water bag from her shoulder and opened it. "Drink. You need to stay hydrated."

She drank. When she was finished, he drank as much as he could. He sealed it back up and tossed it next to the packs and rifle. He still had his canteen on his web belt in addition to his ammunition clips.

He covered everything with foliage. He took a quick look around and found a strange-looking tree stump that would be his marker for when he returned. He picked up his rifle and slung it backward, so it hung on his chest. "This is the hard part," he said, moving to her side and placing one of her arms on his shoulder. "Climb on my back and hang on."

She didn't understand but got the gist of what he wanted. She grabbed his shirt and pulled herself around to his back. He helped her up by reaching under her butt with his hands and lifted her up and around. It was awkward, and she groaned in pain. "Ready?" he said, stabilizing her.

She tapped him on the top of the head. He took off down the trail, running the best he could. She was light but still weighed over a hundred pounds. He tried to keep his hand holding her leg away from the wound as best as possible. He knew that the trail would take less time but was riskier. His eyes stayed focus on the path ahead, searching for more tripwires. As he ran, she groaned. He could feel her leg throbbing. He didn't want her to go into shock, but he didn't want her to fall asleep because of blood loss either. As long as she was groaning, she was awake and alive.

Granier was drenched in sweat from running and carrying Spitting Woman. He was exhausted and stumbled more than usual. It was a huge effort to pick up his feet to keep them from dragging across the ground with each step. His legs were burning, and his chest was heaving for air. He was angry that his body was failing him. He felt Spitting Woman loosen her grip around his neck. "Hey, wake up!" he said.

She snapped awake and tightened her grip. "It can't be that much farther. It just can't," said Granier, hoping.

Granier saw a small stream in his path. He increased his speed using all his remaining strength and leaped over the flowing water. He cleared the stream and landed on the opposite bank with a thud. Spitting Woman groaned in pain. He was surprised when his legs collapsed, and he crumbled to his knees. He tried to steady himself. He was on an incline and leaned forward as much as possible. It wasn't enough, especially with the extra weight on his back. He could feel the weight carrying him backward. He fell backward into the water landing on top of Spitting Woman. Water flowed over her head as she struggled for breath and gulped for air. He rolled off her and grabbed her by the shoulders, lifting her. She gasped, the wind knocked out of her. "I'm sorry. I'm sorry," he said, almost in tears. "This is all my fault. I wasn't paying attention. I should have seen the tripwire. It's not like me. I don't know what's wrong."

She regained her breath and could see he was suffering. She patted him on the shoulder and nodded like it was okay. He chuckled, "We're a sorry pair, aren't we?"

He looked down at the stream. The water was red. Whatever clotting had slowed her bleeding had been knocked loose when she fell. Blood was flowing. "God, no," said Granier as he tightened the cord around her thigh. She winced. He scooped up a handful of water and offered it to her. "You've got to drink. You've got to stay hydrated."

She smelled the water and pushed his hand away. "What's wrong? It's bad?" he said.

He opened his fingers and let the water drain from his hand. He pulled out his canteen, opened and offered it to her. She refused, pushing it away. "You have to drink," he said, pushing it back toward her. "You don't drink, you die."

She nodded and drank from the canteen. It was sour in her mouth, and she grimaced. "Just drink it," he said.

She took several swallows and finally pushed it away. "Alright," he said and took a couple swallows himself. "We gotta go."

He put her hands around his neck and lifted her from the stream. By carefully pushing and pulling, he maneuvered her onto his back. Then he climbed the embankment. His rifle was wet and covered in mud. "Sorry, Baby," he said to his rifle. "I'll give ya a good cleaning first chance I get."

He climbed to the top of the embankment and started to run again. It wasn't far before the run turned into a trot and then a walk. He was beyond exhausted and could feel himself getting dizzy. *Knock it off, you pussy,* he thought to himself. *She deserves better. She deserves the best of you.* He shook off his dizziness and kept moving.

The sun set. The forest darkened. Granier looked down and saw his pants wet with Spitting Woman's blood. He doubted she would live until morning at the rate she was losing blood. There was no time to rest. He kept moving, one foot in front of the other, stumbling, catching himself, using his rifle as a walking stick when he needed it. His legs burned beyond any pain he had felt. His pride was gone. He did whatever he needed to do to keep going — giving himself pep talks. He could feel the woman's grip lessening again. "Hey, none of that," he said.

She let go and fell to the side of the trail. He stopped and knelt beside her. She was unconscious. He pulled out his canteen and sprinkled the remaining water in his hand, then patted it on her forehead and cheeks. "Wake up. You have to stay awake," he said.

There was no response. She was out cold. "Hey, don't do this. Wake up. You have to wake up," he said, shaking her. "Come on. I need your help. I need you."

Desperate, he slapped her hard on the cheek. Nothing. "No, no, no…" He raised his hand again. Her eyes blinked open, and she looked up at him like she was hurt that he had hit her. "I'm sorry. I didn't know what to do," he said, leaning back, falling on his butt in the bushes. "I don't know what to do. I don't know how to save you," he said, helpless.

She smiled a little. "Yeah. You okay?" he said, cheering up. "You gonna be okay?"

She nodded toward the trail in the direction they were headed. "Yeah, we should get going. I know it can't be far. We can make. I'm sure of it. We just gotta keep going," he said, reaching for her hand to wrap around his neck.

She pulled her hand back, refusing. "What's wrong? We gotta go," he said, confused.

She motioned to herself and shook her hand flat like she wouldn't go with him. "No, no. It's not that much further. We can make it together."

She pointed to him, then the trail. He was too tired to

argue. "Alright. I'll go. You stay here and rest," he said as he checked the cord around her thigh. "Keep the cord tight."

He handed her his rifle, "You take care of my rifle, okay?"

She took it, but the weight was too much for her to hold. He laid it beside her in the bushes. "Don't shoot me when I come back, okay?" he said. "I'm going."

He got up, released his web belt, and set it down beside her. Everything was lighter now. He felt different, freer. He started to walk down the trail leaving her. She watched him go, a sadness in her eyes. He picked up the pace into a jog. He could move again; the extra weigh gone. He broke into a run. His eyes were combing the dark path ahead. He could barely see in the twilight. He knew it would get better after the sun's afterglow was completely gone and his eyes were adjusted. There was no time to wait. Her life depended on him reaching the Chinese. He kept running, stumbling over rocks and roots, catching himself.

He had run almost two miles up a hill when he came to the crest of the trail and looked down into the valley below. He thought he saw a flickering light in the distance. *A village,* he thought. *I can get help. She's gonna be okay.*

Even that little flicker of light had closed his retinas a bit, making it hard to see. He didn't want to wait until his eyes adjusted. *It's downhill. It will be easier,* he thought. *I just gotta keep going. It'll be over soon enough.*

He started down the hill moving sideways, using his legs as brakes, twisting from side to side. It was working well, alternating. He picked up speed. He was making good time. The village was getting closer. The trail steepened. He decided to slow down. He straightened his legs more, using them as brakes but they didn't cooperate. He kept moving downhill, picking up speed. Whenever he tried to slow, his knees gave out, and he stumbled. He couldn't stop himself. He just went with it, moving faster and faster down the trail. It was impossible to see. He felt his boot hit something hard. A rock or root, he didn't know. His momentum carried him forward. He was flying downhill headfirst trying to regain his footing. It was no use. He was at the mercy of gravity. He pushed his arm upward to protect his head. He landed with a thud and bounced. His legs toppled over him, and he somersaulted down the trail, landing, bouncing back into the air, landing again. At one point, he landed on his feet again, but they could not hold his weight, and he tumbled again. There was nothing he could do but ride it out, hitting roots, flattening bushes, scraping across the ground.

Near the bottom of the hill, he finally rolled to a stop. He groaned. His entire body hurt, and he wondered if anything was broken. He waited a few moments to catch his breath before struggling to his knees. He felt something tapping his shoulder. He turned to see a long bayonet. It startled him, but he didn't move. He slowly pushed his hands out in front of himself to show he was unarmed. He turned to see the face of a soldier looking down at him. It was an Asian face, round, skin light. The eyes weren't Vietnamese or Japanese. They were Chinese. A soldier, scared, like he was looking at something that he didn't understand. "American," said Granier, opening his eyes wide to show they were different. "Nothing to worry about here. We're on the same side."

The soldier frowned, not understanding. He shouted something in Mandarin and motioned for Granier to get up. Granier rose to his feet carefully, the pointed end of the bayonet's blade easily within striking distance of his vitals. He could see the soldier was young and didn't comprehend the idea of an American. *Probably never seen an American,* thought Granier. *Maybe from a farm, no newspapers or magazines to show him the outside world.*

"It's alright. I'm a good guy. We both fighting the Japanese. I'm on your side," said Granier in a reassuring tone.

The soldier wasn't buying it. He motioned for Granier

to continue down the trail first. "I'd like to do that, but I have a friend. A woman (motioning breasts.) She's hurt. Grenade (motioning explosion.) Shrapnel hit her leg (motioning shrapnel flying and hitting his leg.) She's back up that trail a couple of miles (pointing in the opposite direction.) She needs help. She needs a doctor. You can go with me and help carry her (motioning to carry her.)"

The soldier wasn't having it. He grew angry and pointed down the trail in the direction of the village. "There's no time. She's hurt bad. We need to go back," said Granier standing his ground.

The soldier pressed his bayonet against Granier's chest. "Alright. God damn it. I'll go," said Granier moving to walk down the trail. As Granier moved past the soldier, he pushed the rifle away and elbowed him in the face. The soldier dropped his rifle and grabbed his broken nose. Granier grabbed the rifle and pointed it at the soldier. "You're coming with me. We're going back," said Granier in the meanest tone he could muster.

The Chinese soldier nodded his compliance and walked up the hill. Granier followed close behind with the rifle pointed at the soldier's back.

They made good time going back. They found Spitting Woman unconscious, her breathing imperceptible. Granier knew there was no time to waste. "Pick her up," he said motioning to the guard.

The guard shrugged like what's the point. "Pick her the fuck up, or I'm gonna stick you like a wild pig," he said, angrily.

The soldier nodded and picked her up, cradling her in his arms. Granier motioned for him to head back toward the village. The soldier started back down the trail. Granier picked up his sniper rifle and followed the soldier.

Granier was careful not to let the soldier pick up too much speed as they hiked down the hillside. At the bottom, they encountered a squad of Chinese soldiers on the trail. Granier immediately set down both rifles and let them take Spitting Woman and him captive. They hiked toward the village.

In the village, a Chinese lieutenant questioned Granier as the platoon's medic tended to Spitting Woman. She was still alive, but barely. With hand motions and tone of voice, Granier explained he needed to find the Americans and give them a message. The lieutenant nodded his understanding and radioed his headquarters.

After the medic rebandaged Spitting Woman's wound and made her drink some freshwater, she came around. Granier knelt beside her. "Hey, you scared the shit out of me. I thought you were a goner for sure."

She smiled weakly and said something in her dialect. Granier didn't understand the words, but understood the meaning and said, "You're welcome."

THREE

The American commander sent a jeep to pick up Granier. Granier insisted that Spitting Woman goes with him, even though she was still weak. "I ain't leaving her," he said to the corporal driving the jeep. "She goes where I go."

The corporal drove all night to an airbase where the Americans were headquartered. The base doctor treated Spitting Woman. She was given transfusions to replace her lost blood. Her wound was cleaned and rebandaged again. Granier stayed by her side until he was told the OSS commander had arrived and would like to see him as soon as possible. Granier explained to Spitting Woman with hand motions that he would be back soon and that she should sleep if she could so she would become strong again. She looked worried that Granier was going to leave her in this strange place. He tried to reassure her with a smile. It didn't help. He left.

Granier, mud still caked on his torn and battered uniform, sat in a room with Lieutenant Colonel Archimedes Patti, the commander of OSS Operations in Vietnam. Patti could see that Granier was exhausted, but he needed the information only he possessed. He ordered a large pot of coffee and some biscuits in hopes of keeping Granier attentive. "Where is Colonel Dewey?" said Patti.

"Pac Bo in Cao Bang Province near the border. It's the Viet Minh headquarters. Dewey was wounded during the drop. Not bad, but couldn't make the trip himself. He sent me," said Granier.

"Then Dewey made contact with their leader?"

"Yes. His name is Mr. Hoo. He's very sick – Dysentery and Malaria. Hoagland's tending to him."

"And their military leader?"

"Yes. They call him, 'Mr. Van'."

"And how is he? What's he like?"

"He's smart and confident. His men respect him."

"That's good. How big are their forces?"

"The camp has about two thousand men, women, and children. But only one hundred soldiers."

"Why so few?"

"Most of the men are forced to forage for food and supplies. They can't grow or make anything for fear of being spotted by the Japanese reconnaissance planes. Everything has to be brought in. Even with most of their men scavenging, their people are starving and sick."

"I see. How bad is it?"

"Very. They're barely a fighting force. But those that can fight are brave and capable."

"Capable enough to take on the Japanese?"

"After we landed, we stumbled on a Japanese patrol – fifty well-armed soldiers. The Viet Minh ambushed them and took them out. All of them."

"Really? Then they can attack the Japanese supply routes?"

"Maybe after we get them some food and medicine."

"We're not running a charity."

"I understand that, but they're too few and too weak to take on the Japs in force."

Patti considered for a moment and then asked, "If we were to supply the Viet Minh what they need, how many men could they put in the field?"

"Five to six hundred, maybe more. Their women fight too. Some just as good as the men. The woman that helped me get here, she's one hell of a scout. I'd fight alongside her any day."

"How long before they would be ready?"

"If we get them medicine and supplies, I would guess two weeks. They fight good just the way they are, but we'd need to train them in tactics, especially if we are going after the trains."

"And you believe they would be successful?"

"Yes."

"Well, I suppose we could augment the weapons and ammunition drop with food and medicine."

"Yeah, about that…"

"About food and medicine?"

"No. Weapons and ammunition."

"I assure you, we are sending the latest weapons we have."

"That's the thing… you shouldn't."

"Why in the devil not?"

"If you send them new weapons, they'll need to learn how to use them. Almost everything they have was stolen from the Japanese during raids. They already know how to use and maintain the Japanese rifles."

"You're not suggesting we send them Japanese weapons?"

"I am. It makes sense. We don't need to train them. They already know how they work. They will also be able to resupply their ammunition by stealing it from the Japanese shipments they raid."

"Where are we supposed to get five hundred Japanese rifles with ammunition?"

"At the rate we've been capturing Japanese on the Pacific Islands, I would imagine we have tons of them stashed someplace."

"I suppose it's possible."

"Look. You want the Viet Minh up and running as soon as possible. This is the way to do it."

"Yes, but what about heavy weapons – mortars, machine guns, recoilless rifles?"

"Heavy weapons are a mistake. The two biggest

advantages the Viet Minh have are stealth and mobility. If you give them heavy weapons, I can assure you they'll take them. But they carry everything. They don't use pack animals, let alone any vehicles. Heavy weapons will weigh them down. They'll need to rest more. The thirty miles they can currently travel in a day will be cut in half."

"They can travel thirty miles in a day through jungle?"

"It's not really jungle. It's more like dense forest. And yes, they can travel thirty miles using their Japanese weapons."

"That's incredible. They'll at least want a few mortars, won't they?"

"Japanese knee mortars would be best. They're light-weight and don't require a heavy base plate. Plus they're simple to use and can be set up and ready to fire in under fifteen seconds."

"Yes, but they use grenades, not mortar shells. There's no punch to them."

"They don't need punch. They're not fighting tanks or armored cars. They're fighting men. With knee mortars they can take better advantage of the terrain. When you're fighting in the forest you can't see beyond one to two hundred yards. A 60mm mortar would overshoot most enemy positions."

"Alright. Knee mortars then."

"They could also use fifty Japanese light machine guns."

"Type 96s?"

"Yeah. And lots of ammunition."

"Of course. Alright. You shall have your Japanese arms. I must say this actually averts a potential problem with our allies."

"How's that?"

"We're arming rebels. The French will not be too happy about it if they find out. Giving the Viet Minh Japanese weapons decreases that possibility. The French still believe Indochina is theirs to control after the war."

"And is it?"

"If it were up to me… no. And I think most officers agree with me. We're here to fight the Japanese, not to support colonialism."

"So, what will happen when the shooting stops?"

"Who says it's going to stop?"

"I'll need to coordinate the supply drops. The Viet Minh don't want them anywhere near their base camp."

"The Air Force is General Chennault's wheelhouse. I'll see that they assign someone to meet with you. Now get some rest. You only have four days before the first supply drop. I'm sending you back."

"What about the woman that came with me?"

"She'll stay until she is recovered from her wound."

"Then what?"

"I don't know. I suppose we'll jump off that bridge when we get to it. In the meantime, we'll see that she is well cared for," said Patti, seeing the concern on Granier's face. "Why is she so important to you?"

"She's a good fighter and a scout. I'd hate to lose her. We need her."

"We'll drop her with some supplies as soon as she is well enough."

"She won't like that. I doubt she's ever even seen a plane up close, let alone jumped from one."

"There's a first time for everything."

"Of course. I'll let her know."

Patti called in a sergeant, "Sergeant, make sure this man has something to eat, a hot shower and a cot. A new set of fatigues might also be appropriate. His are a bit worn. See to it he visits the quartermaster."

"Yes, sir," said the sergeant, saluting.

Granier saluted and followed the sergeant out.

Wearing a new uniform and freshly shaven, Granier sat outside watching planes take off and land while sipping a coke. A jeep pulled up. Mc Goon stepped out. "Oh, shit," said Granier to himself.

"You, Granier?" said McGoon, unhappy.

"Yeah," said Granier.

"You mean 'yes, sir,' don't you... Sergeant?"

"Yes, sir," said Granier standing and saluting. "Sorry, we don't have much use for rank in Special Services."

"Well, this ain't Special Services, Sergeant."

"My mistake."

"See you don't repeat it. It ain't my call, but you and I are gonna need to work together if things are gonna run smoothly supplying the Viet Minh. I do my best thinking over a cold beer. You got a problem with that?"

"No, sir. A beer sounds good."

"I gotta report in. I'll meet you at the officer's club in fifteen."

"I ain't an officer."

"Tell 'em Captain McGovern sent you."

"Alright."

"And tell 'em to make sure our beers are cold. Nothing worse than warm beer. Don't know how the Brits put up with it."

"Barbarians."

McGoon laughed and moved off toward headquarters. "Don't let them hear you say that. They'd give ya a thirty-minute lecture on western civilization," said McGoon without turning around.

Four empty beer bottles sat on the table in the officer's club. Two more half-empty bottles were being consumed by McGoon and Granier. "My brain is now properly lubricated to solve your problem," said McGoon. "You don't want the Japs figuring out the location of the drops or the Viet Minh camp. So, each time we need to change the drop zone, and we need to make sure there is no discernible pattern. That's easy enough. The problem is communicating the drop zone location without the Japs cracking the code. We have to assume they will be listening to every radio transmission."

"If we use an American military code, it is only a matter of time before the Japs break it. Once that happens, they will know the time of the drop and our location. They'll attack the Viet Minh with overwhelming force," said Granier.

"Got it. So, we need to use our own code. Something the Japs ain't gonna use lots of resources to break cuz it's only about supplies and it ain't that important."

"Right."

"We need something that we are both familiar with, but the Japs ain't."

"So, what are you thinking?"

"I am thinking… we need another round."

"Good thinking."

McGoon motioned for the bartender to bring two more beers. "What about baseball?" said Granier. "We could use runs as miles and the bases to indicate compass direction."

"Japs like baseball. They might figure it out."

"Yeah, right. I like hunting and fishing. How about that?"

"Maybe, but it doesn't really lend itself to numbers."

"I suppose."

"I've memorized the measurements of all the movie stars. You know… Ava Gardner 34-20-33, Rita Hayworth 37-24-36, Veronica Lake 35-22-35. How about you?"

"Haven't got around to it."

"Shame. That one's kinda fun just thinking about it."

"How about cars? Do you know engines?"

"Of course."

"We could talk about engines. Things like horsepower, cylinder displacement, and flow rates of carburetors."

"That'd work. I doubt the Japs follow American cars. What would we use for direction?"

"I don't know. Maybe the gear shift – first for south, second for north, third for east and reverse for west."

"That works. But let's mix 'em, so they're not in order."

"Alright. I could make a list."

"Okay, but ya gotta memorize it. No documents that could fall into the enemy's hands if you get caught."

"Agreed."

"Now, the next problem… food is bulky. If we're gonna be dropping foodstuffs, it's gonna take some time getting it all out the aircraft door. I can take the plane into a hard banking turn, so everything is dropped in the same location, but any Jap patrol in the area is gonna be able to figure out where the drop zone is located. You could be in a world of hurt if they move in on ya while you're weighed down like that."

"Yeah. You're right. But it's a risk we'll have to take. They need food and medicine more than they need guns and ammo."

"Well, you OSS boys seem to know what you're doing. I'll leave it to you."

Granier walked into the base hospital. Spitting Woman was awake and sitting up with an IV in her arm. The nurses had been pumping her full of fluids. She looked surprisingly good. "You look pretty chipper for a woman that almost died," said Granier. "Tough as nails, I guess."

She was happy to see him. He was the only person she knew in this strange place. She started to get out of bed as if she was going to go with him. Granier put his hands out to stop her, "No, no. You've got to stay in bed. The IVs. You need fluids."

He helped her get back in bed. She didn't like it. He used his hand motions to explain his words, "Look. I've got to go back with the supplies and report to Dewey. You'll stay here and get better. Get strong again. I'll send someone back and get you. They'll bring you back to your people."

She did not like the look of him leaving her. She climbed out of bed again and pulled at the IV tubing in her arm. "No. Wait. Stop. Don't that. You need that," said Granier panicking.

He tried to push her back into bed, but she wouldn't go. "You can't go with me. I'm jumping from a plane. You're wounded. You'll get hurt," he said.

She again reached for the tubing, and he stopped her, "Okay. Okay. If you stay in bed and let them treat you, you can go with me. We still got a couple of days. Just get better."

She calmed down. "I'll come back and get you when it's time to go," he said, turning to go.

She reached out, grabbed his shirt, and pulled him back. "What? You don't trust me?" he said, angry. "If I give you my word, I'm gonna keep it. I'm not a liar."

She wouldn't let go of his shirt and pulled him down to sit on the bed. She said nothing but seemed to be happier that he was near. "Alright, fine. But I ain't sleeping on the floor. Maybe they got an extra cot or something."

McGoon was doing his preflight check when Granier showed up with Spitting Woman in tow. She had recovered, apart from a limp. Granier wore a parachute and carried his leg pack and rifle case. He had a coil of rope over his shoulder. "Who the hell is this?" said McGoon.

"She's jumping with me," said Granier.

"You only got one chute."

"Yeah, well. I got rope. I'll just strap her on."

"Oh, that sounds like a real good idea. What about your reserve chute? Ya can't pull it if she's sitting on it."

"That's a risk we'll just have to take."

McGoon shook his head, "Ya ain't got the sense God gave ya."

"Nope. None at all. But believe me… it's better than fighting with her."

"Has she ever been in a plane?"

"I doubt it."

"You better keep plenty of barf bags on hand then."

"Roger that. Permission to come aboard?"

"It's against my better judgment, but yeah. Permission granted."

Granier helped her walk up the stairs and through the open doorway. The plane's hold was filled with supply containers with parachutes attached. Granier climbed in. "You sit over here," he said motioning to a seat next to the cargo crew. She sat across from the open doorway.

McGoon and Smitty started the plane's twin engines, taxied the plane onto the runway and stopped. It was a short runway, and he was carrying a heavy load. He set the brake and throttled up the engines. The aircraft shook, straining against the brakes.

In the hold, Spitting Woman's eyes went wide. "It's okay. It's supposed to shake like that before we take off," shouted Granier, trying to reassure her. She didn't understand a word.

McGoon released the brake.

The plane lunged forward and sped down the runway. Spitting Woman watched out the open doorway as the grass rushed past and the plane accelerated. She had never traveled faster than a canoe in a fast-flowing river. This was a lot faster than that. She was frightened and exhilarated. She reached over and grabbed Granier's hand. "You're alright. You're okay. You might wanna close your eyes for this next part."

He closed his eyes to show her what to do. She didn't understand and kept watching out the doorway.

The plane hit its rotation speed. McGoon lifted it into the air.

Spitting Woman watched in horror as the plane tilted and the ground fell away in the distance. "Oh, well. Too late now," said Granier with a bit of a smile. "That'll teach you to be ornery with me."

She looked at him for assurance. He laughed. She smiled and relaxed a little. Short of being shot at by the Japanese, this was the most exciting thing she had ever done.

Dewey, the Americans, and the Viet Minh waited in the forest below. They could hear the plane's distant engine. Dewey wanted visual contact before popping smoke. The C-3 disguised as a Japanese Showa appeared over the mountain. "That's them," said Dewey. "Pop smoke."

Green pulled the pin on a smoke grenade and threw it into a small clearing in the forest. The smoke rose.

In the cockpit, McGoon spotted the smoke below. "That's them," he said, pointing, as Smitty flipped the signal switch to green.

In the hold, the cargo crew saw the light change from red to green. They pushed the supply containers, their static lines already connected to the overhead wire, out the open doorway as fast as they could.

The containers' parachutes opened as they dropped and they floated gently down to the forest canopy.

Dewey and his men kept their distance and watched. Dewey called out a number and pointed to each container as it descended. Each man or woman in the group took note of where their assigned container fell.

Once the last container crashed through the forest canopy, the Viet Minh took off, each searching for their assigned container hidden among the trees like a giant

Easter Egg hunt.

McGoon banked the plane and came around for a final pass. He watched the terrain passing below and timed his signal so Granier would hit his drop zone near the small clearing.

Inside the hold, Granier finished tying Spitting Woman to his harness. He checked his knots and tugged at the rope to ensure it was secure. Hooking his static line to the overhead wire, he waddled toward the open door.

Spitting Woman was facing him with her arms around his neck as he had shown her. She glanced over her shoulder and saw that he was backing her toward the open door. She panicked. He was trying to kill her. She was sure of it. She grabbed both sides of the doorway. "No. You can't do that," said Granier pulling her hands away. "You said you wanted to jump with me. This is how we do it. It's gonna be okay. Trust me."

She didn't listen and grabbed again for the doorway. The light turned green. Granier kicked his leg bag with rifle bag out the doorway, grabbed her hands, and leaned forward. She yelped as she fell backward out the door with Granier.

She screamed in terror as they fell. The static line pulled the parachute out. There was a flurry of white cloth and suspension cords. She didn't know what was happening. Everything was coming apart as they fell. The parachute popped open with a jerk, and they were floating downward. Slower. Granier was relieved, knowing he would never be able to reach his reserve chute if the main had failed. She looked around, then up at Granier's face. "I told ya it was gonna be okay, didn't I?" said Granier with a reassuring smile.

She relaxed and looked around. She was flying like a bird. Her head jerked from side to side as floated down. She wanted to see everything. She laughed.

It was that moment that Granier knew he was in love with her – a savage – like him. He, showing her the world, she, enchanted like a child on a merry-go-round for the first time. He didn't care what other people thought; only her thoughts were important. He wanted to make her happy.

They crashed through the leafy canopy, and their chute caught on a tree branch dangling them twenty feet above the forest floor. He released the line holding his leg bag, and it dropped a few feet to the ground. He carefully unwrapped the rope as Spitting Woman held onto his neck. He threw one end of the rope around a nearby tree branch and tied it off in a knot. He handed the rope to Spitting Woman. She knew what to do and lowered herself to the ground. Granier released his harness and lowered himself to the ground using the same rope. "You made it," said Dewey appearing through the trees.

"We did. Barely," said Granier.

Dewey could see Spitting Woman limping. "Is she okay?"

"Yeah. She's fine. Just a little mishap with a grenade."

"A grenade?"

"Yeah. No big deal. She's tough."

"And the supplies and weapons?"

"As you ordered, plus food and medicine. There will be a weekly drop."

"Excellent."

"Commander Patti wants that Jap supply train stopped."

"As do we all. So, let's not disappoint him."

The Viet Minh did not open the containers, even though they knew there was food inside them. They were disciplined and knew they needed to get out of the area before the Japanese showed up. They unhooked the parachutes and carried the parachutes and containers back to the village. Dewey was fairly certain his efforts to collect and return the chutes to headquarters would be thwarted once they returned to the village. The Viet Minh liked the way the parachutes felt and would make good use of the material. The way Dewey saw it, the parachutes would be a small price to pay as long as the Viet Minh stopped the Japanese supplies from crossing the border.

The people in the village feasted on the supplies delivered by the Americans. The aroma of rice once again cooking in their pots replaced the sour smell. The people seemed more energetic, even playful. Hoagland dispensed medicine to those that needed it, which was most of the Viet Minh. "How long before they recover?" said Dewey.

"Not long. A week for some. Longer for others. The food will help build up their immune systems. It'll give them a fighting chance," said Hoagland.

"And Mr. Hoo?"

"He's doing much better. He should be up and around in a few days. He could use the fresh air. That cave is like a tomb."

"And is he still onboard?"

"I think so. He hates the Japanese for what they have done to his people."

"His people?"

"Well, they are. I've never seen such loyalty. They revere him like a god."

"I suppose that's good... as long as he's on our side. Honestly, Hoagland, you're beginning to sound like a fan of Mr. Hoo."

"I suppose I am. He's very intelligent and genuinely cares about his people."

"He's a communist."

"Yes, but I don't think it is as much about the ideology as a way to feed his people. I think that is what is important to him. He may be convinced there is another way if it can accomplish his objectives."

"Honestly, I don't care what they believe as long as they help us stop the Japanese. We're fortunate we are soldiers. We can leave the politics to the diplomats."

"He asked me for a copy of the Declaration of Independence."

"I don't see the harm. Give it to him."

"It might do some good."

"You're a dreamer, Hoagland."

Hoagland smiled at the thought.

With a bowl of rice in her hand, Spitting Woman sat down near Granier. She didn't say anything. She didn't need to. Just the fact that she chose to sit near him gave Granier hope. He smiled shyly. She smiled back. He wondered if it was possible to have a real relationship without ever speaking. How could they share their past experiences? How could they explore their common beliefs? He was sure they had figured out how to argue. He knew when she was mad... and even how to calm her. They communicated in their own way, and it worked for now. That was enough. It was a beginning.

The Viet Minh fought well in small fire teams of three or four, especially if the other members of the team were from the same tribe. They could communicate effectively, and they never left a wounded comrade on the battlefield. But the Japanese usually fought in larger units – platoons, companies, and even battalions.

Dewey understood the need to train the Viet Minh as a fighting unit at the company level. They had been lucky in their assault on the Japanese platoon. The Japanese were outnumbered and taken by surprise. Granier's killing the platoon commander at the beginning of the firefight gave the Viet Minh a decisive edge. But the placement of the

Viet Minh forces was unimaginative. They were positioned in one line hidden in the trees. There was no flanking force or reserve. That was a mistake. If the Japanese had survived longer than they did, they could have outflanked the Viet Minh and turned the tide of the battle.

Most Viet Minh were farmers and tradesmen; they knew little about fighting. The idea behind the training was that this core group could teach the other Viet Minh the skills and techniques they had learned – the student continually becoming the teacher until an entire army was trained and ready to fight the Japanese. Dewey was unsure how long the war with the Japanese would last, but he would carry out his orders in this little corner of the world to the best of his ability.

Dewey put himself in charge of training the Viet Minh unit commanders. He would teach his classes under the forest canopy near the village, drawing diagrams in the dirt with a stick to show correct unit formations and tactics.

Giap paid particular attention and translated for the commanders in the group. He had no formal military training and yet was the military leader of the Viet Minh. He had read many historical military books on tactics but most involved much larger armies than the Viet Minh force currently available. As he listened to Dewey, pieces of a puzzle snapped together in his head. His questions were pointed and probing. He caught on quickly, and would often walk back to the village with Dewey after the class to ask more questions. "What determines victory from defeat?" asked Giap as he walked with Dewey.

"Many things. But it is important to remember the goal of battle. It's not to wipe out the enemy entirely. It's to eliminate his will to fight. Battle often gets down to will. Who is willing to continue fighting when all is lost. There are many stories of battles that seemed lost but were eventually won because the soldiers would not give up," said Dewey. "When you fight, and both sides are thrashing each other, remember that your opponent is suffering just as you suffer. They may seem strong in one moment only to become weak and fatigued a few moments later. Victory is won in moments. Sometimes, one final push is all it takes."

"Then, one should never retreat or surrender?"

"No. I wouldn't say that. At times it is better to survive to fight another day. That's what makes a great leader – the ability to know when to press on and when to call it a day and save what you can. You must be brave but also use your head. Always be measuring and calculating. The commander must not fight, but think for his men."

"You have fought in many battles?"

"No. Not many. I served in Europe in the early part of the war. My unit parachuted behind enemy lines during the occupation of Paris. We worked with the French underground to disrupt the German lines of communication and supply. We had a few scraps with the Nazis, but mostly we just skulked around trying not to be discovered while we blew things up. To be honest, war is mostly boredom punctuated by a few moments of terror. At least mine was."

"When the war is won, where will you go?"

"Wherever they tell me. Back to the States, I would imagine. No sense in keeping millions of soldiers on the payroll with no war to fight. And you... when the war is over?"

"I would like to go back to teaching history. But we must defeat the French first if they chose to fight. Do you think they will fight us once the Japanese leave?"

"I don't know. I know they feel Indochina is still theirs, but the war has taken a great toll on France. They may have more important things to tend to... like rebuilding their country."

"I hope so. War is a terrible thing. But we will fight if we must. Independence must be won before I can return to a normal life. We may not get another chance."

Dewey had put Granier in charge of weapons training. Each day he would march one hundred Viet Minh five miles away from the camp, so the practice gunshots would not lead the Japanese to the Viet Minh. Guards were posted in all directions while he instructed them on how to properly fire and maintain their rifles.

Granier showed them how to strip down, clean, and reassemble their rifles. He made them practice the procedure until it was second nature. He would have preferred to blindfold each soldier, so they learned how to disassemble and reassemble their weapons in the dark, but there wasn't time.

There were a lot of Viet Minh to train. Each man was allowed twenty practice shells to improve his accuracy. Granier ensured that the precious ammunition was not wasted. He taught them the five keys to accurate shooting – determining the distance to target, lining up the iron sight while properly adjusting for distance and wind, proper breathing techniques, keeping both eyes open, and squeezing the trigger rather than pulling or jerking it. He broke them into groups of five and watched closely as each soldier took his practice shots. He taught them to quickly clear jams and load their weapon, tapping the shells in a clip on a hard surface to align them properly.

Granier was not a gentle teacher and often cursed at them, but his instructions were clear and correct. By the end of his mini-course, his students knew the basics and could practice on their own. He made himself available whenever anyone had a question. He knew that his life and the lives of his team members would depend on his pupils properly firing their weapons. He wasn't taking any chances.

Soldiers with the best accuracy were singled out for further training as snipers. He had requested seven sniper rifles with scopes to be delivered in one of the upcoming supply drops. In the meantime, he let them practice with his rifle and made damn sure they didn't damage it or drop it in the dirt. Mishandling of his rifle was punished by a swift kick in the ass with his boot. The Viet Minh learned quickly to respect their firearms.

Green taught courses in self-defense and knife-fighting techniques. Santana instructed them in hand signals and small unit tactics. Hoagland trained them in basic first aid and picked out several of the better students to receive further training as medics. Davis broke off a group of what seemed like the most intelligent Viet Minh and taught them in the use of explosives and simple engineering techniques. They would become a team of sappers. And everyone participated in teaching the Viet Minh to march correctly. They were drilled for an hour each morning and an hour at night. Drilling taught them to maneuver as a group, discipline, and unit pride. The Viet Minh would need to become an army, not just a band of rebels, if they were going to defeat the Japanese.

The sun was a diffused ball of light in a gray sky. It was muggy. It had rained most of the afternoon and had just stopped. The grass was wet, and the ground soggy. *Bad footing,* thought Granier as he laid on his belly on the top of a hill, peering through his rifle's scope at the valley below.

A typical Vietnamese village filled much of the valley. Rice farmers tended their crops, pulling young plants from one part of a field and re-planting them in another. Well-trodden paths compressed the top of the dikes that kept the precious rainwater from flowing away. Water buffalo cooled off in knee-deep water. Children played, mostly pretending to be soldiers, using sticks as guns and rocks as grenades. That's what they knew... war. There were huts with thatched roofs and fences made of tree branches to keep the animals out of the gardens. Railroad tracks stretched across the valley floor and split the countryside.

There was a small Japanese outpost with a squad of six soldiers at one end of the valley. Taking it out would be like running over a shallow pothole, an inconvenience at most. Everything was as Granier was told it would be by the Viet Minh scouts. They had excellent intelligence. That's what bothered Granier. It seemed too good. But then again, this was their country.

The supply train will be coming soon, he thought as he shifted his scope's view to a section of track in the middle of the valley. Davis, led by Spitting Woman and escorted by two Viet Minh soldiers, made his way over the dikes and through the fields, keeping out of sight as much as possible. Granier had objected when Dewey ordered a Viet Minh scout rather than him to escort Davis. Dewey's thinking was that the Viet Minh could more easily reassure any Vietnamese that they came in contact with as they approached the target. Granier couldn't do that. He didn't speak Vietnamese and was a foreigner. Granier's assignment was still vital to the success of the mission. He was the overwatch. He could take out any target within the valley with his sniper rifle. If the shit hit the fan, he would become God. Their lives would be in his hands.

Davis waited until nobody was in sight before he emerged from a nearby rice field and ran to the railroad tracks. He removed his pack and opened the top flap. He pulled out his bayonet and dug a hole beneath a rail. The gravel beneath the rails and ties was highly compressed, which made the digging difficult but would make the explosion more powerful by reversing the concussion waves back into the rail. The TNT explosive charges were half-pound rectangular blocks. He had decided that three charges were the appropriate amount to cut the rail efficiently and he added an additional charge for good measure. He didn't like wasting explosives because he never knew when he might be asked to blow something up and he hated to run out. He placed a blasting cap in each of the four charges.

The blasting caps already had electrical wires connected. It was just a matter of twisting the ends of the electrical wires together and connecting to a long wire that would eventually connect to an electronic detonator a safe distance away from the explosion.

When he was satisfied with the wiring, he slid the four TNT blocks beneath the rail. They seemed a perfect size – the width of a rail. The Viet Minh had suggested removing the rail to instigate the train crash, but he knew that to be risky. Although not probable, it was possible that the train would just keep on going, even without the rail, and jump back onto the rail on the other end. They couldn't risk it. An explosion would sever the rail and, just as importantly, curve the severed ends upward so that the broken rail hit the train's wheels as they passed. The train was guaranteed to derail. He buried the four TNT blocks and the wires with the gravel he had dug from the hole so that everything looked normal from a short distance, in case the Japanese squad at the end of the valley decided to inspect the rail before the train passed through. He doubted they would be so diligent, but he didn't want to take any unnecessary chances.

He unspooled the electric wire as he crawled back over the nearest dike and into the rice fields with the two Viet Minh and Spitting Woman. Laying against the opposite slope of the dike, Davis took out the detonator from his pack, gave the handle a half wind, licked his fingers, placed them on the terminals and pushed the detonator's handle to release the charge. It shocked him, burning the tips of his wet fingers. He jerked his hand away. The detonator was working properly. He placed the exposed ends of the wire into the terminals. He would wait to arm it with several twists of the handle. If the train was close and the detonator went off by accident, all would not be lost. He gave a hand signal to Granier who he knew would be watching. He was ready.

Granier was watching through his scope and relayed the message to Dewey and the others with a hand signal. They did not want to attract any attention that might alert the Japanese squad in the valley who might, in turn, warn the engineer when the train arrived.

Dewey checked the Viet Minh positions. There were over four hundred Viet Minh, armed with Japanese rifles, hidden in the trees on the hillside. There were twelve light machine gunners that would take out any enemy machine gun or mortar positions plus lay down covering fire if the demolition team needed to retreat quickly for whatever reason.

A squad of twenty Viet Minh armed with knee mortars was formed into a makeshift artillery battery. They would break from the woods and run down the hillside until they were within range of the train before letting loose their rocket-shaped grenades. Their job was to pin down any Japanese troops that attempted to advance from the train or outpost. Dewey signaled back that the Viet Minh were ready. Now all they needed was the train, due to arrive any minute.

Granier decided to take another peek at the Japanese outpost. He panned his rifle sight over and scanned the area for Japanese soldiers. They were where he had last seen them, milling around the outpost, talking and joking like nothing was amiss. *Good,* thought Granier. *Stay oblivious just a little while longer.*

As he moved his rifle sight back toward the demolition team, something caught his eyes. Five water buffalo were exiting the village. A little girl with a stick directed them to cross the railroad tracks to the side the demolition team was on. She was singing to the water buffalo reassuring them, keeping them calm. It was strange to see the hulking beasts obeying the little girl as if she was their undisputed master. Any one of them could have easily trampled her, but she was unafraid. When one of them veered from the path she wanted them to take, she scolded the disobedient animal and threatened it by shaking her stick. The animal changed its course, and she praised it for being a good water buffalo.

What concerned Granier was that the water buffalo were dragging their hooves on the dirt and gravel alongside the tracks. If they crossed the area where the wire had been buried, they might pull up the wire and even break it. At that moment, Granier heard the sound of the train whistle as it entered the far end of the valley. "Damn it," he said to himself.

He thought for a moment and decided his only option was to shoot the water buffalo if they got too close. That would alert the Japanese outpost, who would alert the train and the whole operation would go down in flames. It might even endanger Spitting Woman and the demolition team who were far closer to the Japanese outpost than any of the other Viet Minh. He decided to make this Davis' problem and let him handle the new threat. The only problem was that Davis and the rest of the demolition team were looking in the direction the approaching train, not at Granier. This was also in the opposite direction to the water buffalo, making them unaware of the approaching animals. There wasn't much time. Granier considered crawling down there and dealing with the problem himself, but he was concerned he might accidentally tip off the Japanese outpost and reveal the demolition team's position.

The train appeared through the trees in the distance. There were nine heavy machine guns surrounded by sandbags on top of the cars pulled by the locomotive. Over one hundred Japanese troops rode on top of the cars where the air was cooler. More were inside the troop cars, reinforcements for the Japanese army in China.

Granier looked around for a way of getting Davis' attention without drawing the attention of the soldiers at the outpost. He spotted one of the Viet Minh riflemen among the trees. He had a bow and a quiver of arrows on his back. Granier was unsure what the man was thinking by bringing the ancient weapon into battle, but then decided it wasn't a half-bad idea. It was a long-range weapon that was silent. He motioned for the bowman to come over by him. The bowman crawled over. Granier pointed to the demolition team, then to the man's arrows. He made the motion for the man to shoot an arrow at the team, but then made the motion not to hit them. He motioned for the arrow to land beside them and get their attention. The bowman nodded that he understood and nocked an arrow onto his bow. He took careful aim and launched the arrow into the sky. To Granier's surprise, the arrow came down exactly where he had motioned, just two feet away from Davis. "Nice shot," said Granier. "He's gonna be pissed."

Davis jerked around when he saw the arrow land next to him. He thought it might have come from the outpost, but he didn't see anyone with a bow. He looked back up the hill and saw Granier signaling him about the approaching water buffalo. He looked over at the water buffalo and nodded that he received the message, then flipped Granier off for shooting an arrow so close to him.

Spitting Woman saw the approaching water buffalo and the little girl. She looked back at the approaching train and decided she must do something. She grabbed Davis empty pack and ran stooped down fifty feet along the dike toward the little girl. "Where the hell you going?" said Davis.

She picked a large rock and placed it in Davis' pack. She moved as far as the intersecting dike wall fifty feet away from the spot where the explosives were placed. She waited until the water buffalo, then the little girl passed. Spitting Woman popped up holding the pack and looking inside like there was something of interest. She made noises like she was very happy and surprised by whatever was in the pack. The little girl stopped and looked at Spitting Woman and the pack. Spitting Woman looked over at the little girl and then pointed into the pack. The little girl stood on her toes to see what was in the pack. Spitting Woman teased her by tilting the pack forward but kept her from seeing the contents. The water buffalo slowed to within ten yards of where the wire was buried and started munching on the grass along the side of the tracks. Spitting Woman motioned for the little girl to look inside the pack. Curiosity got the best of the little girl, and she walked over, climbing up the opposite side of the dike. Spitting Woman leaned the pack forward so the little girl could see the rock inside. The little girl frowned disappointedly. Too late, Spitting Woman reached out and grabbed the little girl pulling her over the dike and to the opposite side. The little girl struggled and screamed. The water buffalo looked over at the commotion for a moment then went back to eating the grass.

The train sped past the Japanese outpost and blew its whistle. The Japanese soldiers at the outpost waved it off like it was nothing, just another routine supply train. The train sped toward the demolition team's position.

One of the water buffalo saw a nice patch of grass next to the train tracks directly across the demolition team's hiding place. It walked over, dragging its hooves.

Granier watched through his scope, horrified. "God damn it," he said to himself as he chambered a round into the rifle and took aim at the water buffalo.

Davis saw the water buffalo too. He glanced at the approaching train. "Close enough," he said, picking up the detonator, twisting the handle three times and yelling, "FIRE IN THE HOLE."

Everyone ducked including Spitting Woman, still holding the little girl.

Davis pushed the handle downward releasing the

spring-loaded magneto and sending a charge through the wire.

The TNT exploded. The water buffalo disappeared in a mist of red. The ground shook. The rail sheered and bent toward the sky. Perfect.

The train engineer saw the explosion and hit the brake. Too late. The engine hit the mangled rail. Its wheels were pulled to the side and derailed, digging into the gravel and wooden ties. The locomotive twisted onto its side, plowed into the soft soil. Spitting Woman heard it coming and looked up. It was heading straight for her and the little girl. She cradled the little girl in her arms and ran through the knee-deep water as fast as she could, the mud below the water sucking at her feet, holding her back, slowing her down.

Granier watched from the hilltop, helpless, through his rifle's scope. He rose up and said, "Oh, God. No!"

The locomotive plowed up the earth as it careened forward. It hit the dike like it was nothing. Tons of soil and water flew into the air. Spitting Woman could feel the earth underneath her feet, moving like some unseen force was reaching up to grab her feet, slow her down, doom her and the little girl. She felt the water rising in the paddy as the locomotive charged forward creating a muddy wave. She leaped as far as she could to one side and dove into the water with the little girl. The locomotive plowed forward to where she had disappeared below the shallow water. It stopped with the loud groan of contracting metal and the hiss of steam rising from the water. The iron beast was dead.

"Please, God. Please," said Granier, almost in tears.

Spitting Woman emerged from the water with the little girl in her arms. She turned to Granier up on the hillside and grinned at him like it was fun and exciting.

Granier fell to his knees, relieved. "Kill me now," he said to nobody in particular.

Davis looked over at Spitting Woman and the little girl and shouted, "Are you alright?"

Spitting Woman nodded, until bits and pieces of water buffalo rained down, pelting everyone.

The Japanese at the outpost, ran forward, wide-eyed. The first seven cars had crashed into the back of the locomotive in a pile-up and fallen on their sides. The rest of the train was jolted to a stop, still on the tracks, useable. The machine gunners on top of the surviving cars had been slammed up against the sandbags but were unhurt. They re-manned their guns and started looking for targets.

Many of the Japanese troops on top of the train tumbled off as the train slammed to a stop. The troops inside the cars didn't fare much better as they were thrown from their seats. There were a few broken arms and legs but most had survived the crash without major injury. Their unit commanders shouted out orders. The soldiers retrieved their rifles and readied themselves for an attack they were sure would follow the derailment.

Granier snapped out of his panic-driven haze, laid back down with his rifle, and used his scope to scan for potential targets near the front of the train where the demolition team was still hidden.

The battery of knee mortar soldiers sprang from their hiding places and ran down the hill to get within range of the train. Once in their final firing positions behind a small rise, they placed the curved-base of their mortars on the ground and lined up their mortars' direction using the simple sight marking on the mortar tube and checked the bubble indicator to ensure their mortars were at the 45-degree angle required. They loaded a grenade-style shell into the top of their mortar tubes and slipped their fingers into the safety rings on their grenade-shells.

On Giap's signal, the Viet Minh opened fire. Four hundred rifles fired in unison, then separately. The light machine gunners hammered out the first thirty rounds in their magazines before reloading. Their focus was the heavy machine gun teams on top of the train.

The knee mortar soldiers pulled the pins on their first grenade-shells and launched them into the sky.

Bullets rained down on the Japanese soldiers in and around the train. Grenade-shells dropped from the sky and exploded. The Japanese returned fire at the hillside. The Viet Minh were hidden and difficult to see; only their muzzle flashes revealed their positions. The Japanese heavy machine guns sprayed the hillside with a barrage of bullets each gun pounding out a tremendous rate of fire.

Granier opened fire, targeting the Japanese soldiers closest to the front of the train. He was systematic – one bullet, one kill. His aim was deadly. Eight Japanese were killed or seriously wounded in the first ten seconds. His rifle's bolt locked back; an empty clip sprang out of the internal magazine. He pushed in another clip, released the rifle's bolt chambering the next shell, sighted his next target with the scope and opened fire once again. The entire process of reloading took less than three seconds. Rehearsed butchery. With each discharge of his weapon, more Japanese dropped, out of the fight.

The squad of Japanese soldiers at the outpost took cover and joined their comrades firing on the hillside. They did not notice the Viet Minh moving upon their flank. Green and Santana led the Viet Minh soldiers, each commanding an oversized platoon of fifty soldiers. With the Japanese pinned down and focused on the hillside, their mission was to roll up the flank. It was a simple tactic but very effective – by attacking the side of the enemy's line, their opponents could not mass fire like a frontal attack. The two platoons would fire on ten to twenty Japanese soldiers instead of hundreds. Once the enemy's resistance faded, they moved to the next cluster of enemy troops and renewed their assault. Classic. Deadly. The Japanese outpost was wiped out in less than a minute. The Viet Minh advanced on the back of the train.

Granier ran low on targets at the front of the train. He had lost count, but he imagined he had taken out twenty-one to twenty-four Japanese soldiers based on the bodies lying around the train and the empty clips on the ground beside him. Granier didn't think about the lives he had extinguished. He was too focused on his mission. He was given a goal, he developed a plan of action, and he carried it out until success was achieved. Humanity had nothing to do with it. He wasn't cold-hearted or vindictive. He was efficient.

Glancing over at the Viet Minh on the hillside, he could see that they were taking a beating from the Japanese heavy machine guns. Over a dozen Viet Minh lay dead. He changed his target-acquisition to the heavy machine gun teams on top of the train cars. They were well protected by sandbags. They were more difficult targets than the riflemen near the front of the train. Each machine gun team had three members – a gunner, a feeder, and a loader. He needed to take out two to disable the crew and silence the weapon. A single soldier could fire the machine gun, but it would quickly jam unless the bullet belts were fed into the bolt correctly. The gun's oil reservoir also needed a constant resupply of oil, or it would overheat and jam. That, and lugging over the heavy ammunition boxes, were the loader's job.

Granier recalibrated his scope. Each of the machine

gun positions was farther and farther away, making each shot more and more difficult. He began. His first three shots found their targets, successfully killing all three Japanese soldiers operating the closest machine gun. He moved to the next machine gun position and took aim at the gunner. He felt a slight breeze on the side of his face. *Wind. Not good. Changes things,* he thought. The problem was that he didn't know how much it would affect his aim. He fired. The first shot missed. He readjusted. Fired again. Hit the loader in the back several feet behind the gunner. He cursed. That wasn't where he was aiming. But now at least he knew where his bullet had landed. His scope was way off. He adjusted the knobs. He fired again and hit the gunner in the eye. *About time,* he thought. He decided to kill the feeder too since he couldn't tell how bad the loader was hit. He was still moving behind the gunner, now dead. As the feeder pulled the gunner off the weapon, Granier fired again, hitting him in the side of the neck. He went down behind the sandbags. *Good enough,* he thought. *Move on.*

Granier continued aiming, firing, adjusting, firing again, until he had taken out four of the machine guns. The machine guns positioned on the back of the train were an additional one hundred yards in distance and very difficult to hit. He became frustrated. Sweating, his fingers became slippery. His confidence waned, cursing after each shot he missed. He stopped. It took a moment to calm himself. He took two deep breaths and started again. He aimed and fired, hitting the feeder. He wasn't aiming for him, but at that point, any kill was a win. He continued to fire until he hit the gunner. *Good. Move on,* he thought.

He reloaded. It occurred to him he hadn't checked on the demolition team in a few minutes. He moved his scope back to their position. They were gone. He swung it over to where Spitting Woman and the little girl had hidden. They were gone too. He tried not to panic. He scanned the area and saw the little girl frantically trying to herd the surviving water buffalo away from the train wreck and back to her village. She was alright. The Japanese weren't interested in her.

He let his eye leave the scope and raised his head to look down at the rice paddies below the hill where he spotted the demolition team. One of the two Viet Minh soldiers had been hit badly in the back. Spitting Woman and the other soldier were helping him run through a rice field. They stayed low. Davis was behind them defending the rear with his rifle. He was firing his weapon at three Japanese soldiers laying on the opposite side of the dike, firing their weapons at the fleeing demolition team. *Damn it. They must've been hiding,* he thought.

Granier looked back through his scope and aimed. He knew his aim would be off because the scope was set for a farther distance. He fired and watched for a bullet hit anywhere so he could make the proper adjustments. He saw nothing. His scope was way off. He adjusted the sight to where he thought it should be set, took aim, and fired again. He saw a bit of mud kick up like a tiny explosion. A bullet hit. He adjusted his scope again.

Granier took aim, took a breath, let half of it out, and squeezed the trigger. He watched through the scope as the head of one of the Japanese slumped down into the mud. *One.* He moved to the next soldier, took aim and fired. *Two.* The third soldier had seen enough as his two comrades had died in a matter of seconds from each other. He jumped up from his position and ran back toward the cover of the train. Granier fired. The man's back arched and he fell. *Three.*

Spitting Woman and Davis looked back at the dike and the three dead Japanese. They looked up at the hillside and saw Granier behind his rifle, watching over them. They were safe. They made their way back to the Viet Minh lines.

With the demolition team safe, Granier once again went back to taking out the Japanese machine gun positions on the train. He readjusted his scope and fired until he killed two more Japanese soldiers – a gunner and a loader. The machine gun went silent.

The gunfire from the train had slackened. There were a lot of Japanese bodies hanging from windows and laying on the ground.

Giap and Dewey watched from the hillside. "Affix bayonets!" yelled Giap to his men.

The Viet Minh riflemen stopped firing their rifles and attached their bayonets to the end of their barrels.

The light machine gunners and knee mortar grenadiers continued to keep the Japanese pinned down.

Green and Santana continued with the Viet Minh to attack the Japanese flank, chipping away, cutting them down.

When the riflemen on the hillside were ready, Giap yelled, "Bayonets at the ready! Advance!"

Four hundred Viet Minh rose up and emerged from the trees with their rifles held forward at the ready. It was an awesome sight.

Many of the surviving Japanese stopped firing and looked to each other, wondering what to do. They were vastly outnumbered. The remaining heavy machines guns continued to fire, but they too were being picked off one by one by some unseen force.

Giap yelled again as the Viet Minh reached the bottom of the hill and moved into the rice fields, "Double time!"

The Viet Minh increased their speed to a moderate trot, splashing up water and mud, moving forward, unstoppable.

Giap could see the Japanese in the distance, staring at his advancing troops. He could feel them breaking. "Charge!" he yelled at last.

The Viet Minh yelled an angry cry as they broke into a

run toward the train, determined and terrifying.

At first, only a few Japanese abandoned their positions and ran in the opposite direction, hoping to reach the safety of the mountains before the Viet Minh caught up with them. Moments later, it was a complete rout. Even the machine gun teams jumped down from the train and ran.

The Viet Minh overran the train, killing anyone brave enough to stand and fight. There weren't many. The Viet Minh ran after the Japanese for another two hundred yards and stopped as their commanders had instructed them. They fired their rifles, hitting a few stragglers. The rest were left to flee. They would fight another day. The Viet Minh had their victory. That was enough. The Viet Minh cheered. Giap and Dewey didn't want to take any unnecessary risks with their fledgling army. They knew that Japanese planes could show up at any minute and tip the scales of the battle. They needed to empty the train of supplies and move back into the safety of the forest.

Granier stood up and walked down the hill. Spitting Woman was sitting, catching her breath. She rose up. Their eyes met – hers grateful, his relieved. Granier was through playing games. He walked over and hugged her. She hugged him back. Neither wanted to let go.

FOUR

It was night, but the Viet Minh were in no mood to sleep, even after the long day. They were celebrating. Dancing. Drinking. Recounting the stories of their victory. Laughing and joking. With the weapons and supplies they had looted from the train, they could grow their army to three times its current size. There was a feeling that this was just the beginning. They were taking back their country.

Giap had agreed to one single fire in the center of the village so they could roast the pigs they had looted from the train. It was risky, but it had been so long since these people had something to celebrate. He allowed the fire, but only if they kept several containers of water nearby in case they heard a plane's engine and needed to put it out in a hurry.

Dewey was walking through the camp when he saw Santana and Green squatting on the ground with twenty Viet Minh crowded around six squares drawn in the dirt. In each square was a simple drawing of a crab, a deer, a chicken, a fish, a shrimp or a gourd. The Americans and Viet Minh tossed down cigarettes or clay pipes filled with smoking herbs as bets on the squares. A dealer rolled three dice. "Santana, a word," said Dewey.

Santana retrieved his bet of a cigarette from one of the squares and rose. "Yes, commander?" said Santana.

"What are you doing?"

"It's a Viet game called 'Bau Cua.' Kinda like roulette."

"Are you winning?"

"Not so far."

"Then you are unlucky."

"Yeah, I guess so."

"How do you expect to keep the respect of the Viet Minh if they see you as unlucky?"

"I don't know. I guess I really hadn't thought about it that way. We were just celebrating and trying to make friends. I thought it would be good for morale."

"The Viet Minh are not our friends. They are our allies. Very important allies we need to complete our mission. We must keep their respect. The Viet Minh are very superstitious. They hold strong beliefs in things like ghosts, omens, and luck."

"Yes, Commander. I see your point."

"Good. Let Green know my thoughts, will you?"

"Of course, Commander. Right away."

"It's okay to have a little fun. We just need to be careful of the image we project to these people... for the sake of the mission."

Santana nodded, and Dewey moved off.

Hoagland climbed up to the cave. He had several pieces of barbequed pork that he hoped Ho could eat. Ho was getting stronger by the day, but he still was fighting malaria. The medic found his patient awake, listening to the celebration. "It was a great victory," said Hoagland as he entered.

"You were there?" said Ho.

"I watched from the hillside. Your Viet Minh fought bravely."

"Of course. It is what is expected of them."

"How do you do that?"

"Do what?"

"Expectations. They don't want to disappoint you. They'd die for you."

"They would die for the cause. It's not about me."

"Somehow I think you're wrong."

"I am a symbol. Nothing more."

"You're the one that's holding them together. You give them hope. You inspire them."

"If it weren't me, it would be someone else. They hope because that is all they have. What future do their children have without freedom?"

"They've lived under the French for almost two hundred years."

"They've died under the French for almost two hundred years. Enough. My people have paid the price for freedom. It's time."

"I hope you get it... freedom."

"We shall. It is only a matter of time and will. The time has come, and we have the will."

"I doubt the French will just up and leave."

"We don't plan on giving them a choice."

"More blood?"

"If need be. When this war ends, we will have a great opportunity to drive all the invaders from our land. We will not let it pass even if it means more blood will be spilled. We will reach out and grab our liberty like a great golden ring. It is ours for the taking."

Hoagland smiled, "As I said, you offer them such inspiration."

"I am afraid it will take more than inspiration. But still... I do what I can. Will you help me up, Doctor?"

"Of course."

Hoagland helped Ho from his bed and walked with his arm around the small man's waist toward the cave entrance. "Are you sure you are up to this?" said Hoagland feeling how frail Ho was, his steps tentative.

"In war and politics, timing is everything."

"Which is this?"

"Both."

The cave was above the river and village. Ho stopped at the opening. "Thank you, Doctor. I will take it from here."

"Of course. I will be right back here if you need me," said Hoagland.

"I know you will, and it gives me strength just knowing that you are there."

Ho walked slowly out onto the ledge in front of the cave. The fire in the village illuminated his face as he looked down.

A woman saw him first. She stopped dancing, and her eyes went wide. "Uncle," she said in a hushed tone, looking up at the frail man.

The people around her turned on hearing those words and looked up. They repeated the word, "Uncle," some cried, many knelt. The news rippled through the village like a rock in a lake. A great silence settled over the crowd as all eyes looked up.

Ho just stood there, looking out as his people, the proud eyes of a father. "Victory," he said as loud as he possibly could, raising both his hands above his head. He could feel himself shaking.

The crowd roared and chanted "Uncle" at the top of their lungs.

Hoagland could see that Ho was unsteady and moved forward to help him, to keep him from falling into the river below. Ho warned him off with a shake of his head and steadied himself, smiling.

Dewey moved up beside Giap and said, "That man is who the Japanese should fear most."

"That man is who everyone should fear most," said Giap, grinning, joining the chant, yelling "Uncle. Uncle. Uncle."

Granier was away from the celebration, alone. He was kneeling on a blanket, cleaning and reassembling his rifle as he always did after a mission. Finished, he pulled the action back two times to check its function. Perfect. He smiled to himself, satisfied. He looked up to see Spitting

Woman standing before him, her back to the celebration. She glowed from the fire behind her in the distance. She didn't move. He set his rifle down on the blanket and rose his feet. Their eyes met. She looked strangely shy like she was unsure of what he wanted. He stepped forward and kissed her deeply. She kissed back, wrapping her arms around his neck as she had done when they parachuted together. She was wearing her pack. She stopped kissing him, let go of his neck and walked into the forest, looking back as if inviting him. He picked up his rifle and followed her.

She led him to a clearing covered with ferns deep in the forest. The moon was visible through an opening in the canopy. She removed her pack and pulled out a blanket. She spread it on the ground. She looked at him as if asking if this was okay. He said nothing, unsure what she meant. She opened the top of her shirt and let it drop to the ground. Then she loosened the string around her waist and stepped out of the bottoms of her black pajamas, revealing her naked body. She had scars, some from battle, others from life.

Granier thought her beautiful. She stepped forward and unbuttoned his shirt and kissed him on his chest. He too had scars. She pulled him down onto the blanket, and they made love.

Dewey and the Deer Team met with Giap and his commanders in the forest under a camouflaged net. They wanted privacy. Giap trusted his people. Dewey was more skeptical. "Anyone can betray their country given the right set of circumstances and motivation. Better to be safe than sorry," he would say. They decided to locate their planning conferences away from the village and post guards. Giap was the only English-speaker among the Viet Minh and translated between the Americans and his commanders. It made the process slower, but prevented confusion. "What is the latest troop count?" said Dewey.

"Nine hundred and fifty-two are combat-ready. Another seven hundred and forty-six are still in basic training or waiting for weapons," said Giap's Executive Officer.

"That's good. That's very good. We should be able to expand our operations to attack more targets. The problem, of course, is officers. Have you made any progress in the development of officers?"

"It is difficult. Our people are brave and good warriors, but they are not educated."

"I understand. Hoagland, how is your translation of the training manuals coming along?"

"As good as can be expected. Very few Vietnamese speak, and even fewer write rudimentary English. Most of the work still falls in my lap. Mr. Hoo helps when he can, but his duties often call him elsewhere. A typewriter with Vietnamese characters would speed up the work," said Hoagland.

"I didn't know you typed."

"I don't, but I will learn."

"We'll add it to our supply request, but it may take the quartermaster some time to find one. In the meantime, keep at it."

"Yes, sir. Oh, and please don't forget to ask for extra typewriter ribbon and carbon paper."

"Of course. Mr. Green, how go your small unit tactic lectures?"

"Good. They're naturals and catch on quick. It's like someone already taught them this stuff, and I'm just reminding them," said Green.

"Someone did," said Giap. "The Chinese were training us in our struggle against the French."

The members of the Deer Team were uneasy on hearing of the Viet Minh war with their French allies. "What happened?" said Dewey.

"The Japanese invaded, and the focus of the Chinese

shifted elsewhere. As you say, they had their own problems."

"Right," said Dewey. "Well, it certainly shows. Many of your men are experienced fighters. They can teach others. You might consider breaking up your core group and placing the veterans in with the new recruits. It would help with training and boost morale."

"We have already begun the process," said Giap. "It is our culture that the old teach the young."

"Excellent. Alright, I think that about wraps it up. Please forward your supply requests to Mr. Santana. He is compiling our list for the next drop. Mr. Van and I will be finishing our plans for the next mission shortly. You will be informed individually as to your units' assignments."

The meeting broke up with a salute between the Americans and the Viet Minh commanders.

McGoon and Smitty piloted the C-3 disguised as a Japanese transport plane. The dense forest swept below them. Smitty pointed to the smoke from the Deer Team on the ground. "Here we go, boys," McGoon said over the plane's intercom.

In the hold, the cargo crew lined up the supply containers checking to ensure their static lines were not tangled. The drop light changed from red to green. It was a race to get the containers out the open doorway at the back of the plane.

Through the forest canopy below, the Deer Team and the Viet Minh watched as the supply containers left the plane and popped their chutes. They floated down until they crashed through the branches and leaves of the canopy. Many were stuck high in the trees. The Viet Minh scrambled up the tree trunks and cut the container free from their parachutes. The containers crashed to the ground. The Viet Minh picked them up, gathering them together in a forest clearing.

In the distance, a Japanese scout watched the circling plane dropping containers into the forest. The Japanese markings on the plane didn't fool him. He knew it was American. He had been sent to find it. He radioed his discovery.

Dewey supervised the container count. They were still short three containers according to the manifest he had been radioed. Viet Minh teams were out looking for them. Granier and the other Deer Team members were providing security, keeping their eyes on the surrounding forest.

Something caught Granier's eye. He turned and studied the trees. Something moved again. "The remaining Viet Minh teams are to the west, aren't they?" said Granier, his eyes never leaving the area he was watching.

"Yes. Why?" said Dewey.

"I've got movement."

Dewey stopped what he was doing and moved up to Granier's side. "Where?"

"Two o'clock. One hundred and fifty yards out."

Dewey looked out, squinting. "I don't see it."

"Wait for it."

Dewey continued watching. After a few moments, he saw something move and then something else. It was hard to make out, but it didn't matter. Anything that moved was a threat. "Santana, call in the Viet Minh search teams. We'll come back for the containers later. Hoagland, ask the commander to bring his men up and take—"

Dewey never finished his sentence before all hell broke loose. Several light machine guns opened fire on the Deer Team. Everyone hit the ground and scrambled for whatever cover they could find – a fallen tree trunk, overgrown roots, groupings of rocks - anything that would stop a bullet. Mortar rounds rained down, exploding. A Viet Minh soldier suffered a direct hit from a mortar shell.

His arm still holding his rifle landed on the ground. The rest of him was gone.

A company of Japanese soldiers advanced through the trees, firing their weapons. The Deer Team and the Viet Minh returned fire, driving them to cover. "Santana, get that American pilot on the radio and warn him we have made contact with the enemy and are under attack," said Dewey.

"I don't understand. It's a cargo plane. He's unarmed," said Santana.

"The Japanese will be hunting for him."

"Right. I didn't think about that. I'm on it."

"Hoagland, are the Viet Minh teams back yet?"

"They're on their way. Three minutes," said Hoagland firing his rifle.

"They damn well better hurry. We're outnumbered. The Japs'll flank us if we wait much longer. Tell the Viet Minh to leave the containers when we pull back."

"I don't think they'll do it."

"What do you mean?"

"It's food for their families. They won't leave it."

"Tell 'em we'll get them more food."

"I'll try."

Hoagland moved back to find the Viet Minh commander. He found him on the ground, badly wounded, out of the fight. Hoagland moved to tend to him. He relayed the order to leave the containers to the next in command. The commander shook his head 'no.' Hoagland cursed and threatened him. He nodded okay.

Dewey crawled to the firing positions, checking on each member of his team. He came to Granier, firing, aiming, firing. "Buck, find the Jap commanders and take 'em out."

"I'm on it," said Granier firing his sniper rifle, searching for anyone that resembled an officer or a sergeant, firing again and again, dropping Japanese, holding them at a distance. "Deer Team, we will fall back to the far side of the clearing on my 'Go,' then cover the Viet Minh retreat when the rest of their search teams arrive," said Dewey.

"We can't leave 'em," said Granier. "They wouldn't leave us."

"We are not leaving them. We will cover their withdrawal when they are ready."

"Let me stay. I can hold them off while the Viet Minh withdraw."

"No. You will withdraw with your team. That's an order."

"How are they supposed to trust us if we don't stand by them in a fight?"

"God damn it, Buck. This is not up for debate. It's their fight. You will withdraw on my order."

Granier locked eyes with Dewey, both men were angry. Granier begrudgingly nodded his acceptance and went back to firing his rifle, killing as many enemies as he could before he was forced to leave. "Deer Team, GO!" said Dewey.

The members of the Deer Team withdrew, firing their weapons. Hoagland lifted the Viet Minh commander to his feet and helped him retreat. Granier stayed for a moment longer, not firing, waiting, peering through his scope...

He had spotted the Japanese company commander far back from the front line hidden behind a tree. Granier watched as his head popped out for a moment, then disappeared again. "Buck, move your ass!" said Dewey.

"Just a sec," said Granier, staying focused.

"I said NOW!"

Granier watched as the commander's head again popped from behind the tree. Granier squeezed the trigger, and his rifle fired. Through his scope, he watched as the commander's head disappeared in a spray of red mist. Granier crawled backward with his rifle then climbed into a squat and retreated with the other Deer Team members. They continued to fire their weapon as they moved back to the edge of the clearing.

Dewey was furious. "I thought I made myself clear."

"You ordered me to kill the Jap company commander."

"You got him?"

"As ordered."

"Right. Good work."

The Japanese assault lost energy once their company commander was killed. They did not advance further.

The Viet Minh search teams rejoined their main force. Ignoring Dewey's orders, they grabbed the supply containers and carried them back through the clearing past the Americans providing covering fire. Hoagland shrugged to Dewey.

"Hell of a way to run an army," said Dewey.

The Viet Minh and the Deer Team pulled back and traveled in the opposite direction of the village. When they were certain that the Japanese were not following, they changed direction and made their way back to the Viet Minh village. Granier stayed far behind scouting the rear thoroughly, making sure they were safe.

McGoon and Smitty were three miles to the border when two Japanese Zeros dropped out of the clouds above. They were part of an entire squadron that had been searching for his aircraft, knowing that the transport plane would be short on fuel and would need to cross the border sooner rather than later.

McGoon and Smitty did not see the pair of Japanese fighters as they dove. But they saw the tracer bullets from their machine guns as they flew past the cockpit windows. "Ah, shit!" said McGoon banking the plane sharply, pushing it into a steep dive, increasing its speed. He kept a close watch on the altimeter and airspeed. He needed to cut it as close as he dared, but not too close. "You got 'em?" he said.

"Portside, four o'clock I think," said Smitty.

"Not a good time to be guessing something like that."

"I can't tell. They keep weaving back and forth."

"Sneaky bastards. Alright. You ready?"

"Ready."

"Now," said McGoon pulling out of the dive, Smitty helping with the controls.

They were only a hundred feet above the forest canopy when the plane leveled. The two Zeros easily pulled out of the dive and tailed the transport plane. "They're still behind us," said Smitty.

"Ya know, they should really give us some weapons on these things," said McGoon.

"They're Zeros, McGoon," We can't fight 'em," said Smitty.

"Yeah, well... It's better than getting treated like a pin cushion."

The lead Zero fired. The bullet ripped into the left-wing and hit the engine. A stream of black smoke poured out.

The plane shuttered, losing power. "That can't be good," said McGoon as he tried banking the aircraft to shake off the fighter. "This is ridiculous. I got nothing."

"Maybe we could jump."

"We're too low, and you know it. We'd be squashed flatter than a pancake before our chutes opened."

"It was just a thought."

"Leave the thinking to me, will ya?"

More bullets ripped through the plane's fuselage as the second Zero took its turn. Sparks flew as the avionics in the cockpit were hit. "Mary, mother of Jesus. Give me a minute to think, will ya?" said McGoon angrily. "Even a condemned man is supposed to get a last wish."

McGoon spotted something and said, "And that is mine."

"What's yours?" said Smitty, confused.

"That," said McGoon point through the windshield at a riverbed. "Radio a 'mayday' and warn the boys in back we're landing."

"On that?!" said Smitty, wide-eyed.

"You betcha."

"You want me to deploy the landing gear?"

"Nope. You ever do a belly-flop?"

"No."

"Then this will be your first. Good luck."

Smitty warned the cargo crew that it was going to be a rough landing, then radioed a 'Mayday.' Finished, he turned back to McGoon and said, "So, what's the plan assuming we survive the landing?"

"One bridge at a time, good fellow. I'm gonna need both hands on the wheel, so you're gonna need to cut the engines when I say."

"Alright. You sound like maybe you're done this before."

"Nope. Never."

The Japanese fighters opened fire again as McGoon dove down to the riverbed. More bullets ripped into the wing and hit the one good engine. It caught fire. "See, we were going down anyway. We just beat 'em to the punch," said McGoon. "Alright, cut the engines."

Smitty reduced the throttles to zero.

The engines sputtered to a stop. The propellers kept moving, driven by momentum. The plane dropped to the water. Just before hitting, McGoon pulled the nose up, and the plane's belly hit first. The Japanese Zeros zoomed overhead, surprised by the move. The plane skimmed across the water effortlessly until it hit a sandbar sticking out into the river. The plane came to an abrupt stop, its nose digging into the sand and rock, its tail lifting into the air, then slamming down.

The pilots of the Zeros banked hard and came around to strafe the downed aircraft and its crew.

McGoon and Smitty scrambled out of their seats and

into the cargo hold where the rest of the crew was waiting. "Okay. Next bridge. What do we do?" said Smitty.

"I'm thinking. Let me think," said McGoon.

He ran to the back door and looked out. "Alright. Here's what we are gonna do. They're gonna fire on the plane. Once they start, we're gonna run for those trees over there," he said pointing. "Everybody on board?"

The crew nodded, too afraid to speak. They heard the machine guns rattling as the bullets hit the hold, popping holes through the outer skin, sunlight streaming into the dark hold. "Run!" said McGoon, the first out the door.

The Japanese pilots were unable to adjust their fire as they watched the Americans sprint from the downed aircraft.

McGoon made it to the trees and collapsed out of breath. It was more running than he had done since basic training. The others followed, diving into the trees. Safe. "Yeah. Fuck you, Tojo!" yelled McGoon as the Zeros passed overhead.

The Zeros banked hard again.

"Oh shit, they're coming back," said Smitty.

"You really need to stop with the negative attitude, ya know that?" said McGoon. "Everybody just hunker down. Most Japs are lousy shots."

"Most?" said Smitty.

"Enough with the negativity, Smitty. Can't ya see I'm trying to keep morale high with the crew?"

The Americans watched as the Zeros leveled out of their turn and lined up to shoot into the trees. "Damn. I wish I had a bazooka or something," said McGoon.

The lead Zero opened fire. Bullets hit the sand thirty yards away and sped toward the Americans' hiding place. "Oh, shit," said McGoon.

Suddenly, the lead Zero exploded and crashed into the river. The Zero following pulled out and banked hard, heading back the way it came. A few seconds later, six Hawker fighters with shark's teeth painted on the front of their fuselages zoomed overhead. It was a flight of the Flying Tigers chasing after the remaining Zero.

McGoon jumped up and pumped his fist, "Yeah. Flying Tigers! You'd better run, you nip bastard!"

The crew of the downed plane breathed a collective sigh of relief. "Ya see. Positivity wins out every time," said McGoon with a shit-eating grin.

Nobody cared. They were just happy to still be alive.

When the Viet Minh returned to their camp, Granier went off by himself. He was angry and decided it would be better if he didn't see Spitting Woman right away. He missed her, but he didn't want her to see him in a foul mood. He knew he could be difficult to get along with at times and didn't want to overwhelm her this early in their relationship. *Relationship?* he thought. *Hell, I can't even talk to her. She just grunts in response.*

He grabbed his blanket, gun oil, rag, and screwdriver from his pack and carried his rifle into the woods. He laid out the blanket, knelt and went to work stripping down his rifle for a post-combat cleaning. He did not rush cleaning his weapon. He was meticulous as always, taking his time to make sure each part was cleaned of any gunpowder residue or dirt. He grumbled to himself as he worked. He was pissed at Dewey for abandoning the Viet Minh. He knew Dewey had his reasons, but he didn't like the way it looked. Americans were not cowards, especially these Americans.

After a moment, he felt a hand on his shoulder. He jerked around to see a woman's hand. The dirt under her fingernails looked familiar. It was Spitting Woman. She chose to say nothing as she rubbed his shoulders. It felt good. He calmed. *How did she know?* he thought. She slid her hand beneath his uniform and rubbed his chest. She kissed him on the back of the neck. Cleaning his weapon seemed less important at that moment. He pulled her around into his lap, looked into her eyes, and kissed her. Slowly at first, then passionately. His anger was gone.

Dewey was furious when he met with Giap in the forest. "We were betrayed. You have a spy among your people."

"Why are you so sure the information came from my people?" said Giap. "You radioed your headquarters in China and discussed the location of the drop zone. The Japanese could have been listening."

"We broadcast in code."

"They could have broken your code."

"That's highly unlikely."

"So is betrayal from the Viet Minh. Most of our people come from the same group of villages. If they passed information on to the enemy, they would be endangering their own families."

"Then how do you explain an entire company of Japanese soldiers knowing the exact location of the supply drop? They didn't just stumble upon us."

"No, of course not. I agree. Someone passed on the information. I am just not convinced of the source."

"Well you damn well better find the leak, or we're all dead."

"I would say the same to you."

"This is hopeless. We will not solve the problem if you fail to listen to reason," said Dewey dismissing Giap with a wave of his hand, walking away in frustration.

Granier shaved with a safety razor and a bar of soap. It had been a while. The members of OSS Teams in the field were allowed to grow beards to conserve time and water. When he finished, he wiped away the excess soap and studied his face in the small mirror he used for signaling. His clean-shaven face revealed some scars. They were small but noticeable. He wondered what Spitting Woman saw in him but then decided not to think about it. It was wasted effort. She liked him. That was enough.

Granier walked over a series of rocks to the opposite side of the stream that divided the village. He climbed up a path covered with freshly cut grass that kept it hidden and entered the mouth of a large cave. It was smoky inside. The sun filtered through the tree canopy above and formed shafts of light. There was one fire burning in the center of the cave used for cooking and boiling water, shared by the community that lived inside.

A baby cried for a moment but was silenced when its mother placed her breast in its mouth. It was important to keep the children quiet while in the cave. Over twenty families were living together. They were from the same hill tribe. They stayed together. They trusted one another; they depended on one another. Granier understood this. They were a pack.

Spitting Woman was helping her sister-in-law prepare the evening meal over the fire when she saw Granier. She walked over to him and folded his hand into hers. She said nothing as she escorted him through the cave, past the curious eyes and whispers of the other tribe members. Near the back of the cave was where her immediate family lived. There was no furniture beyond several hand-woven blankets on the ground and a dozen baskets that stored food, medicinal herbs, and extra clothing. The area was neatly organized, and the blankets appeared to have been recently beaten to rid them of dust and dirt. Preparations had been made for their guest – Granier.

Spitting Woman stopped at the edge of the blankets and kicked at Granier's muddy boots. She said something. He didn't know what she was saying, but she seemed pretty adamant about whatever it was. "You want me to take them off?" said Granier.

She kicked his boots again and gave him an angry look. Granier removed his boots. She picked up the dirty boots and set them to one side. She seemed satisfied and led him onto the blankets. She placed Granier in the center of the blankets and backed away so her family could get a good look at him. Nobody said anything. They just stared. Some grunted. He felt naked and uncomfortable. Granier didn't like attention.

After a few moments, Spitting Woman moved next to Granier. She motioned to each of the family members, starting with the oldest and said something that he imagined was their name or their relation to her, or it didn't matter because they meant the same thing. He tried to follow along and memorize each name, but gave up when he discovered they all sounded the same. There were two older women and one older man. He imagined they were her parents, but he wasn't sure which one was her mother, or maybe she considered both of them her mothers or one was her mother and the other her grandmother. It was hard to tell. They were very wrinkled. He was pretty sure the man was her father although he could have been her grandfather because his face resembled a leather bag and he was missing most of his teeth. There were brothers and brothers-in-law, sisters and sisters-in-law, what seemed to be cousins, nephews and nieces. He was totally confused until she came to the final two children to be introduced – a boy about five and a girl about three. She took each by the hand and placed them in front of her. "Oh, my God. You're their mother," said Granier, completely surprised.

Spitting Woman frowned. That was not the reaction she was hoping for. He recognized his faux pau and squatted before them. He studied their faces. The little girl looked very much like her mother, but the boy looked like someone else. It occurred him that they had a father and he wondered where he was. "Their father...? Are you married?" he asked a bit frighten by the potential answer.

Spitting Woman struggled to understand what he wanted. After a moment, it occurred to her that he was asking about their father. She made the motion of Japanese by putting her fingers to her eyes at a forty-five-degree angle, then the gesture of an imaginary rifle firing and finally the gesture of death using her tongue hanging out the side of her mouth and her eyes rolled back. "I'm sorry for your loss," said Granier, even though he wasn't.

He felt bad that he didn't have anything for the children. He wanted them to like him. It occurred to him that he did have a fresh pack of chewing gum, but wondered if they were too young. He decided to risk it. He pulled the pack out, opened it, and offered a stick to the children. "You chew it," said Granier gesturing he was chewing an imaginary stick.

Spitting Woman took one of the sticks and tore it in half, giving each of the children a piece. They put it in their mouths, chewed it four times and swallowed. "No, no. You chew it," said Granier, too late.

Ignoring the crazy American, Spitting Woman took the pack from his hand and offered everyone a piece by tearing the individual sticks in halves and thirds depending on the seniority of the family member with the father-figure getting a whole piece. They all followed the children's example, chewed each piece four times and swallowed. "That's not the way you do it," said Granier, frustrated. "Nevermind."

It didn't matter. Everyone was happy, and he was a good guest for bringing desert. The women said something to the group, and everyone sat in a circle on the blankets. Spitting Woman's son and daughter sat next Granier. He wasn't sure what he should do but figured they were little and couldn't be that hard to watch while their mother and her sister-in-law went to the fire to retrieve the food. The two children sat patiently. He was surprised by how well behaved they were even when their mother wasn't within swatting distance.

A clay pot filled with hot stew was placed in the center on three rocks that kept the blankets from burning. Joining the stew was a large green leaf on which sat two dozen skewers of roasted insect larvae and bugs. A large wooden bowl of rice was the last dish. The starch aroma rose with the steam and gave everyone a good appetite. The family used wooden bowls and their fingers to grab what they wanted. A wooden spoon was used to ladle the stew onto the rice in each bowl.

Granier saw a chicken head along with what looked like root-type vegetables and congealed blood cut into cubes scooped into his bowl on top of a healthy portion of rice. He was also given two skewers - roasted grasshoppers and silkworm larvae. He was their guest and deserved the best. He had considered what he might be served and what was in his bowl was a pleasant surprise. He had an active imagination. He ate everything in his bowl and on the skewers, licking his fingers when he was finished to show that he liked it. Over the short time he had known her, Granier had learned that Spitting Woman had four moods – angry, frustrated, satisfied and leave me alone I am busy. At that moment, she was satisfied. For Granier, that was enough.

Spitting Woman rose early the next morning and walked into the woods with a basket on her arm. It was peaceful. She enjoyed being by herself, away from her children and family. She liked spending time with the American, but even he could not fill her need to be alone in the forest. She believed in the forest and thought the trees and animals had powerful spirits. She only took what her family needed, never anything more, and nothing was wasted.

The Viet Minh had stripped the trees and bushes around the camp of everything that was edible. She knew she would need to travel a bit to find what she was looking to gather. She found it after walking a little more than a mile – longan – a soapberry fruit like lychee, smooth-skinned and light brown in color. It was high in a tree, well beyond the reach of someone standing on the ground. She climbed the tree and balanced herself with her arms out as she walked along a branch. She squatted, then straddled the branch so that the fruit was within easy reach. She pulled out her knife and cut several bunches of the berries from the branch letting them fall to the ground below. Then she climbed back down and gathered the fruit in her basket. It was a nice walk, and she felt good.

Granier and Spitting Woman laid on a large rock in the middle of the river with water flowing on both sides. She pulled a berry from the bunch, bit the outer skin, and peeled the skin from the white fruit inside. She showed Granier how she used her teeth to pull the fruit from the remaining skin. She removed the bare fruit from her teeth with her fingers and placed it in the American's mouth. He chewed it carefully, so as to not crack a tooth on the large seed inside. "It's good," he said, pretending that he had never eaten it before.

He spat out the seed into the water. She ate a longan and spat the seed out. It traveled slightly farther than Granier's seed had traveled. "I think somebody just threw down the gauntlet," he said grabbing a berry, stripping it with his teeth, eating the flesh and spitting the seed out. The seed traveled through the air and bounced off another rock in the water. "Deal with it," said Granier.

She followed suit, eating and spitting the seed out. It became a contest like a game of horse, each finding a target farther than the previous spit-shot, challenging the other to hit it. They were competitive and took the game seriously, testing each other's skills. With a seed ready to launch from her mouth, Spitting Woman suddenly stopped. "What's wrong?" he said... and then he heard it. An airplane engine.

They both looked up searching the sky. A Japanese

scout plane appeared over a mountain ridge. It was heading in their direction and would pass straight over the camp. The Viet Minh scrambled for cover, anything that would keep them from being seen by the plane. Granier knew it would take too long to reach the shore and find cover. He grabbed Spitting Woman wrapping his arms around her and rolled into the river.

The water flowed over them. Granier let go of Spitting Woman with one of his arms and grabbed the side of the big rock to keep them submerged. She grabbed him around the neck to keep from floating away. They looked into each other's eyes for reassurance. There was little. It wasn't that they were afraid of what would happened to them – it was a scout plane and had no weapons. It was what could happen to the others in the camp – the old ones and the children, the ones that could not easily run away if an attack came.

They waited almost a full minute holding their breath below the water, staying hidden. Granier slowly poked his face out of the water and watched as the plane passed overhead. Spitting Woman poked her head out of the water and gasped for air. "Are you alright?" he said.

She nodded that she was okay. Everyone in the village seemed to breathe a sigh of relief… until the plane banked and turned back for a second look.

Granier and Spitting Woman again submerged themselves below the flowing water. His grip was slipping on the moss-covered rock. He let go of Spitting Woman with his other arm and grabbed the rock with both of his hands, trying to hang on. Spitting Woman was fighting to hang on. She was tired. He felt her hands slipping from around his neck… and then she was gone.

It suddenly dawned on Granier that he had no idea if Spitting Woman could swim. He panicked and let go of the rock. The rushing water pushed him down the river. He kept his feet in front of him to bounce off any obstructions below the water. He pushed his head out of the water and looked down river where he spotted Spitting Woman clinging to a tree branch hanging over the water. He steered himself toward the branch and reached out as he passed it. He mostly grabbed leaves with his wet hand. His head was still under water. Spitting Woman had a better grip on the branch. She reached over and grabbed the collar of his shirt. It helped a little. Granier was able to use his other hand to grab the branch and pull himself out of the water. They both looked up. The plane was above the river, right above them. "Shit," said Granier.

"Sit," said Spitting Woman mimicking him.

They waited a couple more minutes until they were sure the plane was gone, then pulled themselves out of the water using the branch.

The Viet Minh emerged from their hiding places and exchanged concerned looks. Dewey ran over to Granier and said, "Do you think he saw us?"

"He wouldn't have made a second pass unless he saw something," said Granier.

"Damn it."

Giap came running and said, "We've got to move the camp."

"Two thousand people. They'll see our tracks even if we try to hide them," said Granier.

"You don't know that," said Dewey.

"Yes. I do. Moving is not an option. At least not quickly."

"So, we prepare for an attack," said Giap.

"They'll surround us, pin us down, then hit us with heavy mortars until we are annihilated," said Dewey, hopeless.

"We can fight," said Giap.

"And we will," said Dewey. "To the last."

"To the last," said Giap.

"There may be another way," said Granier. "Mr. Van, how far is it to the closest Japanese airfield?"

"I don't know," said Giap, then turned to Spitting

Woman and spoke to her in her tribal language. "She says about thirty-two miles to the Southwest."

"A small force could reach it before tomorrow morning."

"For what purpose?" said Dewey.

"Kill everyone."

"You don't even know if that plane came from that airbase."

"Why wouldn't it? It's a short range reconnaissance plane."

"Even if it did, when the pilot reports back his findings, the base commander is sure to notify the army and they'll send a battalion to wipe us out."

"Will he?"

"Will he what?"

"Will the Air Force commander notify the Army commander? What if the pilot wasn't positive what he saw?"

"That's a big 'if'."

"Okay, but why would an Air Force commander share that kind of information. Why wouldn't he keep it to himself? This is a big deal, if you think about it. The commander that destroys the Viet Minh camp is sure to receive a big promotion. Why not just bomb us?"

"What does it matter? The results are the same. The Viet Minh are wiped out."

"Not if we reach them first. It's late afternoon. They probably won't attempt a night attack. Too hard to identify targets. That means first thing in the morning is the earliest they would attempt an aerial assault. If we could reach the airbase before the morning, we could stop the attack."

"That's a lot of 'ifs', Buck," said Dewey.

"Look. Even if I'm wrong, attacking the Japanese will throw them off guard. It may buy us some time. You can prepare better for the attack or try to move the camp and cover your tracks."

"I admit… it's a bold plan, and the Japanese won't be

expecting it. How many men will you need?"

"Six men and one woman to show us the way," said Granier. "I'd like Davis to go with us. We'll need explosives for the planes if we reach the field in time."

"Are you sure seven will be enough?"

"No. But we need to travel fast if we are going to reach the airbase by dawn. Seven seems like a manageable number."

"Alright. I agree."

"Mr. Van, I will need your best runners."

Spitting Woman led the way as the sabotage team jogged through the forest. It was a marathon, not a sprint. They didn't stop while there was sunlight. It would be more difficult at night. They wanted to get as far as possible while they could still see the forest floor. All eyes searched for tripwires as they traveled. They stayed off the trails even when they found them.

The closer the team moved toward the Japanese bases, the more dangerous it became. The Japanese had patrols searching for anything amiss around their bases. They were more concerned with a Chinese invasion than a Viet Minh attack. The Japanese commanders still saw the Viet Minh as a rabble, not worthy of their concern.

When a Japanese patrol was spotted, the sabotage team dove into the ferns and bushes. They waited until the patrol passed. They did not want to make contact. They did not want to fight. Not now. Not yet. The brief rest did them good and when they resumed, they were able to pick up their pace. Their leg muscles burned. They would periodically raise their hands to let the blood flow back toward their lungs and heart. Anything to keep going.

After the sun set, one of the Viet Minh tripped over an exposed root and injured his ankle badly. Granier examined it quickly and determined that he wouldn't be able to keep up. They had no choice but to leave him to find his own way back to the Viet Minh camp or die trying. The injured man understood and wished them luck. One of the Viet Minh promised to come back and find him if he could. It was a lie to a dead man. You never go back the way you came after an attack. It was a sure way to get ambushed. There was little doubt the Japanese would find him and take their revenge. The team kept going.

As the surrounding landscape lightened, Granier knew dawn was approaching. They weren't there yet. He was pushing the team as hard as he dared. They would still need to fight once they got to the airfield. Everyone was exhausted, including himself. They had been jogging for over twelve hours with few breaks. It was sheer willpower that kept them going. He was proud of his little team of saboteurs. They had heart. They were giving all to protect their pack – the Viet Minh camp.

As far as he could tell, they had avoided detection. That was a miracle in itself because of the number of Japanese patrols and outposts they had encountered. Success was a longshot and everyone on the team knew it. They needed to be lucky.

Granier heard the sound of a truck engine in the distance. The team crested the hill they were climbing and saw the Japanese airbase below.

A fuel truck was driving back to a maintenance building. There were six Zeros parked along the runway, already armed. The two bombs and the two 7.7mm machine guns that each plane carried would devastate the Viet Minh, especially those not fast enough to seek cover – the old, the young, the wounded and the sick. The Zeros looked ready for takeoff.

There was little time to deploy the team if they were going to stop the air attack. Granier was unsure if it was just an air attack or if the Japanese fighters were providing a pre-emptive strike for a ground assault. He considered the preparation required for a ground assault and the distance a large force would need to travel to reach the Viet Minh camp. It seemed like there hadn't been enough time, but he couldn't be sure. It was always possible that the Japanese had forces in the area. There was nothing Granier and his team could do about a ground force at the moment. Their mission was to prevent the air strike. There were two options – destroy the planes or kill the pilots. They would try to do both. A third requirement was to destroy the airbase communications so they could not inform others of their discovery of the Viet Minh camp. It might have already been too late for that, but the team had to try, nonetheless.

The team was positioned behind the runway, where the command post and maintenance buildings gave them good cover. There were Japanese guards patrolling the entire compound and heavy machine gun positions on both sides of the airfield used for both air and ground defense.

The team Granier had chosen was made up of two snipers and two sappers. One of the sappers had been left behind in the forest with an injured ankle. Spitting Woman had taken his pack of explosives. She would need to take his place to carry the pack for Davis and the other sapper to place the explosives. There wasn't much time for instructions or a pep talk, everyone knew what they had to do. Granier designated a rendezvous point and they split up, keeping low and out of sight.

Davis placed the first explosive package at the base of the command post, tying a bundle of TNT to the wooden post used as a foundation. He would have preferred to place an explosive on all four corners to completely destroy the building and ensure those inside were killed, but there wasn't enough time and he didn't have enough explosives to be overly efficient. The fuse was a five-minute pencil detonator which he crimped with a pair of pliers to activate. He would use pencil detonators with shorter fuses for the other explosives he would plant. This would allow the devices to detonate close together. But it wasn't an exact measurement. There was variance built into the system.

At the same time, the Viet Minh sapper placed another explosive package by the fuel tank near the maintenance building. He was a veteran fighter, but this was his first time using explosives in combat. He was nervous and didn't want to let his instructor down. He too crimped a pencil detonator as Davis had shown him during training, then ran, keeping low, to the next target – a communications hut with a radio antenna sticking up from the end on a pole.

It was dawn and the outline of the surrounding mountains was clear. The darkness no longer masked the movements of the team. Granier deployed his two snipers in the forest near the machine gun positions. Although he hadn't had time to train them in concealment, the Viet Minh snipers were good shots and reliable. He believed that if they could take out the heavy machine gun crews, the sabotage team would stand a much better chance of completing its mission and surviving.

He decided to climb the tallest tree he could find that overlooked the airfield. He slung his rifle on his back and used a doubled-over piece of rope to shimmy up the tree's trunk, like a logger. He reached the branches and continue upward until he was thirty feet off the ground. He straddled a branch and looked out. He had a clear line of sight over most of the airfield. In the distance sat the runway and the six Zeros. He hoped to kill any pilots before they reached their planes. He unslung his rifle and adjusted his legs and elbows until he felt stable. Chambering a round, he surveyed the area with his scope. He studied the Japanese patrols around the perimeter of the airfield and the machine gun positions. He found each of his team members and checked on their progress.

Davis was planting an explosive device on what looked like the officer's quarters. He wondered if the pilots were still in their quarters or in the command post being briefed by their commander. He imagined the later and decided that is where he would focus his attention once the first explosion went off. That was the team's cue to begin the attack – the first explosion.

Granier could feel his legs throbbing from the night's journey. If they cramped, he would be in trouble. He would not be able to hang on. It was a long drop to the forest floor. But what worried him even more were the muscle tremors. Even the slightest tremor could throw his aim off. *Water will help,* he thought. He took his canteen from his belt, opened it, drank two swallows and put it back.

It was calm, even peaceful, as he waited. He had no real idea when the first explosion would occur. Davis didn't like mechanical timers. He preferred a chemical reaction to ignite his detonators. Mechanisms could malfunction or even jam. Chemicals were more reliable. The problem was that he couldn't set everything to go off at the same time with pencil detonators. It was a tradeoff – reliability against timing. Davis chose reliability. It didn't make sense to Granier, but he wasn't an explosives expert and had to defer to Davis. Davis and Spitting Woman were still planting devices, so Granier thought it must not be time yet. All he could do was wait.

He used the time to see how the other team members were doing. His snipers were in place and ready, each aiming at a machine gunner as they had been taught – gunner, feeder, loader – that was the order of execution. *Execution,* he thought. *It sounds criminal. Assassination's not much better. It don't matter. I do my job. Dead is dead.* The Viet Minh sapper had placed his last device and was moving to his firing position near the edge of the forest. *Good,* thought Granier. *Just like an orchestra – everybody up and ready to begin.* He moved his scope over to find Davis. He found him next to a Showa transportation plane rigging an explosive charge on its front landing gear. Spitting Woman wasn't beside him. A slight panic tweaked his nervous system. *Where is she?* He looked around the area and spotted a guard moving toward the area. "Shit," said Granier to himself. "Where the hell are you?"

He kept looking through his scope, searching for Spitting Woman, moving from place to place. He found her squatting next to a supply truck. "Oh, thank, God," said Granier, relieved.

Spitting Woman was facing Davis and not keeping watch on the area behind her. Granier moved his scope back to where the guard was patrolling. He was gone. "Fuck," he said, moving his scope around, searching for the soldier.

He found him just a few feet from the back of the supply truck, he hadn't seen Spitting Woman yet, but it was just a matter of time. Granier put his scope's sight on the Japanese guard's left temple. Everything seemed to be going so well and now it was falling apart. If he fired and killed the guard, it would warn the Japanese, including the pilots. They might not get caught in the explosion. But Granier didn't have a choice. It wasn't even a matter of choosing between Spitting Woman and the mission. The guard's rifle shot would have the same effect of warning the other Japanese soldiers. Granier would take the first shot if it came to it. His line of sight was clear. He wouldn't miss.

The guard approached the end of the truck and stopped. He took out a cigarette and lit it. "Come on, girl. Smell the smoke," said Granier watching through his scope.

Davis finished planting the device on the nose gear of the plane and glanced at his watch. He was out of time. He motioned to Spitting Woman to follow him as they moved toward their firing position, a safe distance from the explosions. Spitting Woman moved, her feet crunched against the gravel. The guard heard the noise, unslung his rifle, and moved around the truck. He saw her. He had only raised his rifle two inches before Granier put a bullet through his head and he fell to the ground.

The Japanese were alerted, and the rest of the saboteur team opened fire. The machine gunners both went down with bullets through their skulls.

Granier was no longer concerned with Davis and Spitting Woman. They could take care of themselves now that the assault had begun. Instead, he swung his scope around to where he thought the pilots would appear – the doorway of the command post. He was right. The commander and the pilots ran out. The commander ordered them to their planes and barked orders to the other soldiers. Granier put a bullet in his head. He fell dead. The pilots started running for their planes. The building exploded from Davis' first device. Piece of wood flew in all directions. One of the pilots was caught in the ball of flame and his uniform ignited. Another pilot screamed in shock as he looked down. A two-foot-long wooden shard had speared him in the side. "Two down," said Granier sighting a third, pulling the trigger, and watching him fall. "Three."

The surviving pilots regained their footing and ran toward their planes, yelling for the ground crews to start their engines.

The crew members ran to each plane and fired up their engines. As the first pilot approached the tail of the first plane, Granier put him face down in the dirt with a bullet to the back of his head. "Four."

Granier swung over to the last two pilots. He sighted the first one to reach his plane. The pilot climbed onto the wing and slipped just as Granier fired. The bullet zinged over his head and ricocheted off the rotating propeller. "Shit," said Granier, again taking aim.

The second bullet didn't miss. The front of the pilot's uniform exploded in red as the bullet traveled through his body and exited on the left side of his chest. He fell to the wing and tumbled to the ground.

Granier swung his rifle around searching for the final

pilot. He found him with one foot already in the cockpit. He centered his sight on his back and fired just as the pilot dropped into his seat. The bullet smashed through the front windshield missing the pilot's shoulder by an inch. It was a rushed shot. Granier realigned his sight to fire through the cockpit and hit the back of the pilot's head, but the plane's canopy support blocked his shot. "God, damn it," said Granier.

He fired anyway, hoping it would go through the windshield and the support. The bullet made it through the back of the windshield but was stopped by the metal support. The plane started to move. "No. No. No," said Granier slinging his rifle onto his back, climbing down the tree, jumping the last ten feet, landing, falling forward to not damage his weapon. He rose to his feet and ran toward the runway.

Spitting Woman saw Granier break from the cover of the trees. She looked around and saw two Japanese soldiers directly in Granier's path, bringing their rifles around to shoot him. She took aim and fired. The bullet hit one of the soldiers in the shoulder and sent him to the ground. But Granier was almost upon them. There wasn't any time. She took aim at the second and fired again. She missed.

The Japanese soldier fired at Granier, who was running straight at him like a charging bull. The bullet hit Granier on the side of the neck and sliced through his flesh. Blood ran down the side of his neck, but it didn't stop him. He used his sniper rifle barrel to knock the soldier's rifle aside, then hit the soldier in the head with the butt of his rifle as he ran passed. The soldier fell, more surprised by the move than the glancing blow of the rifle butt. He quickly regained his senses and aimed at Granier's back as he ran down the side of the runway. The soldier squeezed the trigger, but his head exploded before his weapon fired.

Spitting Woman didn't miss the second time. Satisfied Granier was out of danger for the moment; she looked for another target.

One of the Viet Minh snipers was on his last member of the machine gun crew when the loader swung the machine gun around and fired a burst. It was a wild shot, but the stream of bullets took off the sniper's head. The loader fired the machine gun at Spitting Woman and Davis until it jammed. He tried to clear it when Davis rose up from behind his covered position and shot him. He slumped over the machine gun's hot barrel.

Another Japanese soldier, seeing what happened, aimed and shot Davis in the back. Davis went down, wounded, out of the fight. In the process of reloading his rifle, the sapper saw his instructor hit. Without waiting to reload, he sprang from his hidden firing position, ran out of the trees. The Japanese soldier saw the sapper advancing and swung his weapon around. It was too late. The sapper reached him before he could fire and hit him in the eye with the tip of his rifle barrel. The soldier screamed in pain. The sapper silenced him with his rifle's butt.

Spitting Woman ran to Davis and tended to his back wound. It was painful and bleeding but not fatal. One of Davis' ribs had stopped the bullet from piercing his lungs. The rib was broken, and it was hard for him to breath, but he would live. She put pressure on the wound and wrapped a bandage around him to stop the bleeding as Hoagland had taught her. She was not gentle, but she was fast. As soon as she thought he was okay, she picked her rifle back up and rejoined the fight.

Back on the runway, the Japanese pilot increased the throttle, and his plane picked up speed.

Granier ran down the side of the runway with every ounce of energy he had left in his body. He needed enough of an angle to hit the pilot through the windshield and avoid the metal support. He calculated how long it would take him to unsling his rifle, aim, and fire. He figured he might be able to fire twice before the plane took off. He unslung his rifle as he slowed, then stopped running. He brought his rifle around and aimed with the iron sight, not the scope. The scope would take too long to align. He needed two rapid shots. He saw the edge of the pilot's face and aligned his sight, giving the target a slight lead to compensate for the forward motion. He squeezed the trigger, and his rifle fired. He saw the empty clip flip into the air. His gun was out of ammunition. He had lost count in all the commotion. A rooky mistake. He frantically reached for another clip and reloaded. But it was too late; he had lost the angle. He was crestfallen as he watched the plane's wheels lift off. It was gone.

The plane took a sudden dive, and its wheels banged down on the ground again. The tail of the plane rose into the air. The propeller dug into the ground. The Zero flipped up into the air, turning end over end, smashing down again on the cockpit, exploding in flames as one of the wing tanks ignited.

"YES," screamed Granier pumping his fist in the air.

The plane's two bombs detonated in secondary explosions blowing the remains of the plane to pieces. Granier dove to the ground as the plane's left wheel and landing gear flew past him, barely missing his head.

Seeing Granier down the runway waving at her, Spitting Woman broke off her attack, slung her rifle, put her arm around David and helped him retreat into the woods. The surviving Viet Minh sniper provided covering fire as the sapper threw grenades into the open cockpits of the remaining Zeros, destroying them. They retreated together, disappearing into the woods.

Without an officer to lead them, the surviving Japanese soldiers had no interest in pursuing the saboteurs. Their commander was dead, they had dozens of wounded, and their entire airbase was on fire. They were beyond demoralized. They tended to their wounded and saved what they could from the flames.

Granier was the last to leave the airfield. He couldn't believe his plan had worked. But it had. He disappeared into the safety of the trees and rendezvoused with the surviving team members. They would find a safe place to rest. Their bodies had given all. They would sleep for several hours and tend to Davis' wound the best they could before heading back to the Viet Minh camp.

Two days later the sabotage team arrived back in the Viet Minh camp. They were relieved to find that no ground attack had occurred. The Viet Minh and the Americans were safe for the time being. As a precautionary measure, Ho had ordered the camp to move to another location five miles away. It would be a gradual move, and they would be careful to cover their tracks. In the meantime, Giap had ordered the patrols around the camp doubled and the scouts to perform long-range reconnaissance of the surrounding mountains and forests. He wanted plenty of warning if a Japanese force was encountered.

The members of the team were surprised to find that the Viet Minh sapper that they had left in the forest had made it back and his ankle was recovering well.

Hoagland tended to Davis' wound and reported his status to Dewey. "We should get Davis to a hospital as soon as possible," said Hoagland.

"That bad?" said Dewey.

"It's hard to say. I removed any bullet fragments I could find and irrigated the wound. But the odds of infection are high."

"Transporting a wounded man through Japanese lines is not going to be easy. He would probably be safer if he stayed put."

"He could die."

"He could just as easily die crossing the border."

"Buck did it."

"Buck didn't have a wounded man in tow."

"If I am going to tend to him, I'm going to need more medicine and a proper set of medical instruments to probe the wound more efficiently."

"Of course. I'll see to it personally."

"And Davis is down for the count. He's got to rest."

"Yes. Yes. He'll be missed, but we will do alright without him. What he and Buck did was quite extraordinary, wouldn't you say?"

"They had help."

"And I don't want to take away from that. The Viet Minh did their duty, and then some, but it was our team members that led them. I'm thinking of recommending them both for a citation."

"I'm sure they would appreciate it. God knows they deserve our gratitude. Any idea when the Viet Minh will move the camp?"

"Soon, I hope. It's not easy moving three thousand people through the forest without being detected."

"Three thousand?"

"Their little army is growing by the day. Giap says we could have as many as fifteen hundred soldiers operational by the end of the month."

"That'll put a dent in the Japanese supply lines."

"I should hope so. We're getting a lot of pressure from HQ to step up our raids and take some of the burden off the Chinese forces. The Japs have been very aggressive."

"They're spending a lot of resources supporting the Viet Minh. I'm sure they want to get their money's worth."

"Exactly."

The Viet Minh mourned their losses. The two soldiers that died during the mission were heroes and would be remembered by their families every year with a visit to their gravesites.

FIVE

Spitting Woman was given a day to rest, then sent out on long-range reconnaissance for several days at a time. Granier saw little of her and worried when she was gone. He knew it was stupid. She could take care of herself. That's one of the reasons he loved her. She didn't need him. She wanted him. That made him feel good. He wanted her too. He was excited each time she returned. He waited for her by the edge of the forest like a dog waits for its master.

When she arrived, he picked her up and made her kiss him before letting her down. She didn't like it. She had just spent several days in the bush and wanted to clean herself in the river first. She liked to smell good for him even though he didn't seem to care. She relented, kissed him, and he set her down. She motioned for him to go away. He obeyed.

Just seeing that she was okay made Granier feel better. He had work to do and knew he would see her later that night in the forest where they could have some privacy. Spitting Woman never seemed too concerned about privacy or even the appropriateness of their relationship. Granier didn't feel any pressure like she wanted more. It was what it was, and it would last as long as it lasted. Just being with each other was enough.

When he looked back on his previous relationships – there were very few – the women always wanted to know where it was all going after only a few times of seeing each other. *How the hell did he know?* The relationships usually ended when he was deployed to some far off place and told them that he wouldn't be able to communicate for several weeks or months. They never believed him and ended things in a fight. It was more convenient that way.

With Spitting Woman it was different. They didn't talk, so there was no real way of knowing what was on her mind or even if this was a relationship. He had no choice and neither did she. They just had to go with it. Surprisingly, it worked.

He walked back to the area where the Americans were camped below the cliffs on a rise above the river. The Team's camp was surrounded by large rocks that could be used for cover in the event of an attack. They had set up a camouflaged lean-to that hid their position from passing planes and shielded them from the rain. It also allowed them to have a small fire to heat their coffee and roast fish caught by villagers in the river and exchanged for American cigarettes.

Giap was talking with Dewey when Granier entered the camp. "Colonel Patti has requested that you attack the Japanese garrison at Tan Trao," said Dewey.

"And the size of the Japanese force?" said Giap.

"At least a company. But I have been assured there are no more than two hundred and fifty soldiers in all. The old fortress is considered a key strategic point."

"It should not be an issue. We'll need a few days to prepare."

"Of course. I will inform him that you accept the assignment."

"I will send scouts to reaffirm the number of troops and assess the fortress defenses. I imagine a night attack would be best."

"Perhaps. But let's wait for the reconnaissance report before deciding on a plan of attack. It's always better to plan with intelligence, especially when dealing with fixed defenses."

Hoagland was tending to Davis' wound. Green and

Santana were playing poker with a well-worn deck of cards. "Buck, you want in?" said Santana throwing a cigarette into the betting pot.

"You playing for cigarettes?" said Granier.

"What else?"

"Dewey wants one of us to go with the Viet Minh to inspect the new village site," said Green.

"One of you should go," said Granier.

"Hot date?" said Santana.

Granier said nothing. Dewey and Giap were nearby. It wasn't that he was hiding his relationship with Spitting Woman, but he didn't want to draw attention to it either.

"We figured we'd cut cards for it," said Green.

Granier looked down at the deck. It was hard to tell if it was marked or just so worn that the backs of certain cards were distinguishable. He trusted these two men with his life, but he didn't trust them at cards. "How about we flip for it?" said Granier pulling his grandfather's gold coin from his pocket.

"Is that a two-headed coin?" said Green suspicious.

Granier flipped it to him for approval. "Nice," said Green inspecting the coin. "Where did you get that?"

"It was my grandfather's. Are you satisfied?"

"Sure. Why not? But how do we make it fair? Someone has to flip twice."

"Each of us gets a flip. Odd man out."

"That works. I'll flip it first."

"No. I'll flip it. You'll drop it."

Green tossed the coin back to Granier. He flipped the coin three times, once for each man. Granier and Santana both got tails. "Shit," said Green.

Giap had overheard the three men talking. He glanced at the gold coin as Granier gave both sides of the coin a rub on his shirtsleeve before placing it back in his pocket. There was something about the coin that seemed familiar to Giap. He had seen it before. He said nothing.

When Giap returned to his cave, he moved to his homemade bookshelf. His books were his most precious possessions. Most were history books, many autobiographies of great military leaders – Alexander the Great, Julius Caesar, Sun Tzu, and of course, Napoleon Bonaparte.

He pulled out the volume on Napoleon and thumbed through the pages. Somewhere in the middle, he came upon a drawing of a coin. The coin had been minted in Turin after Napoleon's victory against the Austrians. Napoleon's profile was imprinted on one side and the three fleur-de-lie, the symbol of France, on the other. It was gold and had an original value of twenty francs. He imagined it would have increased in worth substantially. *"Why would an American keep such a valuable coin in the pocket of his trousers?* thought Giap.

It was late in the afternoon. Spitting Woman stood before Giap giving him a reconnaissance report in his command headquarters – a small wooden desk and a couple of crudely-built chairs beneath a camouflaged canopy. She had waited over an hour for him. He was a very busy man. She felt honored that he would take the time to hear her report directly. It made her feel like what she had to say was important.

They spoke in her tribal dialect. Giap had learned it when he first arrived. Few in the tribes spoke good Vietnamese, let alone any other language. They were primitive and uneducated. As a learned man that spoke their language, Giap was revered by their tribal leader, and Spitting Woman respected that.

When she was finished, Giap asked her to join him for some tea. She found it strange that such an important man would want to spend any more time with her beyond her report, but she didn't dare refuse. He offered her a seat and poured her a cup of tea in a fine porcelain cup. She was afraid she might break it when she picked it up and handled it carefully using both hands so she wouldn't drop it. She sipped the hot liquid. It burned her tongue, but she kept drinking it. She wanted to get out of there as fast as possible. She didn't want to get into trouble.

She and her family needed the protection of the Viet Minh camp. Without it, they would be forced to return to her tribal village which had already been raided twice by the Japanese, each time resulting in the death or rape of tribal members, including herself. She had considered suicide after the second rape but knew her family, especially her children, would not survive without her. The rapes were a painful memory she tried to push out of her mind. She and her family couldn't go back to their village, not until the war was over and the Japanese were gone for good.

Giap poured himself a cup of tea. The cup was also made of porcelain, but not matching. Nothing matched, not even the teapot. It was a hodgepodge of fine china looted from incursions against the Japanese and 'borrowed' from the Chinese. "The American called 'Buck'... you are his lover?" said Giap taking his first sip.

"Yes," said Spitting Woman, sheepishly. "Is it allowed?"

"Of course. It may be useful."

"How?"

"He has a coin he keeps in his pocket. I'd like to see it."

"It is gold. Are you going to steal it?"

"We are communists. We do not steal."

"Do you want me to ask him for you?"

"No. I think it would be better if you removed it while he was asleep and brought it to me so I could examine it. You could return it before he wakes. He wouldn't know it was gone."

"Is there something wrong?"

"I believe I have seen that coin before... in a book. I

want to confirm it is the same. Tonight would be good."

"Yes, sir. May I go?"

"Of course. But please finish your tea first."

She emptied her cup in one swallow, rose, saluted, politely bowed twice, and left. Giap scared her. Not because he was mean or vicious. He was a good commander. But he was also powerful, like one of the gods that lived in the woods. Her life and the life of her family were in his hands.

Granier was by the river waiting for her return when she saw him. He had protected her in the past and she was sure he would do so again. She ran to him, threw her arms around his neck, and pulled him down for a kiss. Granier seemed genuinely surprised by her outburst of emotion. "Is everything okay?" he said.

She didn't understand the words, but the concern in his voice told her what he was asking. She looked into his eyes – her protector. She took his hand and pulled him toward the woods. "Okay. I ain't gonna argue, but don't you want to eat first?" he said gesturing eating with his free hand.

She didn't. He picked up his rifle, leaning against the rock, and followed her into the trees.

They moved off a distance from the camp. She pulled · him down into the grass on top of her. She wanted to feel his weight. She wanted to know he was big and strong; that he could protect her and her family. She kissed him passionately as she unbuttoned his trousers. He responded.

It was after sunset by the time they finished making love. It had been a long session, fiery. She felt a little guilty for having ravaged him the way she had. But not too guilty. He had ravaged her back. She felt a little sore and was sure there would be bruises. She laid beside him, staring, studying his face. He was asleep and looked surprisingly peaceful for a man of war. She wanted to wake him but decided she shouldn't. He needed his rest, and she needed to do what Giap had ordered.

She felt bad taking the coin without asking. She thought Giap's request strange, but he was their military leader, and she knew better than to disobey an order from one so mighty. She put on her uniform, careful not to wake the American. Granier's trousers were laying in a bunch at his feet. She remembered pulling them off in a hurry. She quietly picked them up, reached into the pocket, and retrieved the coin. It was heavy, a sure sign that it was gold. She had never held something so valuable in her hand. She didn't know how valuable it was, but she was pretty sure it could buy several piglets. Maybe even a full-grown pig that her family could roast and share with their neighbors in the cave. But it wasn't hers. She was just borrowing it as Giap had said. She glanced back at Granier, still asleep. She needed to hurry. She moved through the trees back toward the camp.

She found Giap at the edge of the forest waiting. "You were successful?" said Giap.

"Yes," she said, handing him the coin.

"He sleeps?"

"Yes, but I don't know how long."

"It should only take a moment."

Giap pulled out a cigarette lighter and broke his own rules by igniting it. This was important and worth the risk. He held the coin to the light from the lighter's flame and studied it. It was Napoleon's image he was most interested in seeing. The emperor's profile was surprisingly detailed for a coin so old. It was beautiful, and Giap admired it. "Who was he?" she asked also starring at the beautiful man on one side of the coin.

"An emperor... like a king."

"A king?"

"A leader like Uncle Ho."

"And like you?"

"Yes. I suppose you are right. Like me."

He closed the lid of the lighter extinguishing the flame and with it the light. He thought for a moment then handed her back the coin."

"Is that all?"

"For now. You have done well."

"May I go?"

"Yes."

She saluted and bowed twice as before. She left Giap standing in the darkness deep in thought. She didn't like it when men thought too much. It was dangerous.

As she moved deeper into the forest, she saw the black outline of someone standing, watching her. She could not see the person's face. It was too dark. She was cautious and slowed. It could have been a Japanese soldier, but she thought not. The Japanese traveled in groups. This person was alone. She moved closer until she could see the hint of a face from a shaft of moonlight that made it through the forest canopy. It was the American – her lover. She froze. *He knows,* she thought. She tried not to panic. "I woke, and you were gone. I was worried," he said.

She didn't understand the words but thought she knew what he meant. She made a gesture touching her stomach like she was hungry, then gestured eating food. "Oh. Did you bring me some?"

She couldn't figure that one out, but she could tell by his tone he wasn't mad. She moved beside him, then moved around to his back. She wrapped her hands around his waist placed one of her hands in his trouser pocket like she was searching for something. She released the coin and let it drop inside his pocket.

"What are you looking for?" he said.

Her fingers slipped around his penis. "Oh. I see. I thought maybe you had enough."

She squeezed him. "Round two, I guess," he said turning into her, kissing her, pushing her up against a nearby tree.

She felt good. She had done what Giap had asked. Her family was safe. She was in her lover's arms.

Granier and three Viet Minh soldiers hiked through the heavily forested mountains surrounding the Pho Day River. They did their best to keep out of sight even from the Vietnamese in the area. They did not want the Japanese to discover their interest in the village of Tan Trao.

Dewey had decided he wanted his own reconnaissance of the French fortress that guarded the mountain pass and river. It wasn't that he didn't trust the Viet Minh scouts to give an accurate report. He did. They were very good scouts. It was more an issue of experience. The Viet Minh were accustomed to attacking Japanese patrols and camps. They had never assaulted a fortified position like the fortress at Tan Trao. Dewey wanted one of his own to survey the area and assess the Japanese defenses. He chose his best man – Granier.

Granier had changed, and it concerned him. He knew he was getting soft. He no longer yearned to be on his own. He liked spending time with Spitting Woman and resented when he was given assignments that took him away from her. He didn't complain. He knew better. He was a soldier, after all, and he had duties. He just didn't relish those duties as he did before he met her. She had changed him, and he liked it. It was comfortable. He was truly happy for the first time in his life. He wondered if he would get fat but didn't seem too concerned about it… as long as she didn't mind.

The reconnaissance team came to the top of a ridge. One of the Viet Minh pointed to the village below and said, "Tan Trao."

Granier pulled out his binoculars and surveyed the valley and the village. Like most valleys in the Highlands, rice fields surrounded by dikes occupied every available foot of land outside the village. The Vietnamese farmers needed to plant their rice in flat areas where the rainwater would pool. If they ran out of space in the valley, they would build terraces which required a lot more work and needed to be maintained every year; rebuilding the mud walls after the monsoon season.

The village was located on the far end of the valley and straddled the river. Several monkey bridges made of bamboo supports and wooden planks stretched across the slow-flowing water allowing the people on both sides of the river easy access to their neighbors. It was hard to tell how many people lived in the village, but Granier estimated two to three hundred.

The old French fortress was at the mouth of the valley where the river disappeared into the mountains. It was a control point that allowed the French to collect taxes and enforce French law. It had been this way for over a hundred years until the Japanese invaded. Now the Japanese held the fortress.

The Japanese weren't interested in collecting taxes or even enforcing their laws. They took what they wanted which was everything, including the entire rice crop when it was harvested. The Japanese needed to support their army fighting the Chinese. The Vietnamese would have to fend for themselves. Without rice, their diet's staple, the Vietnamese starved. The Vietnamese had dealt with invaders before, but none had been so cruel and greedy as the Japanese. Complaining was met with the blades of their swords.

Granier could see Japanese patrols of four or five men working their way through the village and strolling along the top of the rice field dikes. They didn't seem too concerned. In their eyes, the Vietnamese were docile, like sheep. It was the Chinese that worried the Japanese the most. The sheer number of Chinese troops that could invade kept the Japanese commanders awake at night. But this outpost was far from the border, and the Japanese soldiers would be given fair warning if that day ever came. In the meantime, boredom ruled the day, and rape of the Vietnamese women in the village ruled the night.

Granier decided he needed to have a closer look at the fortress and the number of troops inside. It was only noon, and he would need to wait until dark before he could attempt to infiltrate the fortress. He and the other team members took their time eating their lunch of dried mangos, balls of rice in green leaves and fish sauce. After lunch, Granier had them take turns keeping watch while the rest of the team got some shuteye. It was going to be a long night.

A few hours after sunset, Granier woke when a small centipede fell from a tree branch and attempted to crawl into his nose. It wasn't poisonous like the big ones, but it did send a chill down his spine. He had learned to deal with ticks, leeches, snakes, poisonous frogs, and giant spiders, but centipedes just creeped him out; all those legs. He may have been trespassing in the animal's territory, but that didn't give it the right to be rude. He mushed the creature into the ground with his boot.

He took out his binoculars and scanned the village and the fortress again. It looked fairly quiet. There were still patrols, but the Japanese soldiers were more interested in joking with each other than watching the surrounding area. *That's good,* he thought. *Lazy makes my job easier.* He reapplied his camouflage paint on his face, neck, and hands.

He gathered the team, and they made their way down into the valley, staying hidden in the forest, keeping quiet. If they were discovered, the Japanese would surely chase them. That didn't worry Granier. What worried him was that the Japanese would know a reconnaissance team was scouting their position. They would have time to prepare, perhaps even request reinforcements. Stealth was just as important as the information they would gather.

At the base of the mountain, beside the old fortress wall, Granier gestured to the team members; they were to stay hidden while he went into the fortress. They nodded that they understood. The fortress was surrounded by a ten-foot brick and plaster wall that was originally painted yellow but had faded over the years and was stained black with mold. Granier scaled the perimeter wall and laid flat on the top as he looked into the compound.

There was a two-story building that was the command headquarters, five one-story barracks, a smaller building that looked like a sickbay, a kitchen, a storage hut and an open-air dining area with a roof. He counted twenty-four soldiers in the dining room, some finishing their evening meal, others playing cards and showing photos of their wives, children, and girlfriends. It was still early, and at that time of night, there should have been more.

There were two thirty-five-foot guard towers built on thick wooden poles; one at the front of the compound and one at the rear. A guard post was stationed at the front gateway in the wall, and a heavy machine gun nest with a three-man crew was set back thirty feet from the entrance and had a good field of fire over most of the compound. There was also an 81mm mortar set up near the command headquarters, but it wasn't manned at the moment. He imagined the machine gun crew was tasked with watching over it unless there was an assault.

In all, Granier estimated that there were probably fifty to sixty soldiers guarding the fortress and patrolling the village. That was much less than expected. He wondered where the other soldiers might be. Some were probably on long-range patrol in the surrounding mountains; others might have been tasked for a mission of some sort. It was possible that the remaining soldiers just weren't in the fortress at this time and would return in a few days. But Granier didn't like guessing. He wanted to know for sure. The lives of the Viet Minh and Americans would depend on the number of enemies they would be fighting. A miscalculation could be very costly. He quietly dropped down to the inside of the compound and moved along the wall staying in the shadows whenever possible.

As he approached the first building – the storage hut for the kitchen – he saw a guard patrolling the area. He ducked deep into the shadows. As the guard came closer, Granier closed his eyelids so the whites of his eyes would not reveal him. He completely disappeared in the blackness of the shadow. He listened to guard's steps to ensure there was no change in the rhythm that might indicate he had seen something and was stopping to investigate. The guard passed without noticing anything. Granier opened his eyes.

He moved along the wall and entered the storage room. He was alone. He took out his flashlight and examined the supplies. He had been taught to measure the amount of food to indicate the number of people consuming it. Rice was the main clue; so many cups per day per man. They should have had plenty on hand since this was a rice farming area. But they didn't. Not for several hundred men. He checked the cans of umeboshi – salted plums – that were part of every Japanese soldier's daily ration. Again, too few. It seemed that the garrison was lightly manned, even including the outstanding patrols in the area.

He exited the storage hut and moved to the troop barracks. The barracks were windowless so the air could flow through keeping them cool at night. They were built on heavy poles to prevent flooding during monsoon season. He doubted that any of the soldiers would be sleeping this early in the evening. But two of the barracks had their lights on. He would avoid those two. He climbed a set of stairs and entered the closest hut.

It was pitch dark. He listened for the sound of breathing. Nothing. He was alone. He walked into the room. His footsteps creaked against the flimsy wooden floor. He moved along the cots. There were fifty, but only fifteen had mosquito nets set up and their bedrolls laid out. More evidence. *Why not stretch out?* he thought. *Room to spare.*

He heard voices, then footsteps on the stairs outside. He dove between two cots. Two Japanese soldiers entered the barracks and flipped on the light switch. The room illuminated. *So much for stealth,* he thought as the two soldiers walked in his direction. *Shit.* He slid under one of the cots and waited until they passed before sliding out the opposite side. The soldiers were walking away from him. He realized he had a very narrow window to escape undetected. He rose and walked out. He didn't run. The soldier's footsteps covered the noise of his footsteps. The soldiers stopped in front of their beds just as he slipped through the doorway into the darkness outside.

He checked the other two dark barracks to confirm the bed count. They were the same as the first with only fifteen occupied cots in each. Add an additional five officers and the Japanese garrison was only manned by seventy-five soldiers total. *Light. Very light.* He had seen enough and returned to his team on the opposite side of the compound wall.

Dewey walked across the stepping stones in the river to reach the opposite side. It was precarious because the buildup of river moss made the rocks slippery. There was no bridge. Giap and the other Viet Minh commanders were concerned that the Japanese could see a bridge from the air and it would reveal the location of the camp. Instead, they had placed flat stones in the shallowest part of the river.

Reaching the opposing bank, Dewey walked up the hillside to the caves. He entered the open doorway and said, "Hello," to warn anyone inside of his presence.

"Please, Commander, come in and have a seat," said a man's voice.

He entered the small cave and found both Ho and Giap already inside. There was an empty chair made of tree branches and thick strips of bamboo for the seat. "Both of you. This is quite an honor," said Dewey. "I'm not sure I've ever seen you two in the same room before."

"It concerns a matter of great urgency on which we need to speak with you," said Giap.

"Alright. Well... I'm here. How may I help you?"

"It has come to our attention that there is a spy in our camp. As you had suggested," said Ho.

"And you found who it is?" said Dewey, hopeful.

"We have."

"Excellent. I assume you will execute the bugger."

"We do not feel it is our place."

"Why is that?"

"It is one of your men. The one you call 'Buck.'"

"What?! That's not possible."

"It is possible. He is French."

"He's not French. He's an American."

"He is French, and we are insulted that you chose to bring him into our camp. You have put the lives of our people in jeopardy."

"This is ridiculous. He's an American like me. Not to mention, he has risked his life several times to defend your people."

"Yes. That is what spies do. Pretend to be on your side while stabbing you in the back."

"Hang on a minute. What evidence do you have to support your accusation?"

"The gold coin he carries. It is French."

"You're accusing him because he carries a gold coin?"

"A French gold coin."

"It's a good luck charm like a rabbit's foot. I have one myself. My father gave it to me before I went off to college."

"A French gold coin?"

"No. Of course not. It's a double eagle."

"An American coin. Quite understandable. But it doesn't answer why your sniper carries a French coin."

"His grandfather gave it to him as a momentum."

"His grandfather was French?"

"Yes. I suppose he was. But Buck is not French. He became an American citizen with the rest of his family when they immigrated."

"From France?"

"He was twelve years old."

"A young man."

"A boy."

"A French boy."

"That doesn't make him a traitor. In America, we don't judge a person by their heritage. We judge them by their actions."

"In Vietnam, we don't have that luxury."

"He is a good man. Loyal."

"He is a spy for the French."

"You don't know that."

"Mr. Dewey, try to see this from our perspective. If there is even the faintest chance that your man is a spy, he must be dealt with."

"What do you mean 'dealt with'?"

"He knows too much to be released."

"You're suggesting you will assassinate him?"

"No. It is not our duty. It is yours. You brought him into our camp. It was your mistake, not ours."

"Alright. I've heard quite enough. There will be no assassination of Americans while I am in command. We are a people of laws. We believe in innocence before guilt."

"Nobody has to know. But he must be dealt with... and soon."

"If you persist, my team and I will leave... and American support goes with us."

"I see. I wonder if your commander Patti will see the situation the same way."

"I assure you he will."

"Perhaps. Or maybe he will see our attacks against the Japanese as a higher duty than one man's life?"

"I have nothing further to discuss."

"Very well. Enjoy your evening."

Dewey left in a huff. "What would you have me do?" said Giap to Ho.

"Do what is necessary to deal with the problem."

"Yes, Uncle."

Dewey walked into the American camp, his mind racing, mumbling to himself. He saw Hoagland finishing up tending to Davis' wound. Dewey waited until Hoagland was finished and Davis was resting quietly. "How is Davis?" said Dewey.

"Much better. The infection is nearly gone. He's healing well," said Hoagland.

"Excellent. When can he travel?"

"Travel?"

"Back across the border. I'm going to send him back with Buck. He'll make sure they get through."

Hoagland sensed by Dewey's urgent speech that something was wrong. "Commander, excuse me for asking, but is everything alright?"

"No. But when it is ever? We're dealing with barbarians."

"What happened?"

"That's none of your business, Hoagland."

"Of course not. But you're talking about sending one-third of our team back to headquarters. Is that wise? Especially at this juncture."

"We do what we have to do... for the success of the mission."

"Alright. I imagine it would be a week before Davis is ready."

"A week?"

"Yes. It's a long journey on foot. He has to regain his strength."

"I see. Very well. Keep me advised on his progress."

"Of course."

Dewey moved off, distraught. He stopped at a spot overlooking the river. He considered the events and marveled how things had unraveled so quickly. He could not let the mission fail, not if he wanted to continue with his career in the OSS, not if he wanted to serve his country.

Granier and his team hiked through the forest at a good clip. He was anxious to get back to the Viet Minh camp. He thought about what he had discovered and what he would tell Dewey. His report could cost American and Viet Minh lives if he was wrong. He wasn't wrong, but he was unsure how right he was. It all depended on how one interpreted the information. It was up to him to provide a clear picture of what was happening on the ground and not to exaggerate its meaning. Dewey would interpret the information how he saw fit. They didn't always agree, and that was okay, but there were a lot of lives at stake.

This would be the most difficult raid yet for the Viet Minh. The Viet Minh had surprise on their side, but the Japanese were entrenched in a well-armed fortress. Standard military doctrine suggested that the attacking force would need to be three times that of the defending force in a fortified position. That was not a comforting thought for Granier. A lot of Viet Minh could die.

Dewey went back to Ho's cave and entered. Giap and Ho were still there discussing the problems in the camp. "If I may interrupt?" said Dewey.

"Of course," said Ho. "Please sit down."

"I shall stand. This will only take a moment. I have reconsidered our discussion and... although I think it very unlikely, I suppose it is possible that Buck is a potential threat to you and your people. At least I understand the reasoning behind your conclusions. I will send him back across the border with our wounded man, Davis, as soon as he is well enough to travel. In the meantime, we will move forward with the raid on the Japanese garrison at Tan Trao."

"This is not what we asked for," said Ho.

"No. This is a compromise. It's an effort not to abandon the progress we have made. We still fight a common enemy."

"And what will happen to your man in the meantime?"

"I will watch him personally."

"You will be responsible for him and his actions?"

"Yes… as always."

"And during the raid?"

"He will be with my men and me. I will keep a close eye on him. When we return, he will leave with Davis."

"Would you accept an alternative?"

"I would not. I am informing you of my intentions. I am not asking for your permission."

"Then I see we have little choice. Thank you for informing us. See that you watch him closely. He is your responsibility."

"Right. Well… good day," said Dewey, turning and leaving.

Spitting Woman was not happy when a messenger said Giap wanted to meet with her again that evening after sunset. In her mind, Giap was trouble she didn't need. It was always better to stay away from powerful men, especially if you were a Viet Minh woman. She entered the forest where they had met before. Giap was waiting with another man, Spitting Woman's unit commander, Mr. Doa. "Am I in trouble?" she asked, sheepishly.

"No, my daughter," said Giap. "You have proven your loyalty and your usefulness. There is a matter we need to discuss with you."

She said nothing in response. She listened. Giap's accent in her native tongue was not good. At times she had trouble understanding him, and she wondered if he had trouble understanding her.

"The American... your lover... he is a spy for the French," said Giap, careful, knowing it would be a blow.

"That's not possible. I know him. He is a good man."

"He is a traitor."

"He has fought for us. He saved my life many times."

"Yes. A spy does that so that you trust him. So you will tell him your secrets."

"How do you know this?"

"The coin you took from him and showed to me. It is French. A gift from his grandfather. His family is French. He was born in France. He became American when he and his family went to the United States."

"He told you this?"

"No. The American commander, Dewey, told me when I confronted him about the coin. But all that doesn't matter. Your lover is a spy for the French. Uncle Ho and I are sure."

"Uncle knows?"

"Yes. I had no choice but to tell him."

"Oh, no..."

"Uncle does not blame you. The Americans and we were fooled too. It is not your fault. The French man is deceitful."

Spitting Woman felt her legs giving out. Her power was gone. She squatted on the ground, knowing it was disrespectful, but she couldn't stand anymore. She felt faint. "This can't be true. What will happen to him? Is he being sent back to China?"

"No. That is not an option. He knows too much about us. He is endangering all of us; your tribe, your family, your children. He cannot be allowed to leave and rejoin the French."

"What are you saying?"

"He must die. His death must seem an accident. We cannot afford to lose the American's support. They will not accept his assassination by our hand or their own. He must die in battle. During the upcoming raid on the old fortress at Tan Trao. Commander Doa will help you."

"You want me to kill him?!"

"Yes, but it must seem that the Japanese did it. You and Commander Doa will create the situation to ensure his death."

"I can't."

"This is an order. You must obey. The Viet Minh have protected you, your family, and your tribe. We wish to continue this arrangement, but we can only do so with your strict obedience. You should think about your children and your parents. You must do what is necessary to keep them safe. Do you understand?"

Spitting Woman was frightened by the thought. She had seen what the Japanese could do to young children. They were barbarians. She loved Granier, and she loved her family. It was a terrible choice to make. She slowly nodded and said, "I will do as you say."

Granier returned to camp and looked for Spitting Woman. He missed her and wanted to hug and kiss her before reporting to Dewey. She was nowhere in sight. The information he had gathered was important, and he knew he must report it immediately.

Granier found Dewey with the other Americans and reported his findings from the mission. "How sure are you that there are only seventy-five soldiers in the garrison?" said Dewey.

"There is no way to be sure. They could receive reinforcements any day. It could also be that they were due for a supply shipment, and that explains the low food stocks. But if I am right, we should attack as soon as possible. With only seventy-five men, we could easily defeat them with minimal losses of our own," said Granier.

"I see. How many men would you suggest as an assault force?"

"Well, I've been giving that some thought. The smaller the force, the faster we can travel without being detected. I think five hundred. That's enough to defeat the garrison even if they do receive reinforcements."

"Alright. Five hundred. Light machine guns and mortars?"

"Absolutely. And plenty of grenades. We'll also need some of Davis' explosives to destroy the fortress when we leave."

"Yes... Davis. There's something else I need to speak with you about."

"What's that?"

"When this mission is completed, I want you to take Davis back across the border."

"You think he's up to it?"

"Hoagland assures me he will be by the time we return."

"Okay. I can hitch a ride back with the next supply drop."

"No. You won't. I've asked for your replacement."

"What?! Why? I can't believe you're disappointed in my performance."

"It's not that. Look I know you've grown fond of the Viet Minh scout. Normally, headquarters frowns on fraternizing with our allies, especially when they are aborigine."

"That's why you're sending me back. Because I'm fraternizing? That's bullshit, Commander. Everybody has been fraternizing."

Dewey felt like a coward and decided to come clean. "It's not that. Mr. Van and Mr. Ho have discovered that you were French."

"What? How?"

"It's not important. What is important is this mission. We are making real progress with the Viet Minh. And they, in turn, are taking the fight to the Japanese just as we planned. They're saving lives."

"Chinese lives."

"The lives of our allies. If we stay the course, it is just a matter of time before the Japanese are forced to withdraw from China and Indochina. But Mr. Ho and Mr. Van are threatening to withdraw their forces if you stay in the camp."

"Look. I can talk to them. I can explain. I'm not a spy."

"I know that. And I think deep down they know it too, but in their minds, they can't risk it. They hate the French. And regardless of your loyalty to America, they see you as French."

"You've got to let me try to explain, Commander."

"No. It's done. The decision has been made. You will be returning to headquarters in China. That's an order."

Granier was stunned. It took him half a minute before he responded, "Yes, sir."

"You've done excellent work here, Buck. Someday, the Viet Minh will recognize that. In the meantime, you will have to accept the gratitude of a grateful nation. I've recommended you for a Bronze Star. Commander Patti assures me that you will get it."

"Yeah. Thanks," said Granier. "May I be excused? I've got a lot to do… to prepare for the raid."

"Of course."

Granier left, downcast and unsure.

Granier found Spitting Woman walking toward the river. He was glad to see her but unsure how he would tell her that he had been ordered to leave. He thought about telling her that he would come back when the war was over. At the rate the Americans and their allies were advancing in the Pacific, he didn't think it would last too much longer, especially if they could cut off the Japanese supply lines. In the meantime, he was sure he could get leave and maybe take her someplace nice like the Philippines or Hawaii. He had saved up a lot of money over the years, and he couldn't think of anything he would rather spend it on than making her smile. "Hey," he said approaching her from behind.

She turned. Their eyes met for a brief moment, and she looked away. Granier was surprised, worried. "What's wrong?" he said. "I thought you'd be glad to see me."

Her eyes filled with tears. "Whoa. Hey, what's wrong? Is it something I said?" Then it dawned on him, "You heard, didn't you?"

She was angry and disappointed. She slapped him across the face and hit him with her fists on the chest and arms. "Wait a minute. It's not my fault. I don't want to leave. I especially don't want to leave you. But I'm a soldier like you. I have to obey my orders."

She stopped and broke down sobbing. He grabbed her and held her close. "Stop. Stop. It's gonna be okay. It's not forever. The war will end soon. I can come back. I will come back. I promise. You're the only woman that has ever made me happy. I wouldn't leave you for the world. You gotta believe me. I love you."

She kicked him until he let her go. She ran off into the woods. He didn't follow her.

SIX

The Viet Minh task force, five hundred soldiers strong, and the American team, minus Davis, wound their way through the mountains and forests. They did not talk unless necessary, and all of their gear was tied down or stowed in their packs to prevent any clanking sound that might tip off an enemy patrol or outpost. They were disciplined and took seriously the instructions of their commanders no matter how inconsequential their orders seemed. Unlike the Americans that seemed more self-assured, the Viet Minh troops believed that because their commanders were more educated, they knew better. It was a soldier's job to listen and obey.

The column did not travel on footpaths. Instead, they stuck to the trees. It was hard going. The forest floor was uneven and thick with groundcover. Exposed tree roots were especially hazardous and caused more than one twisted ankle. It was dark below the forest canopy. The shafts of sunlight that did make it through were not welcome. The soldiers' eyes were forced to readjust between light and dark constantly. Five hundred soldiers left a trail of stomped plants and footprints in the soil. It couldn't be helped. The last three soldiers in the column used tree branches to cover the tracks as best they could. Nobody thought it worked well, but they had to try. Their best method of remaining undiscovered was speed and silence.

Dewey had not told Ho and Giap that the suggested troop levels were Granier's idea. He knew that they would become immediately suspicious if they knew of the intelligence source. Dewey trusted Granier and knew there was little chance he was a spy for the French. But it didn't matter. Granier had to go to keep the peace and to complete the mission successfully. Dewey had ordered Granier to stay with the team and not scout ahead. That job was left to the Viet Minh scouts, including Spitting Woman. The scouts and snipers were competent, especially after having been properly trained by Granier.

Granier carried his rifle in his hands, always at the ready, and the explosives Davis had given him in his backpack. He had been chosen to take Davis' place as the leader of the demolition team since he already knew the compound and where the explosives should be placed. Davis had given him a refresher course on demolition before he left. He had been trained on their use during his OSS training back in America, but when it came to explosives, a refresher course was never unwelcomed. He and Davis had discussed the enemy compound. They outlined a demolition plan. Davis had insisted Granier use the chemical pencil detonators instead of the electronic timers. Granier was going to argue with him but then thought better of it. It was Davis' specialty. He would carry out the mission according to Davis suggestions.

Granier avoided contact with the Viet Minh. He didn't know with whom Giap and Ho had talked about their suspicions. He would be forced to leave soon enough. There was no need to get in an argument with any of the Vietnamese, especially when he planned to come back after the war. He didn't want any grudges.

Spitting Woman was, of course, different. He had to find a way to talk with her before he left. He had to make things right. He had asked Hoagland if he could translate, but Hoagland said he didn't understand her tribe's language and wouldn't be much help. The only other person he knew for sure understood her language was Giap. Granier was sure that was not going to happen. He would have to try to communicate with her as he always had with his gestures, expressions, and the tone of his voice. He considered drawing in the dirt for really hard concepts. It left much to be desired, but it was all he had.

He wanted to give her space so she would calm down. He would talk with her in the evening after the mission before they returned to the Viet Minh camp. He would find her in the forest where she would be keeping watch, alone, and for the first time in his life, let the woman he loved know how he truly felt. He would tell her of the sacrifices he would make for her and that he couldn't think of living without her. He had to find a way to make her understand that she was loved and that he was worth loving.

The Viet Minh had five scouts in front of their column and two on each side guarding their flanks. If the task force were discovered, the Japanese would be tipped off. It was obvious where they were heading. The old French fortress was the only Japanese position in the area worth attacking. The idea behind the scouts in front was more than just spotting the enemy before the enemy spotted the column. In the event of detection, the scouts would try to mislead the Japanese by taking them on a wild goose chase through the forest. Hopefully, that would give the Viet Minh column the time it needed to move past the Japanese patrol without detection and continue their mission. It was a very risky assignment for the scouts who normally did not engage the enemy but rather reported back the enemy position to their commander.

Spitting Woman was part of the five scout team in front of the Viet Minh column. The advanced team of scouts proceeded through the forest spread across a line one hundred yards apart from each other. That gave the column a wide berth in which to travel. They were almost a half-mile in front of the column. Because of their large number, the Viet Minh soldiers needed plenty of time to disperse and hide should they encounter a Japanese patrol.

The scout team came to a fast-moving mountain stream. While a welcome source of refreshment, flowing water made the scouts more cautious. It was difficult to hear approaching footsteps over the sound of water flowing over rocks. The stream was also a natural resting place for the Japanese. The chance of encountering a Japanese patrol was higher near a stream or river.

The scouts stopped at the stream. The two scouts on either end of the line walked down the bank to ensure there were no Japanese patrols nearby. The three center scouts, including Spitting Woman, closed their ranks and took up close defensive positions where they could cover each other in the event of a firefight.

The column would be arriving shortly and would naturally want to drink from the stream. It was the scouts' job to make sure it was safe. Spitting Woman scooped up a handful of water and examined it. It was clear and cool in her hand. She smelled it. It smelled fresh and free of odor. She took a small sip and tasted it. It was fine. She drank and filled her water bag.

Her eyes never left the surrounding forest. She thought about Granier. She was angry with him. He had lied by being nice to her. He wasn't the man he seemed. He was a traitor. He was endangering her and her people just like Giap had said. She forced herself to stop thinking about the stupid American. He was an annoying distraction. She had a job to do and needed to focus.

As she tied a knot over the opening of her water bag, something caught her eye. She motioned to the other two scouts that she was going across the stream to have a look. She set down her pack and carried her rifle at the ready. Stepping on a rock in the middle of the stream, she crossed to the opposite bank and walked up a small slope to a fallen tree. A thin wire attached to one of the exposed roots stretched twenty feet across the forest floor and seemed to end at an upright tree. It was one and a half feet off the ground so that small critters would not accidentally trip it. A boobytrap. She wasn't sure what type – mechanical or explosive, but that didn't concern her at the moment. Were the makers of the boobytrap watching and waiting? She acted like she was unaware of the wire and did not search for the weapon that would be triggered by the wire. If the enemy was watching, she did not want to give them a reason to kill her.

She moved to the fallen tree and around the side that was not boobytrapped. Her eyes continued to scan the area, searching. She had to know if someone was waiting to ambush the column. She would be the bait. She walked deeper into the trees out of sight of the other scouts.

There was a small clump of bushes at the top of a rise that looked like they had been disturbed. She walked around them and approached from the back. She knelt in the clump and pushed the plant leaves back. There were two square marks on the ground and an imprint of a man laying down. *A light machine gunner,* she thought. *They had been waiting to see what they caught. So, where is he?*

She moved through the bushes and trees examining the forest floor, finding evidence of more men – twenty-five in all – a kill squad. She found some cooked rice that someone had eaten and let a few grains fall to the ground. *Sloppy,* she thought. She smelled the grains and rubbed them with her fingers. *One, maybe two days,* she thought. They were gone but had left their boobytrap set the way a hunter leaves a snare.

She walked back to the area where the boobytrap had been set and motioned to the other scouts to stay where they were. She could hear the column approaching. There wasn't much time. She followed the wire to the tree and studied the mechanism. Her eyes followed a second wire up into the trees. She stepped behind the tree and hooked the hard barrel sight in her rifle to the wire that stretched to the fallen tree root. She gave it a hard tug. There was a whipping sound, and a large mud ball with sharpened wooden spikes swung down from the tree canopy. It was designed to swing around a large area, so if the first swing didn't hit anyone, it would swing in a circle until it found a target or ran out of energy. Spitting Woman attached her bayonet to the barrel of her rifle. As the spiked ball swung near the tree, she reached out and cut the rope. The ball crashed to the ground and rolled into the stream.

When the commander of the column arrived, she suggested they take a different path to the fortress. If the Japanese had set a trap here, they might have set them elsewhere in this area of the forest. He agreed and informed Dewey and the Americans of the needed detour.

Granier examined the spiked mud ball in the stream and looked with concern at Spitting Woman. They had brief eye contact before she looked away. There was nothing he could do to protect her, and it made him crazy like ants crawling over his skin. He would have gladly taken her place. She would continue to do her job, no matter how dangerous. It's what he loved about her. She was courageous.

It was just before sundown when the column arrived at the mountain ridge above the old French fortress. Dewey insisted that Granier be brought forward with the other scouts to explain the layout of the village and the fortress to Dewey and the Viet Minh commanders. Hoagland translated. Everyone listened closely. Their lives and the lives of the men under their command depended on it.

Granier squatted down on the forest floor with the others looking out at the valley below. "The Japs keep two patrols, five men each, going at all times. One for the village to the west and one for the rice fields just beyond it. I estimate about two hundred villagers, mostly farmers. Nothing we need to worry about."

"Any chance they might help us?" said Dewey.

"Slim at best. Probably get in the way more than help."

"Alright. No farmers."

"The Japs also keep two fifteen- to twenty-man squads patrolling the surrounding mountains. The group that set up the boobytrap was probably one of those squads. The remaining soldiers are stationed inside the fortress on the east end of the valley. If we attack after midnight most of them will probably be asleep in the barracks. We have enough explosive charges to blow the barracks to smithereens if we can place the charges without being detected. There is a river that runs by both the fortress and the village. The biggest challenge will be approaching the fortress undetected because of those two guard towers. If we take out the towers, our forces can have free movement outside the perimeter walls. There is a heavy machine gun and an 81mm mortar positioned near each other inside the compound."

"Can you take the machine gun and mortar teams out from the ridge?"

"Unfortunately, no. They're too close to the buildings. If we could get some men on the perimeter walls, they would have a clear shot at both positions, but the guards in the towers could easily snipe them."

"So, the guard towers are again the key?"

"Yes. If I can get up into one of the towers, say the front one, I could probably take out the Japs in the back tower plus the heavy machine gun and mortar positions."

"That's a lot to ask of one man."

"I was thinking a man and a woman," said Granier glancing over to Spitting Woman.

"I see. From what I have witnessed, you couldn't ask for better."

"That's true. There's only one problem with this plan... I need to set the explosive charges under the barracks. That's gonna be difficult to do if I'm stuck climbing a tower to play sniper."

"I can handle the explosives. Although you might want to give me a quick refresher course before you leave."

"Right. If you can set the charges and detonate them just as I take over the tower, we should be able to wipe out a majority of the Japs before they even know what hit them. The Viet Minh can focus on the patrols in the village and rice fields, then rush the main gate once I've eliminated the two heavy weapon positions. Once we control the compound, we should be able to provide a strong defense if the patrols from the mountains show up."

"A lot is riding on you, Buck. If you fail, the Viet Minh could be slaughtered by the heavy machine gun and mortar when they breach the front gate."

"Yeah, well... if I fail, I'll be dead, and I won't give a damn."

"Interesting way of looking at it. Commander, what do you think?"

The Viet Minh commander heard the translation and nodded to affirm his answer. "We have a plan then," said Dewey with confidence.

While the Viet Minh and the Americans rested in the afternoon heat, Granier took the time to clean his weapon once again and ensure it was working properly. He no longer needed to think about the process of disassembling and reassembling his weapon. It had become routine. Instead, he thought about his rifle sight plan.

The first demolition explosion would be his cue to open fire. He thought about the flash from the explosion. It would blind him momentarily, and even if he had his eyes closed, his retinas would contract making it difficult to see in the dark. The guard in the tower would move to the side of the tower facing the explosion so he could look out and see what was happening. He would wait until his target stabilized and his retinas returned to normal before taking his first shot. He figured two to three seconds would be required. That was an eternity in a firefight, but it couldn't be helped. Missing was not an option.

The distances he would be shooting from were not far enough to be affected by temperature and moisture in the air. There was no perceivable wind, so that was a plus. But that could change by the time he was ready to shoot, so he made a mental note to check the wind once he was on the tower.

There would be four distances for which he would need to shoot. The first shot was from the front tower to the back tower. He estimated the distance at one hundred and sixty yards. It was a flat trajectory roughly parallel to the bore. He would adjust his scope for that distance since it was the most crucial shot. Since it was a relatively short distance and he wanted to make sure he killed the guard outright, he would go for a headshot.

The second set of targets were the machine gun and mortar positions. Even though the targets would be closer in range, they would prove to be more difficult shots. There were two problems with those sets of shots. First, he would not have time to readjust his scope once the firefight started. He would need to ballpark the alignment of the target to the scope reticle. Second, the Japanese weapon positions were at a sharp downward angle from the tower. That meant that gravity would have a different effect on the bullet's trajectory and he would need to compensate. Third, the second target set was a shorter distance than the first. At seventy-five yards out, the bullet would be at the top of its trajectory when it hit the target. Again, he would need to compensate. He would go for chest shots so that he was sure to hit something even if it wasn't one of the target's vital organs.

The third target set was the Japanese troops inside the compound. They would be at different distances and angles. He would need to ballpark his aim accordingly for each shot. Chest shots again.

The fourth and final target set would be any Japanese

troops approaching from the village, rice paddies or forest. He figured that those distances and angles were such that he could probably use his current scope setting, then adjust fire from there if he missed a shot. He thought he might be able to identify an object that was approximately one hundred and sixty yards out toward the village and use that as an adjustment marker. Again, chest shoots. It was far from a perfect plan.

Granier glanced over at Spitting Woman. He was giving her the space he thought she needed to come to terms with his leaving. She was talking with her commander, Dao. She looked upset. They both looked in Granier's direction as Dao gestured with his hands. Granier couldn't tell what they were talking about, but he imagined it was last minute instructions about the assault. Dao was getting upset and yelling at her. Granier wanted to go over and smack the man upside the head but then thought better of it. Spitting Woman could fight her own battles. Granier didn't like Dao, and he trusted him even less. At least Dao was a good fighter and smart. There was no doubt about that.

It was well past midnight when Dewey, Santana, and Green descended from the forest and approached the old French fortress. Dewey referred to the simple map Granier had drawn of the buildings and weapon positions inside the fortress and the best points of access and egress. They waited until the guard outside the fortress passed before climbing over the perimeter wall and entering the compound. Just as Granier had done, they moved along the wall, staying in the shadows.

Santana and Green kept a close watch as Dewey crept under the first barracks and placed the explosive package. Each package had a chemical pencil detonator of varying length of time – the longest placed first, the shortest last. They weren't exact and required that Dewey place the bombs and activate the detonators at one-minute intervals.

He placed each explosive beneath the center of each barracks for maximum effect, then crimped the pencil detonator with a pair of pliers before scrambling back out from under the building and moving to the next target.

As the explosive charges were placed, Granier, Spitting Woman, and two other Viet Minh maneuvered along the edge of the forest near the front gate and the guard tower overlooking it. Spitting Woman and the two Viet Minh wore Japanese uniforms seized from past raids. Granier wore his camouflaged uniform because he was too big to fit in one of the captured uniforms. Spitting Woman and Granier did not communicate beyond what was required for the mission. They knew that the moments before a battle needed their complete focus. Their personal matters would have to wait.

Two Japanese guards patrolled the entrance to the compound.

The two Viet Minh soldiers exited the forest and walked toward the main gate. They spoke to each other in mumbled tones so nobody could determine the language being spoken. One laughed at the other's joke. Their commandeered uniforms had bloodstains around several bullet holes. It was too dark to see well. One of them pulled out a pack of cigarettes and offered a cigarette to the other. He pulled out a lighter and lit his cigarette and his comrade's cigarette as they drew closer and closer to the entrance. He extinguished the lighter before the Japanese guards could see his face up close.

The Japanese guard in the tower looked down at the two approaching soldiers like it was nothing unusual.

The two Japanese guards on the ground said something to the two approaching soldiers. The soldier with the cigarette pack did not respond but held out the pack as if offering a cigarette to each of the guards. The two Viet Minh closed the distance between themselves and the Japanese guards. The two guards reached out each taking a cigarette and not paying attention to the soldiers' faces hidden in the shadows of their caps.

Granier threw a large rock in the bushes nearby and ducked out of sight.

The sound of the rock caught the attention of the guards on the ground and the guard in the tower. When the guards on the ground turned away, the two Viet Minh placed their hands over the guards' mouths and plunged knives into their hearts, killing them quickly and without a sound. The Viet Minh dragged the guards' bodies underneath the tower and took their places, guarding the front of the main gate.

The guard in the tower was busy investigating the noise from the rock and did not see his two comrades killed. When he finally decided the noise was nothing but an animal moving through the bushes, he looked down at the guards, now smoking cigarettes beside the fortress entrance, and everything looked normal. He went back to surveying the surrounding area.

Granier and Spitting Woman waited until the guard in the tower was looking in the opposite direction. They sprang from the forest and ran quietly to beneath the tower supports where they were out of sight from the guard above.

On cue, the two Viet Minh soldiers started a fight, one reaching into the pocket of the other like he wanted another cigarette. A shoving match broke out.

The tower guard above looked down at the commotion and scolded them for not doing their duty.

Granier and Spitting Woman climbed the ladder on the opposite side of the tower.

The two Viet Minh stopped their argument and resumed guarding the main gate.

The tower guard shook his head in disgust. As he turned back around, he was surprised to find Granier standing directly behind him. Granier placed his hand over the man's mouth and thrust his bayonet through the bottom of the soldier's head between the chin and throat. The guard died with a grunt. Granier kept him from collapsing and let his corpse gently fall to the deck of the tower. Spitting Woman was aiming her rifle at the opposite tower at the back of the compound just in case.

The man in the opposite tower was the only guard with a view of the tower at the front of the compound. He seemed unaware of the death of his comrade.

She switched places with Granier and assumed the position of the front tower guard. Her Japanese uniform was too large for her small frame, but the only person that could see her well enough to notice was a hundred and sixty yards away in the opposite tower, and it was dark. The loose uniform was good enough in the shadows of the tower's roof. Her height was the biggest problem. She was shorter than the dead guard, and that could be a noticeable difference even in the dark at a distance. She stood on the dead guard's corpse to make up for the difference in height.

Granier unslung his rifle, laid down on the tower deck, and quietly chambered a round. He glanced at his watch and took aim. Spitting Woman kept her rifle down so as not to cause alarm from anyone watching. After the first explosion, she would be the first to fire on the machine gunner while Granier took out the back tower guard. It didn't take long.

Dewey was out of breath by the time he'd placed the final explosive package beneath the command post and crushed the pencil detonator. The fuse was only two minutes on the last charge. That wasn't much time for him and his team to find cover from the explosions. As he crawled from beneath the building, Green gave him a hand up. They ran to the perimeter wall and ducked down behind some water barrels Santana had spotted.

Dewey pointed to the different directions he wanted Green and Santana to aim once the firing started. Each man pulled out a grenade and slipped their fingers into the safety rings. The grenades would add to the confusion and hopefully kill more Japanese. They were as ready as they could be, considering the circumstances. Dewey desperately wanted a drink from his canteen to wet his parched throat, but he didn't dare as the time to detonation ticked down.

Granier knew the time was close. He closed his eyes to minimize the effect of the explosion's flash. He took several deep breathes to relax. *Just another day on the shooting range. Ain't no big deal,* he thought. It was a lie he told himself to stay loose and release the tension from his fingers and arms. Even the slightest muscle contraction could throw his aim off. Once the firing started and he took his first shot, he knew he would be okay. It was the waiting that was stressful.

The first explosion lit up the night sky and ripped apart the Japanese barracks killing or badly wounding everyone inside. Fourteen soldiers were put out of action in an instant.

Dewey, Green, and Santana tossed their grenades and opened fire. The grenades exploded in different parts of the compound, caused the confusion and chaos they had been hoping for. The enemy had no idea of the direction of the threats they faced.

Spitting Woman opened fire at the machine gunner below. Her first shot missed. Her second shot hit him in the shoulder. Her third hit him in the throat and killed him. The loader took his place behind the machine gun and gave her a new target.

Granier opened his eyes and peered through his scope. The light from the explosion was dissipating. The guard was moving to the opposite side of the tower just as he had predicted. Granier's retinas expanded. The guard settled. Granier squeezed the trigger. The rifle fired with its usual jolt. The guard's head jerked, and he slumped over the tower's rail. Dead. The second and third barracks blew up. Japanese poured out of the remaining buildings into the compound, looking for the enemy.

Granier moved to the next target – the machine gun position – just in time to see the loader go down. Spitting Woman had things under control. No need to duplicate effort. He looked around and saw three Japanese soldiers running toward the mortar position. "No. No," said Granier mockingly as he opened fire.

He compensated as best he could according to his sighting plan. It took five shots to kill the three Japanese in the mortar crew. No shell made it into the mortar. Others would take their place, but that was for later. Right now, he needed to kill as many Japanese within the compound as he could. His aim was getting better as he compensated a bit more after each shot until he found his sweet spot. Two more shots killed two more soldiers. His empty clip flipped from the open chamber of his rifle. He reloaded and released the bolt loading the next round. He searched for another target and found an officer – a lieutenant yelling at his troops, pointing where to direct their fire. *Bonus,* he thought as he took aim and fired. The officer was hit in the chest. Dead. His troops were leaderless.

A platoon of Viet Minh waiting in the forest ran to the wall where Dewey and his men had climbed into the compound. The first three men bent down, allowing the others to use their backs as a step to climb the wall. They sprang over the wall, dropped down into the compound and opened fire on the Japanese coming out of the buildings.

Granier glanced at Spitting Woman. She was kneeling and shouldering her rifle. Aiming. Firing. Reloading. Repeating the cycle. Completely focused on the task at hand. *Now that's a woman,* he thought proudly.

He heard a barrage of gunshots from behind and turned to see the Viet Minh pouring out of the jungle and into the village, attacking the Japanese patrols. He thought they had the situation in hand until he spotted a large group of Japanese soldiers running across the dikes surrounding the rice fields. It was one of the large patrols returning from the mountain. It was a long shot for Granier, but he decided to demoralize them a bit before they attacked the Viet Minh. He turned around and laid prone. He took aim and compensated for the extended distance as best he could figure. He opened fire. Two shots and he took down his first man. The next shot, another man went down. Two more before the next man was hit in the shoulder. He wasn't dead but probably couldn't fight. Granier moved on – aiming, firing, reloading. Focused.

A few moments later, he watched as a man he was aiming at went down before he could squeeze the trigger. The Viet Minh in the village had joined the fight and were firing on the Japanese in the rice fields. *They're closer. They can have 'em,* thought Granier as he turned back around toward the compound. The Japanese were putting up a fierce fight. Bullets were shredding the tower. Spitting Woman had moved from a kneeling to a prone position to avoid being hit. Granier reloaded and poured into the Japanese below, dropping several.

The two Viet Minh soldiers pretending to be guards at the main gate had rigged an explosive package and detonated it. The wood and iron gate blew to smithereens. The fortress was breached. The two Viet Minh ran inside and opened fire on the Japanese, killing several before they themselves were mowed down by a Japanese corporal firing a light machine gun.

Viet Minh that had been hiding poured out of the forest and entered the compound, firing their weapons, tossing grenades, killing Japanese.

The Japanese recoiled at the onslaught and pulled back into the remaining buildings where they could find some cover. They returned fire, killing and wounding a dozen

Viet Minh.

The fortress commander stood on the steps of the command post, yelling to his troops to stand their ground when another explosion ripped the building apart. He went flying through the air and landed on his face, his back shredded, his uniform smoking. Dying.

The fighting continued as more Viet Minh entered the compound. The Japanese again pulled back. Some escaped out the back entrance. Others fought on. Two Japanese privates tried to retake the heavy machine gun. *Fools' courage,* thought Granier as he ended their effort with two well-placed shots.

The Japanese inside the compound were leaderless and losing the battle. They continued to fight for their survival in small groups of three or four, using whatever they could for cover. They ran low on ammunition and pulled ammo belts and bandoleers from their dead and dying comrades. One of the soldiers ran to a supply hut and dragged a crate of grenades over to his comrades. They scooped the grenades, pulled the pins, and hurled them at the Viet Minh, driving them back.

The explosive package that was meant to take down the communications tower had malfunctioned, and the antenna still stood. Dewey was concerned that the Japanese might have called for reinforcements or air support. Not wanting to see a clear victory end in a Viet Minh massacre, he decided it was time to leave. He ordered the Viet Minh demolition team to place charges along the walls as the fighting continued. The goal was never to occupy the fortress but rather to destroy it to prevent future use and free the locals in the area from Japanese occupation. Dewey signaled Granier that he and the others were leaving.

Granier and Spitting Woman would provide overwatch as the Viet Minh, and the Americans retreated into the forest. Then it would be their turn to climb from the tower and retreat. Dao and his men were to provide cover for

Granier and Spitting Woman when they ran for the forest. The fortress would be destroyed moments after their retreat. It was risky, and the timing was critical. They would all rendezvous on the other side of the mountain ridge.

Dewey and the Americans on the ground covered the Viet Minh as they placed the last of their explosives. They returned to the American's position. There was too much open ground between them and the main gate. Dewey ordered Green and Santana back over the wall. The Japanese were greatly reduced in number but were still fighting back.

Dewey waited until Green and Santana were over the wall. He glanced back at the communications hut. It was still standing, and it bothered him. It was a failure, and he hated failure. He picked up a satchel charge and motioned for the Viet Minh to give him cover. He ran across the compound, pulled the detonator wire, and flung the charge next to the communications hut. He ran back to his covered position and dove behind the water barrels just as the charge exploded, shaking the ground, destroying the hut and bringing the communications antenna down.

Their job was done and little time remained before the wall charges went off. He and the remaining Viet Minh climbed over the wall. He snapped a salute to Granier before jumping down and retreating into the forest. It was Granier's signal that he could now retreat with Spitting Woman.

Granier looked back at the village and could see the Viet Minh already retreating into the forest as they continued to fire at the Japanese patrol. "Our turn," said Granier gesturing to Spitting Woman. "You go down first. I'll follow."

He continued to pour fire down on the Japanese to cover her retreat, but she didn't move. It was time to kill Granier as Giap had ordered. She knew Dao would be watching from the forest and that if she didn't do it, he would accuse her of being a traitor. She would be executed, and her family would be ejected from the camp. Without her, they would surely die. The thought sent a shiver down her spine. She had no choice; the American had to die before leaving the tower. It would look like the Japanese killed him. Even the bullet from her rifle would be Japanese in case his body was ever recovered. He was a spy and a traitor as Giap had told her. He had no reason to want the American dead unless it was true. She had recounted this argument a dozen times in her mind, but something was holding her back...

She had loved the man more than any man she had ever met. He had protected her and even saved her life more than once. Maybe he was a spy and a traitor, but he didn't deserve to die. There was too much good in him. He turned back and saw she hadn't left yet. "What are you waiting for?" he said, rising into a kneeling position in preparation. "I'm starting to run low on ammo. You gotta go now."

She looked back toward the forest and prayed to the forest gods that Dao was not watching. She turned her rifle around and thrust the butt of the weapon into the back of Granier's head with a heavy thud. He went down unconscious. She knew that when he awoke, he would be surrounded and would continue to fight the Japanese until they killed him. She didn't want that.

Granier's eyes fluttered open for a moment, and he tried to focus them. He saw Spitting Woman pick up his sniper rifle and throw it over the side of the tower. *What the hell is she doing?* he thought, his head spinning in a whirlwind of pain.

She pulled out his bayonet and threw it over the side. With no way to fight, the Japanese would capture him. He would live.

He groaned and tried to rise. She hit him again even harder with her rifle. Again he went down, unconscious. She took one last look at his face. Tears welled up in her eyes. She turned away and climbed down the tower.

The Japanese from the village advanced toward the fortress. They opened fire on Spitting Woman as she climbed down and reached the ground. She wanted to fire back, but there wasn't enough time. She ran for the forest. A burst of gunfire from the forest drove the Japanese back. Dao and a platoon of men emerged at the edge of the trees. Dao met Spitting Woman and slapped her across the face. "You are a stupid woman and a traitor," said Dao as he moved past her and ran toward the tower.

Spitting Woman moved into the safety of the trees and returned fire at the Japanese. She watched as Dao slung his rifle over his back and climbed the tower. She was sure he would kill Granier. The Japanese fired at him. She prayed that one of them would hit him before he reached the top, but the idiots were bad shots and kept missing. She considered for a moment, swung her rifle around, took aim, and squeezed the trigger.

Her bullet hit Doa in the lower back. He jerked in pain but held on. He looked back toward the trees as he knew it was her and not the Japanese that had shot him. The anger rose inside him, and he continued to climb.

She could see a growing dark spot on his uniform. He was bleeding badly. She thought she might have hit his liver. She wanted to fire again, but the other men around her were suspicious and would surely know it was her firing at their commander.

Doa approached the top of the ladder and reached for the last rung. He missed it, lost his grip, and fell backward, faint from blood loss. His leg caught on the ladder, and he hung upside down. Streaks of blood ran down his face, his eyes rolled back in their sockets, and he passed out.

She wasn't sure what to do. *What if he woke up before the Japanese reached him?* Seeing their commander beyond saving and the Japanese continuing to advance, the Viet Minh retreated deeper into the forest. Spitting Woman took one last look toward the tower that now held Dao and the American. Like all things, their fate was in the hands of the forest gods. She followed the Viet Minh back into the forest.

Granier's eyes opened. Blood flowed from the wound on his head. At first, he didn't know where he was. Then he remembered Spitting Woman throwing his rifle over the side. He was on the tower, defenseless. She had betrayed him. *But why?*

The explosive charges along the perimeter wall all detonated at the same time. It was a thunderous explosion that killed most of the remaining Japanese within the fortress walls. The perimeter walls on the forest side of the compound collapse into rubble. The supports under the tower were sheared. Dao was killed from the explosion's concussive wave. The tower tipped over and fell. Granier was still conscious and still alive when it crashed to the ground in a heap of timber and sheet metal roofing.

The Viet Minh and Spitting Woman arrived at the rendezvous point on the opposite side of the mountain ridge. One of the Viet Minh explained Dao's heroic death as he went back to save the American. Both died when the perimeter wall was demolished and the tower fell. Hoagland translated the report to Dewey. "Do you think Granier's really dead?" said Hoagland.

"I don't know, but I'm not going to take his word for it. If Granier is dead, I want to see it with my own eyes. On me," said Dewey to the other team members as he started hiking back up the mountain.

The Americans headed over the mountain ridge until they heard the sound of two plane engines. They stopped and looked down into the valley. Two Japanese Zeros were circling over the demolished fortress. If the Americans were discovered, the Zeros would surely attack – or worse... follow them back to the Viet Minh camp. It was a risk Dewey wouldn't take. He abandoned the search for

Granier's body. The disheartened team returned to join the column back to the Viet Minh camp. The death of their companion soured the Americans' great victory.

Spitting Woman took her place with the other scouts out in front of the column. She was unsure of what had happened to Dao and the American, but her guilt was real. She wept quietly as she walked through the forest.

SEVEN

Granier sat upright in a bed, staring at a beetle crawling up a wall. *Someone's dinner,* he thought. According to the French doctor that patched him up, he had a severe concussion, three broken ribs, seventeen cuts that needed stitches, dozens more that didn't and more bruises than a prizefighter. The stitches had been sutured using thread from his uniform and a regular sewing needle. There had been no anesthesia to soothe the pain — not even an aspirin. The Japanese did not give their prisoners medical supplies. They barely gave them food – a half cup of rice with a drizzle of fish sauce per day per prisoner. The prisoners supplemented the protein they needed with bugs and rodents they captured. Water was supplied by nature when it rained, which was often this time of year. The runoff from the rain sliding down the tin roofs was stored in empty food tins, bedpans and whatever else the prisoners could find that didn't leak.

Granier was the only American in the prison camp. All the other prisoners were French. The Japanese that found him unconscious under the rubble of the guard tower discovered the French coin in his pocket when they searched him. His uniform had been torn to shreds and had no visible insignia to identify his country. They naturally assumed he was French.

The commander of the prison camp considered shooting him as a rebel, but when Granier was questioned under torture, he didn't say anything. Nothing. Granier hadn't spoken since he arrived. He just had this blank expression on his face like nothing affected him. The Japanese thought he had suffered such a severe concussion that his brain had been scrambled beyond healing or he was just too stupid to understand the interrogator's questions.

They put him under the care of a French doctor. The doctor was from a hospital in Hanoi before the Japanese changed their mind about the French governing themselves and put them all in prison. Now, the Japanese were waiting for the French to slowly die of starvation and disease so they could be rid of them. Disobedience to the rules or the whim of an officer was met with the edge of a sword usually resulting in decapitation or, at best, dismemberment. As the French prisoners would say... *It was a rough playground.*

Granier didn't care. He didn't care about anything. Not living or dying. Not sickness or health. Not the edge of the Japanese sword. He was a dead man walking, and he was fine with that. He had heard the expression once that 'Betrayal was the willful demise of hope.' *So true,* he thought. It saps one's will to go on... to survive. He wasn't sure why he was still breathing. *Instinct, I guess,* he thought. *The brain must be wired to take a breath because God knows it's not me doing it.*

While recovering from his wounds, Granier thought about what Spitting Woman had done and why. He pondered whether she ever loved him or whether their relationship was just a convenience. He certainly loved her. That was no lie. He concluded that she must have been ordered to betray him. Someone powerful wanted him dead because they thought he was French. *Maybe Ho, maybe Giap.* She would have been faced with an impossible decision – kill him or be killed for disobedience. He knew she was the only person capable of protecting her family, and she had to survive to protect them. She had chosen her pack over an outsider. Granier wondered if he would have done the same. *No,* he thought. *She was my pack. I would have done anything to protect her and her family. She should have trusted me.* He wondered what he would do if he ever saw her again. He fought the need for revenge. *Animals don't seek revenge,* he thought. *Be an animal. Let it go.* But her betrayal was entrenched in Granier's subconscious like a vein of ore deep in a mountain, hidden, but always there, waiting to be revealed.

When Granier was finally released from the sickbay, he joined the other prisoners. They spoke to him in French and assumed he was a French army soldier that had had a hard time of it and didn't feel like talking. They gave him a wide berth. They had seen men like him snap before, and it was best not to be around when it happened. Not everyone in the camp was a soldier. The Japanese had arrested many of the French citizens, especially those in government, and placed them in the prisons alongside the soldiers. They did not mix well, and the soldiers dominated the civilians. The soldiers did whatever it took to survive and weren't afraid to fight with their fists. Some even relished it as a way to pass the time.

A French corporal, Laurent, was assigned by the French commander the job of giving Granier an orientation of how things worked in the camp and getting him situated in his barracks. As they walked through the entrance and down a row of twin bunks, Laurent said in French, "Your uniform… or what's left of it… I haven't seen it before. What unit are you from?"

Granier did not respond.

"I'm not spying for the Japanese if that is what you are thinking. I would rather die. Besides, it is insane to pet the tiger that can eat you, yes?" said Laurent.

Granier still said nothing. "This is your bunk," said Laurent pointing to a top bunk. "It belonged to a civil engineer that hung himself in the toilet a couple of days ago. I guess he couldn't take it. Although I think he may have had a little help from a couple of his roommates that didn't like listening to his crying at night. He is in a better place, I think."

Granier did not react to the story. "You don't speak much, do you?" said Laurent. "That's not good. You need to make friends to survive in a place like this. Look, if you don't want to speak that's your business, but at least smile occasionally, so the others know you don't want to kill them."

Granier just stared straight ahead, no reaction. "Ah, well... it's your neck," said Laurent. "Stay clear of the guards whenever possible. You don't want to piss them off. They're barbarians. They enjoy hurting us. It's like a game to them. Toughest cat in the house gets the mice. That sort of thing. You'll steer clear if you're smart."

Granier said nothing. He climbed up into his bunk and stared at the ceiling, ignoring Laurent. "No, no. No thanks required," said Laurent as he walked toward the exit. "Always pleased to help."

The prisoners not in sickbay were expected to work in the surrounding area. Each morning a work detail of one hundred prisoners was led out of the compound under heavy guard and marched into the forest. They were given saws, axes, wedges, sledgehammers and chains which they would use to cut down trees and drag them across the soft soil. The downed trees were loaded on to trucks and driven to a nearby sawmill where they were cut into lumber. The prisoners operated the equipment in the sawmill too. More than one lost his fingers in the steam-powered machinery that drove the circular saw.

No prisoner was crazy enough to try smuggling a tool that could be used as a weapon back into the camp. Even the slightest infraction, no matter how innocent, was considered a viable reason for immediate execution. There were however broken saw teeth that could be smuggled inside the prisoners' mouths or butt cheeks. The prisoners sharpened the bits of steel the best they could on rocks and nail heads. With patience, the edges could become razor-sharp. It drove the Japanese crazy to see the French show up to roll call with clean-shaven faces. When asked by a Japanese officer, the prisoners responded, "My beard just fell off last night while I was asleep. It sometimes happens to us, French."

It was late in the afternoon, and the day's work was done. Grey clouds rolled in, and it was muggy. A sure sign of rain. Granier was sitting outside on the steps of his barracks, watching as a group of soldiers played football with a hollowed-out coconut. He saw a Japanese lieutenant flipping a coin as he passed in front of the main gate and approached the commander's hut outside the wire. Even at a distance, he recognized the coin. It was his gold coin. He wondered how the lieutenant had come by it. He might have bought it from the soldiers that delivered him to the prison compound but more likely ordered them to hand it over, using some sort of excuse as to why it was required. He might have said that he would keep it for the prisoner to whom it belonged until he was released. *Doesn't matter,* he thought. *It's mine, and I want it back.* Granier knew bringing it up with the lieutenant would only cause trouble. He might even kill him for being insubordinate. He just didn't want that man touching his grandfather's coin. He would bide his time and wait for the right moment.

Granier stood in the line to get his daily ration of rice and fish sauce. His stomach had shrunk over the last few weeks, and the hunger pains had ceased. He knew he would need his strength if he were going to get his coin back. It was a purpose. He needed a purpose to go on. Nothing else seemed to matter.

The Frenchman serving scooped up a half cup and plopped it on Granier's mess tin. There were dead worms in the rice. The Frenchman smiled and said, "Protein."

The next Frenchman in the serving line used a teaspoon to ladle a drizzle of fish sauce over the rice. It would be Granier's breakfast, lunch, and dinner. He stepped out of line and stood eating with his fingers. He didn't mind the dried worms. He watched the lieutenant with his coin as he inspected a platoon of Japanese troops on the opposite side of the wire. He studied his enemy. The lieutenant berated his men for the smallest infraction in their dress, grooming, and maintenance of their weapons. That didn't bother Granier. *Discipline is good,* he thought. *It hardens a soldier. Gives 'em confidence when they get it right.* Granier didn't fault the man for being a tough commander. That was his job. He didn't fault the man for being Japanese. He was doing what his country demanded of him. The man's offense was simply taking his grandfather's coin. For that, Granier would make him pay. He couldn't let that stand. Not after everything that had happened. This justice was within his reach.

The Japanese lieutenant was oblivious to Granier, who was just another French prisoner that should have committed suicide instead of being captured. The lieutenant had his own problems. When he had left for the military academy, he had moved his wife and son to the island of Kyushu to live with his brother and his family. His brother had a good job as a manager at the Mitsubishi Armament factory in the Urakami Valley. His house was big and near the factory. The lieutenant knew that his brother and his wife would take care of his wife and son while he was away serving his country.

Everything had gone well for the first three years of the war. But then the Americans took the island of Okinawa. It was still far from the mainland islands, but unless the Americans could be stopped, it seemed only a matter of time before they invaded the mainland. It was most likely Kyushu island would be the first island invaded. The

Urakami Valley was heavily defended by anti-aircraft batteries which discouraged the American bombers from attacking, and there was a substantial garrison of soldiers there. But the lieutenant knew it was not enough to halt the American advance. He was concerned about the safety of his wife and son. He wrote her a letter and asked her to move to the Northern Island of Hokkaido where her mother lived. There was little heavy industry in Hokkaido and would most likely be the last island the Allies invaded. His wife and son would be safe until the Japanese forces wore the Americans down, drove them back into the sea, and achieved final victory.

He double-checked his letter to ensure that he had not said anything that might prevent the war censors from delivering it to his wife. Even without delay from the censors, it would still take over a week to reach his wife, and even that wasn't for sure. Military correspondence took precedence. Personal mail, even from an officer, got there when it got there.

The French prisoners carried on with life the best they could. They played cards, even though the well-worn deck they had purchased from a guard for a pack of chewing gun was missing a few cards. It didn't matter. It passed the time, and once they figured out which cards were missing, it made the games more interesting.

Fights occasionally broke out between prisoners. The compound was a pressure cooker with too many men in too little space. The Japanese guards let the fights unfold and only stepped in when ordered by their commander. It was good fun to watch the Frenchmen beat the shit out of each other.

The prisoners had flying insect races by tying a thread from one of their uniforms and letting the bug fly around in circles until it collapsed from exhaustion. It felt good to watch the bug suffer more than they did. They were the masters once again. They were in control.

Granier found it all pitiful but said nothing. He acted like he was watching, but his eyes were focused beyond the wire on the lieutenant whenever he would appear. He ruminated on ways of getting his coin back. Stealing it was one option. Maybe creating some sort of issue that would force the lieutenant to enter the compound, then using a diversion while he picked his pocket. It could work if planned and executed correctly. The problem was more psychological. Granier wanted the lieutenant to know that he was taking his coin back. He wanted to face him when he did it. He wanted to dominate him like a beast dominates its prey. He had little regard for the consequences of his actions. It was his way of restoring his worth as a warrior. Fearless. Unbending. That feeling of renewal was more important to Granier than life itself. It was who he was and all he valued. That... and his grandfather's coin. Everything else had fallen away and no longer mattered.

It had been a long day, cutting down trees in the forest under the watchful eye of the guards. Even with the prisoners starving to death, the Japanese still demanded that they work a full day. Granier could feel his body wasting away as it ate away at his muscle. Any fat on his body, of which there was almost none, had been chewed up in the first three weeks in the camp. Next, it would be muscle. Then finally, his organs. Eventually, death, most likely from disease as his immune system shutdown.

Unlike the other prisoners, Granier didn't think about escape. He had no reason to escape. He had given up hope of happiness. Even if he found someone he could love, he would never trust again. Trust was the basis of any good relationship, and it was out of this reach. Because of his nature, his prospects had been slim before he met Spitting Woman, and now they seemed non-existent. There was some satisfaction in knowing he would never love again. It meant that he would never hurt again as he did now.

Better to let it all end in this faraway land. But first… the coin.

As the work team walked back toward the camp, Granier saw something that perked his interest. The lieutenant was exiting the commander's hut and walking in the direction of the entrance to the camp. As usual, the lieutenant wore his Showato – an officer's sword – on his left side so it could be drawn across the body. Granier wondered if the lieutenant was righthanded and if he kept his grandfather's coin in his right pant pocket. The odds were in his favor. The sword concerned him too. Unlike the samurai swords of old made by skilled craftsmen, the Showato was made of cheap steel, stamped using power hammers and tempered with oil. Even so, the officers wore it with pride and kept the blade's edge razor-sharp. Once out of its sheath, it would be deadly. Not such a bad thing, but not before he retrieved what was his. To stand any chance at all, he would need to stay close to his enemy.

It will be a matter of timing, thought Granier. *Will the column of prisoners cut across his path in time and force him to wait until they pass before proceeding? If he stops, this may be the only chance I ever have.* Granier had abandoned his belief in a higher power long ago. But at this moment, he couldn't help himself. He prayed as he drew closer to the lieutenant. *God, if you exist, I will only ask for this one thing before I die. A chance. Just give me one last chance.*

To Granier's amazement, the lieutenant stopped to berate one of the guards near the fence for having loosened the top button on his uniform.

Maybe there is a god. Granier moved closer, one foot in front of the other, his remaining muscles tensing, adrenaline coursing through his veins, the beast within rising once again.

As he was about to enter the entrance to the camp, Granier stepped out of line and walked to the lieutenant. A guard yelled at him. He didn't stop. The lieutenant turned to see why the guard was yelling. A prisoner was walking past him. The lieutenant reached for his sword. He would strike the impudent Frenchman, severing his head from his shoulders as he passed. Granier pivoted behind the lieutenant, reaching out with his left hand to grab the hilt of the sword, keeping the lieutenant from drawing it from its sheath. He swung in back of the lieutenant and slid his right hand into the lieutenant's pocket. The lieutenant struggled to pull his sword out, not realizing the prisoner was stopping him. He looked down and saw the dirty hand on the hilt. His thrust his elbow backward hitting Granier in the chest. Granier was weak and couldn't hold his ground. He fell backward, landing on his ass in the dirt. He raised his hand holding the coin up, locked eyes with the lieutenant and said in English, "Mine."

The French prisoners behind the wire gathered to watch the fight. They had a morbid curiosity of how the lieutenant was going to kill their fellow prisoner.

Guards rushed forward. The lieutenant yelled for them to get back. He would deal with the prisoner alone. He reached for his sword. "Draw that sword, and I'll stick it up your ass," said Granier in English climbing to his feet.

The French prisoners were shocked to hear Granier speak English and exchanged surprised glances.

The lieutenant was surprised by Granier's language. It was in English. He had heard it before. No matter. The prisoner would be dead in a moment. He drew his sword and prepared to strike. "I warned, ya," said Granier with a snarl, tucking the coin in his pocket.

Granier's survival was about luck and a bit of psychology. There would be no second chance. Granier needed to predict the direction of the stroke of the lieutenant's sword. If he was wrong, he was dead. The lieutenant was arrogant, and Granier had embarrassed him in front of the men he commanded. *He'll want my head,* thought Granier. *He's too angry to consider anything else. That's his weakness… pride.*

The lieutenant stepped forward raising his sword above

his head. *A feint,* thought Granier. *Poor predictable bastard.* Granier thrust his arms out to the lieutenant's right side in preparation for a downward side stroke. He guessed correctly. As the sword came down, the lieutenant shifted his arms and swung for the prisoner's head. Granier lunged forward and used both his hands to grab the lieutenant's forearm. Granier twisted counterclockwise into the lieutenant's body while holding his arms, keeping the sword away. The lieutenant was caught off guard by the speed of the prisoner's maneuver. Granier locked his foot behind the lieutenant's boot. He released his right hand from the lieutenant's forearm and drove his elbow into the officer's cheek. The lieutenant stumbled backward from the blow, and as he did, Granier's foot tripped him. The lieutenant let go of his sword as he fell. Granier reached out with his right hand and caught the falling sword by the hilt. He swung the sword around as the lieutenant landed on his ass in the dirt. He stopped the blade an inch from the side of the lieutenant's throat and said, "Pussy."

A corporal ran up and struck Granier in the side of the head with the butt of his rifle. Granier was stunned as he fell sideways and released the sword, letting it fall into the dirt. The lieutenant recovered, picked up his sword, and stood above Granier. He raised his sword to strike. *A simple straight stroke,* thought Granier as he looked up from the ground at the enraged lieutenant. *Nothing fancy. Split my head like a watermelon. Quick. Painless.*

A man's voice called out. The lieutenant froze, his face full of anguish, wanting to proceed with the prisoner's death, but afraid. Granier turned to see a Japanese major standing on the steps of the command hut. He had come out when he heard a commotion. He had seen everything. He walked down the steps and over to the lieutenant and Granier. He scolded the lieutenant in Japanese. The lieutenant bowed obediently and re-sheathed his sword. The major turned to Granier on the ground and said in

English, "You spoke English."

Granier said nothing. "Your accent... you are an American, are you not?" said the major.

Granier remained silent. "I studied economics at the University of San Francisco before the war. Beautiful city. Especially the Golden Gate Bridge," said the major studying the American. "Why are you here in Vietnam?"

Granier kept quiet. The major's face hardened. He wasn't used to being ignored, even by the enemy.

"You assaulted an officer. Be glad you did not kill him. You will be punished. There is no other way," said the major as he motioned for the guards to take the prisoner away. "Perhaps we may talk later when you are ready."

Granier was picked up by the arms and dragged to the hot box – a sheet metal box with barely enough room to fit a man with his legs bent and his head bowed. Once inside, the guards used a wooden mallet to drive wedges in place to hold the door shut. Granier was left to cook in the sun and freeze in the night from his clothes drenched in sweat. No food. No water.

Three days later, Granier was dragged from the hot box and carried to the commander's hut by two Japanese guards. His uniform was even more tattered and stained with salt marks from the sweat. He smelled of urine. His lips were blistered, cracked, and bleeding. His legs were cramped and spasming. He was unable to walk on his own. One more day in the hotbox would have killed him.

The guards sat him in a chair in front of the major. They moved back and stood next to the door. Granier had trouble sitting upright. "It's the dehydration," said the major pouring a small cup of hot tea. "It can make you dizzy, and you can lose your sense of balance. Drink this. It will help."

Granier wanted to refuse anything offered to him by the major, but he was sure he would pass out any minute. He picked up the teacup and moved it toward his lips. His hand was shaking with tremors. He brought his other hand forward, and it was just as bad. The major gave a nod to one of the guards. The guard stepped forward and helped steady Granier's hands as he drank. "You are to be transferred to Tokyo. Your presence, along with the other American prisoners, will help protect the city from being bombed by the allies. You will be shielding the emperor and his family."

"I'd rather die," said Granier, his voice scratchy and hushed.

"That is not an option. While you wait, you will be moved back into the compound with the French. You will no longer be required to work in the forest. Conserve your strength. It will be a long journey to my country. The lieutenant you attacked will not be allowed to seek retribution against you. It is his punishment for losing his sword. You are a lucky man. He has a most foul temper. He has been reprimanded several times for decapitating prisoners. See that you do not cross him again. If you obey, I will let you keep the gold coin you fought so hard to obtain."

"It was mine."

"Nothing is yours. You are a prisoner. If you disobey in any way, I will see that the coin is removed. That will be your punishment. Do you understand?"

Granier took a moment to consider, then nodded.

Granier was escorted back into the compound by the guards. The tea had helped him regain some of his strength. He was able to walk most of the way slowly until the guards became impatient and picked him up by the arms and carried him.

Laurent and another French prisoner took Granier from the guards and helped him to sickbay. "So, you are American. That explains your attitude," said Laurent in French.

Granier smiled. His lips cracked and stung.

"You think this is a joke? That lieutenant almost killed you. Had the major not intervened, you would be missing your head. So, what do we call you while you are still breathing, which I doubt will be long?"

"Buck."

"How do you know French?"

"Born in France. Moved to the States."

"French and American. Passionate and pigheaded. I'm amazed you lasted this long. No matter what you were told by the major, you must stay away from the lieutenant. He's a mean bastard."

"He's a pussy. 'Sides...going to Tokyo... with other Americans."

"Good. The sooner you are out of here, the safer you will be. This war is winding down, and we are winning. It won't be long before the Japanese are forced to surrender. But that's when we really need to worry. Many of the officers will probably commit suicide. It's their way. But before they do they may decide to take a few prisoners with them. Everyone needs to keep their head low or see it loped off."

August 9, 1945

North Field airbase took up almost half of the island of Tinian. It was a six-hour flight to Japan and home to American 313th Bombardment Wing. The 509th Composite Group had been attached to the 313th but was assigned its own area of operations on the Northern tip of the island. The 509th had very little to do with the 313[th,] and almost all contact between the aircrews was prohibited. Their mission was one of the biggest, well-kept secrets of the war.

Major Charles Sweeney sat alone in the mess hall nursing a cup of coffee. His crew was already boarding the B-29

Superfortress nicknamed "Bockscar" after having finished their final briefing in the early hours of the morning. He had given his co-pilot, First Lieutenant Don Albury, an excuse that he had left something in his quarters. In truth, he just needed a few moments alone.

Sweeney had flown the blast measurement instrumentation aircraft, another B-29, during the first atomic bombing of Hiroshima. He knew better than almost anyone the power of the weapon called "Little Boy." Now, it was his turn to pilot the Superfortress that would deliver the second bomb, called "Fat Man." The thought made him queasy. This was the most important mission of his life.

The commander of the atomic bombardment operation, Colonel Paul Tibbets, passed by the doorway and caught a glimpse of Sweeney as he went by. He stopped for a moment in the hallway and thought about whether he should speak to Sweeney. He knew what he was feeling. Tibbets had piloted the Enola Gay when it dropped Little Boy three days earlier. Tibbets turned, entered the mess hall, and said, "Are you okay, Chuck?"

"Oh, yeah. I'm great. Very excited. The whole crew is. I'm just drinking a half a cup of coffee to help me stay awake during the flight," said Sweeney.

"Yeah. You won't need that. Adrenaline will be pumping through your body the entire flight. It did for me. You know it's okay to have reservations?"

"Really? Did you?"

"Yes. Of course. I knew what I was dropping and what it would do."

"And yet…"

"We do our duty. That's why they chose us."

"Yeah. I suppose you're right. I'd better get going," said Sweeney, rising.

"What's on your mind?"

Sweeney stopped and thought for a moment, unsure he should speak, then… "I'm very grateful to be given this honor…"

"I know you are. But time is limited. So. let's cut through the bullshit. Spit it out."

"Why two?"

"Yeah. I thought that might be it."

"I understand why we needed to drop Little Boy. The Japanese had to know it was real and its power. But didn't the deaths of all those people send the message? They're done. We know it, and they know it. Hell, the Russians just entered the war and our marines are already on Okinawa. It's over."

"And yet the Japanese haven't surrendered."

"It's only been three days."

"That's enough time. They could have surrendered if that's what they wanted. They've made the decision to continue fighting."

"That's insane."

"I agree. But it was insane to start the war in the first place, and here we are. One hundred and sixty thousand American soldiers dead. Over twenty million Chinese soldiers and civilians dead and countless wounded. More will die if we are forced to invade Japan, not to mention the millions of Japanese civilians that will most likely die. We need to end this war now. This is the best and fastest way to do it."

"I keep telling myself that. It doesn't make it any easier."

"You're a good soldier, Chuck, and a hell of a pilot. I have no doubt you'll do your duty."

"I will. Now if you will excuse me… I have worlds to destroy."

Tibbets smiled at the reference to Robert Oppenheimer's quote as they saluted each other and Sweeney headed out to the airfield. Tibbet's expression darkened as soon as Sweeney was out of sight. He knew Sweeney would do his duty, but he also knew he would never be the same once his mission was complete. It was the sacrifice they both had decided to make for their country. One cannot commit mass murder, even if it is their duty, without it taking a toll on the soul.

It was a little after three in the morning when Sweeney walked out of the officers' quarters and on to the tarmac. In the distance was "Bockscar" – the aircraft that would drop the second atomic bomb. He could see Albury through the aircraft's windshield checking the switch settings in the cockpit. His crew was top-notch and worked well together. Sweeney was the newest member, having taken over as pilot less than a month ago. Albury had been the pilot before Sweeney. Naturally, Albury was disappointed at the demotion from pilot to co-pilot, even though he knew that just being in the cockpit would assure him a place in history. Albury had great respect for Sweeney. He had watched Sweeney closely during training, and the five practice runs they had flown together. Sweeney knew the mission like the back of his hand and had a firm manner of command. Sweeney's professionalism soothed the blow of being denied the honor of dropping Fat Man. It was the way the brass wanted it – best crew and best pilot. They weren't taking any chances.

Bockscar was a beautiful aircraft and one of the world's largest. Even at night, the work lights reflected off the bomber's highly polished skin. Bockscar was a Silverplate - one of ten B-29 Superfortresses that had been modified by the US Army Air Force to drop an atomic bomb. 'Silverplate' was the codename used for the bomber designed to carry the top-secret devices developed by the Manhattan Project. Unlike the other B-29s, the Silverplates' engines were fuel-injected and had reversible props. All of the gun turrets had been removed to compensate for the additional weight of the atomic bombs. Except for the tail gun position, the Silverplates were defenseless. The aircraft's bomb bays had to be extensively altered to accommodate the new bombs. Each Silverplate was capable of carrying either Little Boy or Fat Man type bombs. They could also carry conventional bombs.

As Sweeney approached, Albury saw him through the cockpit's spherical windshield and gave him a thumbs up. Sweeney performed a visual and physical inspection of the aircraft. He knew Albury would have done his own inspection before entering the plane and would have notified him immediately had he found anything amiss. Albury was that kind of officer – professional and thorough. Sweeney felt privileged to have such an experienced airman as his co-pilot. But even though he trusted Albury with his life, Sweeney would perform his own inspection. Two sets of eyes were better than one, and this mission was too important for anything to be overlooked.

America had spent two billion dollars developing the weapons and modifying the aircraft. It was money hard spent during a war that seemed to consume every nickel available. Everyone from the generals that oversaw the project and the scientists that created and tested the devices, on down to ground crews that maintained the aircraft, had worked hard to reduce any risks to an absolute minimum. They were the best and the brightest America had to offer.

The maintenance crew chief was doing his own last-minute inspection of the mechanisms that would release Fat Man, already loaded in the bomb bay. Sweeney poked his head up through the open bomb bay doors and said, "Any luck with getting that fuel transfer pump working?"

"No, sir. It's still froze up like a nun. We're still 'go' though, right?" said the crew chief.

"Yes. We are still go."

"You know I could still replace that thing in three or four hours."

"No. The decision has already been made. There's not

enough time before the weather front moves in. We're going as is."

"I'm real sorry about it – the transfer pump."

"Stuff breaks, Chief. It's the nature of the beast. We'll be alright."

"Yes, sir. Just don't spend too much time on target. She gobbles fuel like a son of a bitch."

"I am well aware. You and your crew have done a hell of a job keeping her ready. I'm grateful."

"It's been an honor, sir," said the chief, standing inside the bomb bay, snapping to attention and saluting.

Sweeney saluted back and resumed his inspection.

At 3:49 in the morning, Bockscar lifted off from North Field on Tinian. Fifteen minutes into the flight, the aircraft's weaponeer, Commander Fredrick Ashworth, entered the bomb bay and swapped out the electronic safety plugs. Fat Man was armed. The first leg of their journey was to Yakushima Island where Bockscar would rendezvous with two more B-29s – The Great Artiste and The Big Stink – each carrying blast measurement instrumentation and photographic equipment. From there, the three planes would proceed to the city of Kokura – the primary target.

When Bockscar arrived at Yakushima Island, Sweeney began circling at 30,000 feet, as planned in the mission profile. Within a few minutes, The Great Artiste, piloted by Captain Fredrick Bock, arrived and linked up with Bockscar. The Big Stink, piloted by Major James Hopkins, was nowhere to be found. The two aircraft continued to circle the island burning their precious fuel as they waited for The Big Stink.

After the allotted rendezvous time of fifteen minutes came and went, Sweeney grew concerned. Ashworth was in charge of the bomb, but Sweeney was in charge of the plane. It was Sweeney's call whether to continue without The Big Stink. Sweeney called Ashworth on the intercom, "What are you thinking, Dick?"

"I don't know. Maybe we should break radio silence," said Ashworth.

"Absolutely not. Tibbet was very clear on that."

"Then, we should wait. Keep circling and see if Jim shows."

"You know we don't have our reserve fuel?"

"Yeah. But The Big Stink has the camera equipment. Do you really want to drop this thing without any photographic evidence?"

"I think there will be plenty of evidence once it explodes."

"Chuck… it's history."

"Yeah. I know. Alright. We'll wait a while longer, but that means less time over target."

"Let me worry about that. Just keep an eye out for Jim."

While they circled, the Enola Gay and Laggin' Dragon, the two B-29s assigned as weather planes for the mission, reported that the cloud cover was acceptable at both the primary and secondary target areas. "Well, that's good news," said Albury. "For a minute there, I was worried."

Sweeney shook his head with a chuckle at Albury's attempt at levity.

Sweeney waited another twenty-five minutes in search of The Big Stink. It never showed. Fuel was low. "I'm calling it," said Sweeney to Albury. "We're heading for Kokura."

They banked the aircraft and headed north.

In the bomb bay, Ashworth felt the plane's turn and said, "Ah, shit. Fuckin' Hopkins."

Bock, the pilot of The Great Artiste, followed Sweeney's lead, banked his aircraft and headed north.

Kokura was one of Japan's largest shipping ports and a key industrial center. It had been the secondary target for the Enola Gay. If Hiroshima had been clouded over, Kokura would have been hit by Little Boy on the first atomic bombardment. But instead of being let completely off the hook, the city had become the primary target of the second bomb – Fat Man.

When Bockscar and The Great Artiste arrived, only thirty percent of the city was visible. Over two hundred B-29s had firebombed the industrial installations in nearby Yahata the previous day. The smoke from the fires that continued to burn had blown in, and a thick haze had settled over Kokura.

Sweeney piloted Bockscar over Kokura. Flak bursts cracked below the aircraft. With only three minutes remaining before passing over the aiming point - Kokura Arsenal - Sweeney turned the controls over to his bombardier, Captain Kermit Beahan. Sweeney called out to the crew to put on their goggles. He kept his off so he could see what he was doing. He knew the risks.

Beahan watched through his Norden bombing sight and was unable to spot the aiming point through the haze. "I can't see it! There's smoke obscuring the target," shouted Beahan over the hum of the four engines.

"Shit," said Sweeney as they passed over the position of the intended aiming point. "I'm taking control."

"You have the aircraft," said Beahan and released the controls.

The flak was getting closer as the anti-aircraft batteries below dialed in the aircraft's altitude. There was a swift discussion among the crew. The tail gunner reported that flak was bursting at their altitude. The crew was scared. Making a second pass was far more dangerous than the first. The initial surprise of the bomber's attack was gone, and the anti-aircraft battery crews would be ready. "Everybody, shut up," said Sweeney over the intercom. "We're going again. We'll change our altitude to thirty-one thousand and hopefully shake off the ack-ack."

Sweeney swung the aircraft around for another pass. He again turned the controls over to Beahan and called for the crew to put on their goggles. Again, Beahan stared through the sight's reticle and again encountered the heavy haze. "No good. No good," yelled Beahan. "I can't see it."

"Damn it," said Sweeney. "I'm taking control."

"You have the aircraft," said Beahan, again releasing the controls.

"What about using radar?" said Albury.

"No. Visual only. Those were the orders," said Sweeney.

"We got Zeros on their way up," said Sergeant Spitzer, one of the two radio operators, with alarm in his voice.

"We're going again," said Sweeney over the intercom as he banked the aircraft.

"What about the Zeros?" said Albury.

"They can't shoot worth shit at thirty thousand feet. 'Sides, it'll take 'em a few minutes to reach us."

"Good to know. For a second there I thought we might be in real trouble."

Sweeney couldn't help but laugh. "Don, I'm trying to concentrate."

"Is that what you call that?" said Albury, not getting the reaction from Sweeney that he hoped. "I'm sorry. I'll shut up."

The flak was exploding right outside the Bockscar's fuselage, shaking the aircraft violently. It would only take one well-placed shell-burst to ignite their remaining fuel or set off Fat Man. Sweeney changed altitude again, climbing another thousand feet. As they approached the aim point for the third time, Sweeney turned over the aircraft's controls to Beahan and said, "Don't fuck this up, Captain."

Beahan watched the reticle. Nothing but haze. "No go," said Beahan, deflated.

"I'm taking control of the aircraft," said Sweeney,

similarly dejected.

"You've got control."

Sweeney knew that if they went again, he and his crew would die. If the anti-aircraft batteries didn't hit them, then the Zeros surely would. He knew that Bock would never leave without Sweeney and his crew. He would be signing their death warrants too. Sweeney's mind raced.

Albury turned and could see the determination in Sweeney's face. "What about Nagasaki? It can't be any worse than this," said Albury. "We still have enough fuel for one pass if we go now."

Sweeney considered for a moment, then said in the intercom, "We're going to the secondary target."

His crew took a collective sigh of relief as the Bockscar banked and headed south. The people of Kokura never knew how close they had been to annihilation. Nagasaki was only ninety-five miles away.

The flight engineer, Master Sergeant John Kuharek, ran some quick calculations on his slide rule. The blood drained out of his face. "We're not gonna make it," he said to himself.

"What?" said Albury, overhearing him.

"What's up, Master Sergeant?" said Sweeney.

"We don't have enough fuel to make it back, Major," said Kuharek.

"You mean to Tinian?"

"No. Not anywhere. We can't even reach Okinawa."

"What if we go now?" said Albury.

"No. It's already too late," said Kuharek

"It'll be alright. We'll ditch in the sea if we need to. They'll find us," said Sweeney.

"Like they found the crew of the Indianapolis?" said Albury.

"Let's finish the run, and I'll figure something out."

"Finish the run?"

"You're damn right we're gonna finish it."

"Alright. I guess it doesn't matter either way."

"No, it doesn't."

The Bockscar flew on. Sweeney tipped the aircraft's wings to signal Bock. The Great Artiste followed. The Zeros over Kokura assumed they had chased off the two American bombers and returned to their base. The crew of the Bockscar was out of danger from being shot down for the moment. It was little consolation as the news of ditching in the sea rippled through the aircraft. Everyone remained quiet; some said prayers.

Sweeney and Albury watched through the windshield as Nagasaki neared. Cumulus clouds had moved in over the city. "It's socked in. A layer of cumulus at seven thousand feet," said Sweeney.

"If we're gonna do anything, we gotta do it quick," said Kuharek.

"It's gonna be trouble if we try and land with Fat Man still in our belly," said Albury.

"Not to mention the six hundred gallons of reserve fuel we're still carrying," said Kuharek. "We could ditch the device in the sea."

"If we're gonna do that, we should just drop the damn thing over the city. We could get lucky," said Albury.

Sweeney considered for a brief moment, then said, "Dick, what do you think about using radar?"

"But you said—" said Ashworth.

"Forget what I said. Can we hit the target?"

"Yeah. I think so."

"Do it."

The crew in Bockscar readied themselves. The tone was activated, and the radar scanned the valley below. Beahan took one last glance through the Norden bombsight. It was still socked in, then a break in the clouds appeared, and he could see the two Mitsubishi arms factories below. "I got it! I got it! Two factories right below us."

The factories Beahan was looking at were in the

Urakami Valley almost two miles away from the designated aiming point. "Alright, boys. Here we go. Googles on," said Sweeney over the intercom, once again leaving his off. "Captain Beahan, you have the aircraft."

"I have control," said Beahan, his eyes fixed to the target as seen through the bombsight reticle.

At two hundred miles per hour, there wasn't much time before the Bockscar would fly beyond the factories. Beahan flipped the switch to the bomb bay doors. He only had forty-five seconds to set the Norden bombsight on the new aiming point, kill the drift, and kill the closure on target. Once ready, he acted immediately and pickled the bomb release switch. "Bombs away," he said, then caught his mistake. "I mean, bomb away."

The aircraft lurched as Fat Man, a five-ton bomb, was released from its cradle and started its descent. "We did it," said Albury, looking a bit shocked.

"Yeah. We did," said Sweeney with a slight grin. "Well done, Kermit. I'm taking control."

"You have the aircraft," said Beahan, relieved.

During the moments following the release, Sweeney had one job - put as much distance as he could between Fat Man and his crew.

The crew of the Great Artiste saw Fat Man drop from Bockscar. They hustled to release the three instrument packages on parachutes that would measure the explosion. Once released, Bock followed Sweeney with the same mission – get the hell out of Dodge.

Fat Man dropped for forty-two seconds before it detonated at one thousand six hundred and forty feet above the factories. The valley was surrounded by low hills that contained the blast and protected Nagasaki's largest residential neighborhood less than a mile away. But for the people in the valley, it was a different story. Thirty-five thousand factory workers, soldiers and civilians were killed in a matter of seconds, engulfed by the blast and the firestorm that followed. The factories, as well as the surrounding buildings and homes, were demolished. Forty-four percent of Nagasaki laid in ruin. At twenty-two kilotons, Fat Man's explosion was almost twice the size of Little Boy's.

The Japanese lieutenant's wife and son were killed in an instant. They were less than a quarter of a mile from ground zero. She was holding her son as she hung laundry in the backyard of her brother-in-law's house. The bodies of the wife and son disintegrated together. There was no time for surprise or even pain. They were just gone.

Inside Bockscar, Sweeney saw a bright flash beyond anything he had ever seen. White spots exploded across his retinas. For a moment, he wondered if he was blind and considered turning over the controls to Albury who was wearing his goggles. He held the aircraft steady and waited. His vision came back slowly, and within thirty seconds he could see well enough to pilot the plane. "You okay?" said Albury.

"Yeah. I'm fine," said Sweeney.

A few seconds later, three shockwaves hit one right after the other. The plane shook violently, and several crew members were thrown to the floor. For the moment, the worst was over. They had survived. Everyone that could made their way to a window to observe the blast.

The mushroom cloud rose above the city. The top was bright bluish, while the bottom was salmon pink where the firestorm was wreaking havoc. It took the cloud forty-five seconds to reach the same altitude as the two bombers and continued to rise as it grew in size. "Ah, Major... the mushroom cloud is coming at us," said Spitzer.

Sweeney immediately dove Bockscar to pick up speed and banked hard right to avoid the cloud of atomic ash and smoke.

Bock also dove The Great Artiste but banked in the opposite direction. They could rendezvous later when they were out of danger. At the moment, Bock needed to do what he thought best to save his crew and aircraft.

At 30,000 feet both aircraft leveled off. The crew of Bockscar was giddy and hopeful. They talked about the end of the war and returning home. Sweeney and Albury knew that was not likely. They were 457 miles from the nearest US airfield on Okinawa. There wasn't enough fuel to make it. They would have to ditch the aircraft in the sea. Sharks would be attracted to blood from the wounds they would surely suffer. It would take hours for any rescue ships or aircraft to reach them. The only good news was that they had linked up with The Great Artiste again and Bock would be able to identify the location of the crash when he reached Okinawa. It wasn't much, but it was something — a veiled hope.

Sweeney remembered something Tippet had told him when he was instructing the crews on Tinian. It was called "Descending by steps." The idea was simple – use your altitude to increase your speed and shorten the time in the air to reach your destination without using more fuel. Out of options, Sweeney decided to give it a try. Without increasing his throttle, he dove two thousand feet then leveled off. It had worked. He had increased speed without using more fuel. He tried it again with the same results - more speed, no more fuel. He didn't dare go any lower for the time being. They were still above Japan, and the anti-aircraft batteries continued to take potshots at the two aircraft as they passed overhead. There was also the threat of Zeros that might be patrolling the area. Bockscar didn't have any spare fuel for a dogfight, not to mention most of its weaponry had been removed. He needed to fly in a straight line to Okinawa if they were going to have any chance of making it. That meant he couldn't fly around any of the know Japanese airfields. They would have to take the risk and hope all the Japanese squadrons where out on missions.

When Bockscar passed over the last Japanese Island with an airbase, Sweeney proceeded with his steps in descent maneuver. "How we doing on fuel?" said Sweeney.

"We're still short, but it's improving. Just keep doing what you're doing," said Albury. "Do you think it's cold?"

"What?"

"The water. The air's warm."

"Ah, hell, Don. It ain't the water you gotta worry about. It's the sharks."

"I know. I know. But I'm not a big fan of the cold."

"Remind me to bring you a blanket next time."

"You think there will be a next time?"

"Not if you don't stop blabbing and let me focus."

"Right. Right."

When the island of Okinawa came into view, the crew cheered. Bockscar was riding low over the water at two thousand feet. Sweeney had run out of steps. "Fuel?" said Sweeney.

"All main tanks show empty. We're running on fumes," said Albury.

"Sergeant Spitzer, have you reached the airfield's control tower yet?" said Sweeney.

"No luck, Major. I think the blast may have damaged the radio."

"Alright. I want you to fire our flares."

"Which color?"

"All of 'em. Hopefully, we'll get their attention."

Spitzer grabbed the flare gun, opened a porthole on the right side of the aircraft, and fired out the first flare. He reloaded and fired the second. "Mix it up. Side to side," said Sweeney.

Spitzer moved across to the opposite side of the fuselage, opened a portal and fired the third flare. He moved back and forth, reloading, and firing until all the flares had been expended.

Sweeney could see the fire trucks moving out from their hangers and aircraft taxing away from the runway. "Good job, Sergeant. I think you got their attention."

At that moment, engine number two coughed and shutdown. They were still a mile out from the edge of the runway. "We lost number two," said Albury.

"Yep," said Sweeney. "I'm gonna have to keep our airspeed up as much as possible in case we lose another. We're gonna be coming in hot."

"Copy that."

With only three engines still running, Bockscar dropped at an alarming rate. The landing gear lowered, creating even more drag. "You see those B-25s parked on the right side of the runway? Probably don't want to hit those," said Albury.

"Ya think?" said Sweeney.

"Just trying to help."

"Is that what you call that?" said Sweeney with a grin.

Bockscar cleared the end of the runway with less than ten feet of altitude. "Everyone hang on. This is gonna be a little rough," said Sweeney.

Another engine coughed and stopped. "Great," said Sweeney.

Bockscar came down hard on the runway and bounced twenty feet back up in the air. Sweeney and Albury forced the aircraft back down. Another hard landing, but this time the wheels stayed down. "Brakes," said Sweeney as he stood on the brakes and reversed the pitch on the propellers still turning.

Albury also pressed on the brake pedals with everything he had.

The wheels smoked as they heated up, locking, unlocking, locking again. The aircraft whizzed past the B-25s parked along the runway. Disaster averted. The end of the runway was approaching fast, and Sweeney wondered if the brakes would give way. With only twenty-five feet to go and the aircraft moving at a fair clip, Sweeney cranked the steering wheel and turned the plane one hundred and eighty degrees. Bockscar skidded sideways to a stop.

Nobody said anything for a long moment, their eyes wide. Sweeney slowly turned to Albury and burst out laughing. Albury and the rest of the crew joined him.

Albury and Sweeney stepped from the aircraft as a jeep pulled up. General Doolittle, the famed aviator and base commander, stepped out of the driver's seat. "Who the hell are you? And why the hell did you land on my airfield without permission?"

Sweeney and Albury snapped to attention and saluted. "Major Sweeney and First Lieutenant Albury, General. As to why we landed on your airfield… we kinda ran out of gas, and our radio was out," said Sweeney.

"We just dropped Fat Man on Nagasaki," said Albury.

"That's Bockscar?" said Doolittle, surprised.

"Yes, sir," said Albury.

"We thought you crashed."

"So did we, General," said Albury.

"We completed our mission, General. As ordered," said Sweeney, choking up a little.

Doolittle studied them both for a long moment, then said, "Well done."

EIGHT

It took two days in sickbay for Granier to recover. The morning he was released, he sat on the steps of his barracks enjoying the sun. The hotbox had no windows and was dark. While in it, he had wondered if he would ever see the sun again. It was hot facing the sun, and he could feel the skin on his face heating up to the point of being sunburned, but he didn't care.

There were only a small number of Frenchmen in camp. The rest were out on work detail. He watched as a corporal holding a slip of paper emerged from the communications hut with its long antenna sticking out of the roof supported by a bamboo pole. The soldier looked lost for a moment, then regained his sense of direction and ran for the commander's hut. He climbed the stairs and disappeared inside. A few minutes later, the corporal emerged without the message in his hand, ran down the stairs, and ran over to the lieutenant and delivered what seemed to be a message from the commander. The lieutenant turned to his bugler and gave him an order. The bugler sounded assembly. It took a little over a minute for the thirty-two soldiers still in camp to assemble. The guards in the towers, patrolling the perimeter, and at the main gate remained at their posts.

The major walked from his command hut, down the steps and over to the assembled men. At a sergeant's command, the men snapped to attention as their commander stopped and stood in front of them. He ordered them to stand at ease. He took a moment before speaking. He spoke a few words, then read the message the communications corporal had given him. Listening to the message, one of the soldiers screamed in anguish and fell to his knees. The sergeant berated the soldier. The lieutenant was also affected. He stood motionless, numb from the news in the message. The major saw the lieutenant was not reacting to the situation. The major took control, stopped the sergeant and let the soldier continue sobbing. Several other soldiers showed similar emotions, shaking their heads in disbelief. The major finished with a few more words to his men, then ordered them dismissed. Upon being dismissed, the Japanese soldiers gathered in groups as if discussing the major's message. The lieutenant just stood in the same place, staring at the ground.

A Frenchman with a crutch that had also been watching the spectacle hobbled over to Granier and said, "What the hell was that?"

"Something," said Granier, trying to piece it together.

It wasn't until the work detail returned that Granier and the others heard the news passed on by one of the more friendly Japanese guards. The Americans had dropped two mysteriously powerful bombs on Japan, killing tens of thousands, mostly civilians, and demolishing two cities-Hiroshima and Nagasaki.

Many of the Japanese soldiers had friends or families in at least one of the two cities. To prevent retribution, the major forbade any of the soldiers under his command from entering the prison compound except to deliver the daily rice ration. The work details were also stopped until further orders. "Now is when we worry," said Laurent on hearing the news.

August 14, 1945

Since the atomic bomb attacks, Japanese patrols near the Viet Minh camp had slackened. Nobody was sure why, but the reprieve was welcomed. The Viet Minh were more relaxed, but still kept their guards posted around the camp and their scouts out on long-range reconnaissance.

Dewey surmised that the Japanese might be recalling units to defend against the Allied attack on the Japanese mainland that they knew was coming. He was determined to keep the pressure on the Japanese in his little corner of the war until it was done. In his planning conferences with Ho and Giap, they seemed distracted like they were focused on something else besides winning the war. Dewey was frustrated. "We need to attack the Japanese now to keep the pressure on. We need to force them to keep troops here in Indochina or risk losing it."

"Our goal has always been to force the invaders to leave, not stay," said Ho.

"I understand that. But you don't want them to leave and then come back."

"I doubt that will happen. The two atomic bombs and the Russians joining the war have destroyed their hope. The Japanese are finished," said Giap.

"The Allies made the mistake of thinking the Germans were done before the Battle of the Bulge. Never underestimate your enemy's ability to fight back. We need to keep the pressure on," said Dewey.

"We need to conserve our strength," said Ho. "Our struggle will not end with the Japanese. We may still need to deal with the French."

"I am sure all of that will be worked out during the peace negotiations. I would think you would want to demonstrate your loyalty to the Allies since they will hold your fate in their hands."

"No one holds the fate of the Vietnamese people except the Vietnamese. But we understand your point. We do not want to seem ungrateful to the Americans for their help."

"Excellent. I think we should consider another attack on one of the Japanese airfields. If we destroy some of their aircraft, I seriously doubt they will be able to replace them anytime soon. That could free up our movement and allow us to broaden our area of operations."

Santana sat by the radio, listening on earphones. His eyes widened, he tore the earphones off his head and jumped up. "Where's the commander? Where's Dewey?" said Santana.

"I think he's in the caves," said Green, cleaning his BAR rifle.

Santana ran off in the direction of the caves.

Ho, Giap, and Dewey leaned over a map. "I am thinking of a similar-sized force like the one we used on the French fortress. We were able to move quickly without being noticed. I suggest we do the same this time—" Dewey was interrupted by Santana running through the entrance of the cave.

"Commander, I need to speak with you," said Santana, out of breath.

"I'm afraid you'll have to wait until we are finished," said Dewey, annoyed at being interrupted.

"No, sir."

"Excuse me?"

"It's over."

"What's over?"

"The war. The Japanese have accepted the terms of surrender."

Dewey was shocked. "Are you sure?"

"It was on the radio. We are to stand down immediately."

Dewey couldn't help but grin. Ho and Giap seemed less than joyful at the news. "I'll join you and the other men in a few minutes," said Dewey.

"Yeah. Okay. I mean… this is good news, right?" said

Santana.

"Very good news," said Dewey.

Santana left. Ho and Giap had a quick discussion in Vietnamese, then turned to Dewey. "We and the Viet Minh will be leaving for Hanoi. We think you and your men should come with us. It will be safer for you," said Giap.

"What are you talking about?" said Dewey.

"Revolution," said Ho.

The Japanese lieutenant at the prison camp had been allowed to send a cable to enquire about his family. He received a response and was crushed by the deaths of not only his wife and son but his brother and his family. His grief was deep. He went to his quarters and wept. He had done his duty and served his emperor. Even with the war going badly, he had his family to consider. They gave him a purpose. And now they were gone.

The lieutenant had a Tanto – Samurai short sword – buried in the bottom of his footlocker where nobody would find it. He had purchased it for three packs of French cigarettes and two cans of foie gras. The seller was a Japanese corporal that would not say where he had obtained such a beautiful weapon. The lieutenant imagined the corporal had stolen it from an officer of high rank, perhaps after he was wounded or dead. It didn't matter to the lieutenant. It was his now. He knew very well how to use it to commit Seppuku. An old sergeant that had served as a hand servant for a general had instructed him. The key was to be decisive in one's movements – don't stop once you start. Life would never be the same if he failed to die after disemboweling himself.

The lieutenant had decided not to surrender. There were no enemy lines to charge and be gunned down. He would have to do it himself. It made him proud. He had lost face after the American had taken his sword. Seppuku was an acceptable method to restore his honor. The only question was when.

A corporal entered his quarters and informed him that the major had an announcement for the soldiers under his command and the prisoners. The lieutenant thought it strange that the prisoners were to hear any announcement at the same time as the Japanese. It seemed disrespectful to the Japanese soldiers. He rose, tucked the tanto in his belt, and followed the corporal out of his quarters.

The prisoners were assembled inside the wire as close to the commander's hut as possible. They had a translator that would translate the announcement as it was read out loud. The Japanese soldiers were assembled right outside the hut, along with the lieutenant. The Japanese major, solemn and downcast, walked outside and stood on the porch to deliver the message. He was wearing his dress uniform with daisho – a traditional set of matching swords, one short, the other long. "I have been instructed to read to you a message from our heavenly sovereign," said the major unfolding a paper with a quivering hand. "To our good and loyal subjects: After pondering deeply the general trends of the world and the actual conditions obtaining in our Empire today, We have decided to effect a settlement of the present situation by resorting to an extraordinary measure. We have ordered our government to communicate to the governments of the United States, Great Britain, China, and the Soviet Union that our Empire accepts the provisions of their Joint Declaration."

The major stopped for a moment to check his emotions and to let the translator for the French catch-up. It took a moment for the French prisoners to realize what the emperor had said – that Japan was surrendering unconditionally. "It's over. The war is over," said one of the prisoners. "The Japanese have surrendered. We won."

A cheer erupted through the French ranks. They danced and patted each other on the back.

The Japanese soldiers watched, their heads bowed in shame. The major finished the announcement from the emperor and then gave the Japanese guards instructions. "You are free to go," said the major to the French. "But I suggest you stay until transportation can be arranged to take you to Hanoi."

The Japanese guards did as they were instructed and opened the gates to the prison compound. The machine gunners in the towers brought down their weapons, leaving their posts unmanned.

The major realized that it was a very dangerous situation for both sides. There were some Japanese that might seek revenge for Hiroshima or Nagasaki or the firebombing in Tokyo. Some French prisoners had been poorly treated by the Japanese and had watched many of their comrades die from starvation, sickness or beheading. He would talk with the French commander of the prisoners and hopefully come to some accommodation that protected their men. But his orders were clear. The French were allowed to leave anytime they wished. The Japanese soldiers would stay until their commanders gave them new orders.

The major was ashamed and wanted desperately to commit Seppuku. But he still had a duty to perform, and he believed there was no other higher call than duty. Seppuku would have to wait. He ordered that the remaining Red Cross packages that had not already been looted by his men be distributed to the prisoners. The boxes contained canned food, medical supplies, soap, toothbrushes, lice combs, and books to read.

The lieutenant turned and scanned the French prisoners until he found the American, staring straight back at him as if they had unfinished business. The lieutenant smiled a little. There was one last thing he needed to do to restore his honor before joining his wife and child in the afterlife. He would need to wait until the major was busy with the French commander hashing out the details of what would happen next.

Laurent walked up next to Granier and glanced in the direction he was looking. He saw the lieutenant. "He'll come for you," said Laurent.

"I expect he will," said Granier, never taking his eyes off the lieutenant.

"He's a coward. He'll bring others."

Granier grunted in response. "It's stupid to die this close to freedom," said Laurent.

"Freedom is overrated."

"Let it go. The war is over."

"Not mine and not his."

"Don't you want to live?"

"Again, overrated."

Laurent knew that the Japanese lieutenant would most likely kill Granier. Granier was without weapons beyond his hands. He had seen Granier fight and thought him lucky to still have his head. Human flesh was no match for a samurai sword, especially if surprise were taken out of the equation. The lieutenant would be coming for Granier, and he would be prepared. It was possible that the lieutenant could walk up and shoot Granier in the head with his pistol. Fortunately, the Japanese soldiers were deeply tied to their culture, and that meant using the sword the lieutenant carried. Laurent considered for moment… if he could keep the two apart until the transportation came, Granier would live and never have to deal with the lieutenant again.

Laurent told several of the French soldiers the situation and asked for their help. They agreed.

On the opposite side of the fence, the lieutenant approached the Japanese soldiers that he knew had lost loved ones in the bombings of Hiroshima and Nagasaki. His pitch was simple – revenge against the American. He had plenty of support to carry out his plan when the time came.

Laurent approached Granier, his eyes following the lieutenant's every move outside the wire. "So, I have been thinking," said Laurent. "Once the bloodletting starts, it may be impossible to stop it. The Japanese may choose to continue and attack the French prisoners. It would be safer for all concerned if you and the lieutenant were prevented from having a confrontation."

"What?" said Granier while keeping his eyes on his target.

Three prisoners moved up behind Granier. One threw a shirt over his face while the other two grabbed Granier's arms from behind. Granier was caught off guard. He struggled to free himself from their grip. The prisoner directly behind him was a bruiser, the largest man in the camp. He punched Granier several times in the back, knocking the wind out of him. Granier stopped struggling.

They took him to sickbay. The doctor used chloroform from one of the newly opened Red Cross packages to knock him unconscious. He wrapped Granier's face in gauze so nobody would recognize him. The prisoners lashed Granier's hands and feet to the bed frame using torn pieces of cloth. They did not want to hurt Granier. They wanted to keep him alive. They threw a blanket over him to hide his bonds.

Later in the afternoon, after the prisoners had gorged themselves on the food inside the Red Cross packages, the French commander left the compound and walked toward the Japanese commander's hut. The lieutenant watched with interest as the commander and the major saluted each other on the porch then moved inside for their meeting. The lieutenant realized that this could be his only chance to get at the American prisoner before he was transported away from the camp. He signaled the men he had recruited for the task.

Granier woke up in a groggy haze. His hands and legs were tied down. The gauze over his eyes prevented him from seeing anything. He could smell the urine and feces from the patients suffering from dysentery. He was in sickbay. He considered calling out but then thought better. He fingered the bonds on his wrists. They weren't rope or wire. They were made of cloth twisted into a strand. He tugged hard at his wrist to see if they would give way. They didn't. *Okay,* he thought. *I do it the long way.*

The long way involved sorting through the twist of cloth and finding an edge. He felt up and down the edge until he felt a piece that was frayed. He pushed the edge of the cloth against the wooden rail to which it was tied. He used his thumbnail to rub the frayed edge making it bigger. If he could get a tear in the cloth going, he might be able to continue the tear until enough of the cloth was torn so he could break it. He knew the process would probably cost him a thumbnail and would create one hell of a blister on the end of his thumb. *Don't be a pussy,* he thought and pressed on.

The lieutenant entered the prisoner compound with seven soldiers, bayonets already affixed on their rifle barrels. They moved into the crowd of prisoners in search of the American.

Two more soldiers, with their rifles slung, carried three bamboo poles and a long coil of rope. They set up a tripod just outside the entrance to the compound.

Several of the French prisoners yelled at the Japanese soldiers, taunting them. "Where is the American?" said the lieutenant in French.

The prisoners ignored him and continued to shout. One of the prisoners pushed back when one of the Japanese soldiers shoved him aside. The lieutenant rushed forward, drew his sword, and swung with a downward stroke into the prisoner. The blade stopped mid-chest having sliced the upper half of his body in two. The French were in shock as their comrade fell to the ground. The lieutenant cleaned his blade on the dead prisoner's tattered uniform. "Where is the American?" he said again.

Toward the back of the crowd of prisoners now giving the lieutenant a wide berth, two of the prisoners that had helped subdue Granier exchanged a glance and moved back toward the sickbay.

The lieutenant looked at the prisoners and spotted Laurent. "You know the American," he said, pointing his sword at Laurent. "Where is he?"

Two of the Japanese soldiers grabbed Laurent and pulled him forward. He was forced to kneel before the lieutenant. "I will find him with you or without you. The only question is the ownership of your head."

"He's gone. He left an hour after the gates were opened. He said he could make it through the jungle. That it would be safer than waiting here," said Laurent.

"You lie. He would never leave. We have unfinished business," said the lieutenant.

"He was afraid you would kill him with your sword."

"No. The American is many things, but a coward is not one of them. I will ask you one last time, and if I am not satisfied with your answer, I will kill you," said the lieutenant, raising his sword for a horizontal strike across Laurent's neck. "Where is the American?"

Laurent locked eyes with the lieutenant and said nothing.

"I'm right here, ya little pussy," said Granier in English, standing in the doorway of the sickbay with the two prisoners behind him.

Four Japanese soldiers rushed forward. Two grabbed the American while the other two cleared the way, threatening any prisoners that interfered with their bayonets. As they escorted him past the lieutenant, Granier turned and said in French, "I'm surprised you're still alive after that thrashing I gave you. No honor, I guess. Or is hari-kari just too much for you to handle?"

"You talk big, American. We will see how you feel five minutes from now," said the lieutenant in French following them out the main gate and over to the tripod of bamboo poles. On the lieutenant's orders, the soldier closed and locked the gate. Two soldiers stood facing the gate with their rifles leveled in case the French tried to interfere by rushing the gate.

The soldiers held the American tight, preventing him from moving. The lieutenant walked over and slid his sword into one of Granier's shirt sleeves. A quick upward stroke sliced the shirt off. The tip of the blade nicked Granier's ear lobe. "So, sorry. I must be more careful," said the lieutenant. One of the soldiers pulled the rest of the shirt off his opposite arm. Next, the lieutenant slid his sword inside Granier's trouser leg next to his inner thigh and just an inch from his testicles. Granier seemed a bit nervous. "Don't worry, American. Castration would cause too much blood loss. You will need all your blood for what I am about to do to you. Castration doesn't come until the end," said the lieutenant as he sliced outward with a clean stroke and the trousers dropped to the ground, leaving Granier completely naked.

Granier could see where this was going. He knew that once they had him suspended on the bamboo poles, he would be helpless. If he was going to escape and kill the lieutenant, it had to be before he was tied to the tripod. He used all his remaining strength to pull the smaller of the two men holding him around to the front. He kneed him in the groin as hard as he could. He released Granier's arm and fell to his knees. With one hand free, Granier grabbed the other soldier by the throat and squeezed, cutting off his air. Granier did not see the rifle butt that hit him in the side of the head. But he felt it and went down in a daze but still conscious.

The soldiers pushed Granier to the ground and hogtied him – his feet and hands tied together behind his back with a short length of rope. They hoisted him up on the tripod forcing his arms, legs, and back into a painful contortion. "Anything more you want to say before we get started?" said the lieutenant sliding his long sword back into its sheath and drawing his Tanto.

"Just one question, I guess," said Granier.

"What's that?" said the lieutenant laying the short sword's blade on Granier's chest.

"How does it feel being on the losing side of a war?" said Granier.

The lieutenant drew the blade across the American's chest with a clean half-inch deep slice. There was surprisingly little blood. The lieutenant had been careful not to cut too deep where he might have severed an artery. At first, the pain was slight. But as the nerve endings in the flesh were exposed to air, they burned like fire. Granier winced. He couldn't help himself. "That's the first of one thousand," said the lieutenant. "Let's continue. I don't want to be here all night."

A guard on the porch of the commander's hut had seen enough and ran inside.

The second slice was down and diagonal to Granier's rib cage below his chest. Again, the slice was only a half-inch deep, but was enough to expose a few ribs but drew little blood.

"Enough," said the major standing on the porch next to the guard. "Lieutenant, you will release that man at once."

The major ordered his guard to shoot the lieutenant if he touched the American again. The guard raised his rifle and aimed at the lieutenant's back.

"My wife was named 'Katsuko' and my son 'Daishin.' Remember them. They are why you die in such a manner," said the lieutenant making another slice on Granier's left leg.

The guard did nothing. "I gave you an order," said the

major, but still the guard did nothing.

The lieutenant could feel that time was running short. He sheathed his blood-stained short sword and drew his long sword. He raised it above his head in preparation for a long diagonal stroke that would cut through the American's rib cage and disembowel him. A shot rang out. The lieutenant twitched.

The major, holding the guard's rifle, stood on the porch, having just fired.

The lieutenant looked at Granier for his final moments of life. Granier raised his head, looked the lieutenant in the eyes, and said, "Pussy."

The lieutenant fell dead. The French prisoners pushed on the fence in unison, and the lock broke. The Japanese soldiers did nothing to stop them. The gate swung open. They rushed out and surrounded Granier. They had no weapons, but they vastly outnumbered the Japanese. The major ordered his men to stand down. The French used the lieutenant's sword to cut Granier loose carefully. He fell into their arms. They brought him back to sickbay where the doctor went to work stitching him back up. While Granier's wounds were painful, none was fatal. "You're making this a habit, I see," said the doctor as he placed a rag sprinkled with chloroform over his patient's nose and mouth.

Granier took a breath and passed out.

The next day, a convoy of military trucks picked up the prisoners. The Japanese weren't taking any chances at violating the terms of the ceasefire and treated their prisoners humanely. Some even tried to make friends with the French. They were the ones that would now need mercy after surrendering unconditionally. Now that the war had ended, the Japanese didn't want it to start again.

The country was in chaos. The Vietnamese people shouted curses and threw water buffalo dung and rocks at the Japanese trucks as they passed. The French did their best to keep out of sight. They were still unarmed, and the Vietnamese hated them just as much as the Japanese.

Word spread through the trucks that a Chinese commander had been placed in charge of Hanoi by the Allies. He had given orders to place the French in a detention center until a transport ship could be arranged to carry them back to France. They would not be allowed to remain in Vietnam.

Many of the French prisoners didn't want to return to France. Vietnam was their home. Besides, life would be very hard in France as hundreds of thousands of troops returned, looking for work in a war-shattered economy. Millions of civilians would struggle to rebuild their lives from the ruins left by the Nazi occupation. It would not be an easy life.

Vietnam, on the other hand, was relatively untouched. The French plantations could be quickly rebuilt and replanted. It wouldn't take long for life to return to normal for the French as it was before the war started. But for that to happen, they would need to stay and take back what was once theirs. The prisoners began to make plans. If they could show the French politicians in Paris that even after being prisoners, they were not willing to give up Indochina, the French government would have no choice but to send troops to support their effort.

Granier had a bad headache that wasn't helped by the potholes in the road. He could feel the eighty-six stitches he had received tug at his flesh with each bump. The improvement in food from the Red Cross packages helped him fight off infection and heal quickly. He hadn't thought about what would happen once he was freed from the Japanese prison camp. He never expected to live that long.

There was much that he didn't know. The biggest question was if Dewey had known of his betrayal. He doubted that Ho and Giap would have acted without

American support. It was too risky. Dewey was practical and always put the mission first. Sacrificing one man to defeat the Japanese in Indochina would have been a smart move. Maybe even patriotic. But even well-intentioned betrayal was still betrayal. If Dewey had betrayed a member of the pack, that was something Granier couldn't forgive. The only way to find out was to find the Deer Team... to find Dewey.

He wondered if the Deer Team was still with the Viet Minh. Maybe they had been recalled to China once the atomic bombs had been dropped and the end of the war was in sight. Finding them wouldn't be easy. The members of the Deer Team were experts at not being found.

He thought about skipping Dewey and taking his revenge on the Viet Minh by hunting down Ho and Giap. They would be easier to find. They had a following of over 2,000 soldiers. If he was patient, he could kill them both, and nobody would know. But the truth of his betrayal would die with them. He wanted to know the 'why' and just as important the 'who' was behind it.

Once Ho was eliminated, the Viet Minh would most likely collapse, and that would be the end of their rebellion. Men like Ho only came along once in a lifetime. The Viet Minh would not recover. The thought pleased Granier. He had fought to protect them, and they betrayed him without a second thought. He hated the Viet Minh.

He wondered about Spitting Woman and what he would do if he ever saw her again. He was lucky he wasn't dead because of her betrayal. He wondered if she thought he was still alive or if she thought about him at all. As a scout, she needed to be pragmatic and unemotional. Her focus was always on the next step, not the last step. She kept herself in the present and didn't worry about the past. He thought he understood her. How she thought. He was wrong. He had miscalculated her loyalty toward him. He didn't want to think about her anymore. That was the past. He needed to move forward. But not thinking about her was impossible.

What bothered him most was not what she had done to him. It was that he had allowed it to happen. He had let his guard down. He had let emotions gum up his inner compass – his survival instinct. He swore that would never happen again. Never. He would take his emotions out of the equation. It was better that way. He wouldn't get hurt, and he would be more reliable. From that point on, everything would be about the mission. In between missions would just be wasted time. There was a lot that Granier needed to think through. Fortunately, it was a long journey to Hanoi.

A train sped past moonlit rice paddies. It was late, and most of the passengers were asleep. No Japanese troops were guarding the train's cargo. There was no need. The war was over.

The stoker in the locomotive threw a shovel-full of coal into the boiler and closed the iron hatch. He set his shovel down and wiped the coal dust from his face with the dirty rag he always carried with him. He poured himself and the engineer two cups of tea from the clay teapot they kept on top of the boiler. The tea was double-strength black tea and kept them both awake through the night. The engineer took a sip and leaned out the side window to check the track ahead.

There was a bonfire beside the tracks about a mile ahead of the train. The engineer throttled down and applied the brakes. As the train slowed to a stop, the engineer and stoker looked out to see the fire-lit faces of 2,000 Viet Minh armed to the hilt and carrying everything they owned on their backs. The Americans were with them. Giap stepped forward into the light and said, "Thank you, brothers. Do you mind if we hitch a ride?"

The engineer, scared shitless, shook his head, giving his permission. The Viet Minh and the five Americans climbed on board the train. Every inch, including the roof, had someone sitting or standing on it.

When Ho Chi Minh climbed aboard, his personal guard escorted him into one of the passenger cars. Every eye followed him as he walked down the aisle toward the front of the car. Many had thought the old leader of the Viet Minh a myth; he had never been seen after all these years. Everyone knew he was the best hope for an independent Vietnam. Nobody said a word or even whispered. A passenger jumped up, offered his seat, and knelt before him. Ho reached down, took the man's hand, helped him to his feet, and motioned for him to sit back down. The man was almost in tears and said, "Please. It would be my great honor. Please, take it, Uncle."

Ho, moved by the gesture of the stranger, smiled, and said, "I thank you for the seat, brother. I would not be truthful if I said my bones were not weary. It has been a long journey, and I fear it is not yet over."

The train blew its whistle, shattering the stillness of the night, and steamed ahead towards Hanoi.

Dewey and Hoagland made their way through the train cars until they reached the car in which Ho Chi Minh was sitting. As they approached, Dewey said, "You asked to see me, Mr. Hoo. I hope you don't mind, but I brought Hoagland along with me. He wants to check your vital signs."

"Yes, of course. Mr. Hoagland is always welcome, with or without his medical bag," said Ho.

Hoagland went to work, checking Ho's heart and lungs.

"How many I help you, Mr. Hoo?"

"Mr. Dewey, I would like you to review the speech I will present once we reach Hanoi. I believe you will find many of the words familiar."

"Of course."

Ho handed Dewey the typewritten speech. "It promises to be the most important speech I will ever offer. I would be honored if you both stood beside me when I present it."

"Of course," said Dewey. "We would be honored. I will read this and get back to you with my notes."

"Thank you, Mr. Dewey."

Dewey left Hoagland to finish checking on Ho. "Two Americans beside a communist. Are you sure that's what you wish to portray?" said Hoagland.

"That is exactly what I hope to portray," said Ho. "We have fought together. I consider you my friends, and I want the world to see it."

Hoagland smiled and finished up his exam.

Hoagland walked back to where Dewey was seated reading Ho's speech. "And how is the patient?" said Dewey.

"He's fine. Extraordinary actually when you consider three months ago I wasn't sure if he would last through the night," said Hoagland.

"Excellent. Our work here is almost done."

"Commander, do you ever get the feeling that all of this happened a little too easy?"

"Too easy? We lost Buck, remember?"

"Yes. And they lost men too. Good men. But it just seems like Mr. Hoo always says and does the right thing."

"Of course, he does. He's a politician. And a very good one from what I can tell. This speech of his is quite remarkable. He starts off quoting Thomas Jefferson."

"But that's what I mean. It's like he's trying to impress us. Impress America."

"Well, he's doing a pretty good job. I don't think that makes it a conspiracy."

"No, not a conspiracy. More like a well-choreographed ballet. Every word, every nuance has a meaning and a purpose. Like he's trying to accomplish some end goal."

"We all do that, Hoagland. Mr. Hoo seems to have mastered the technique. Good thing for the leader of a new country."

"You think the French will let them go?"

"I don't think Mr. Hoo and Mr. Van are going to give them much choice."

"And what will America do?"

"I don't know. Stay out of it, I hope. They're both our Allies."

"When has America stayed out of anything?"

"Damned if we do and damned if we don't."

"I suppose. I'm glad I'm not a politician."

"You're still young. You never know."

At sunset, the train pulled into the outskirts of Hanoi. Giap studied a hand-drawn map and watched from the window of the locomotive. He showed the engineer the name of a building on the map. The engineer pointed to a tall building rising from the city's skyline. Giap nodded.

As the train approached the city center, Giap watched the building. He signaled the engineer. The engineer slowed the train to a stop in the middle of a neighborhood. Two hundred of the Viet Minh disembarked with Giap.

With his head out a window, Ho gave Giap a thumbs up and wished his soldiers good luck. Hoagland stuck his head out the next window. "Where are they going?" said Hoagland.

"The Japanese may have surrendered, but they continue to take the harvest of our crops from our farmers at gunpoint. Our people are starving," said Ho. "Mr. Van will see that justice is done."

Hoagland had no idea what he was talking about. Giap and the Viet Minh disappeared into the neighborhood.

Giap and his men moved through the streets until they entered an industrial area. Two Japanese guards stood in front of a chain-link fence surrounding several warehouses. As the Viet Minh approached with Giap in the lead, the Japanese unslung their rifles and ordered the group to stop. They didn't. Giap walked up with a Vietnamese translator and informed the two guards that the Viet Minh were taking control of the warehouses and that if they resisted, he would see that they were hung. They exchanged a nervous look, lowered their weapons, and stood aside. One of the Viet Minh took the guard's keys and opened the gate. The Viet Minh flooded inside and opened the warehouses.

Inside the warehouses, space was stacked high with bags of rice. Each Viet Minh picked up a sack and exited the warehouse.

The Viet Minh, their rifles slung over one shoulder, and a bag of rice slung over the other, walked through the residential neighborhoods. The people were frightened. The Viet Minh had been elusive since the start of the war. While many people secretly belonged to or had sympathies for the Viet Minh organization, most Vietnamese had never seen an actual rebel fighter and didn't know what to expect. This was the Viet Minh's way of introducing themselves. No words, just action.

When the Viet Minh came upon a square, park, or market where people gathered, they plopped down several bags of rice and cut them open. The people rushed forward with whatever containers they could find and scooped up the raw rice.

When the rice ran low, more bags were brought in and cut open. This went on for hours during the night until all the warehouses the Viet Minh had raided were empty. Vietnamese mothers and fathers cried with gratitude. They could finally feed their hungry children. Some Vietnamese were so hungry they ate raw rice and died when their stomachs swelled beyond capacity and burst.

The next morning, Granier and the French prisoners continued their journey toward Hanoi, riding in the convoy of Japanese trucks. It was the fifth day since his final run-in with the Japanese lieutenant. His muscles had already stopped aching from being strung up, and his stitches were itching. That was a good sign. He was healing. The severed cells were bonding together at the base of the wound, then contracting to pull the wound together. The contraction caused the itching. He could also feel the string that held his wounds together was getting impacted by the fresh skin that was forming. It gave the skin around the sutures a tugging sensation. He had a bad habit of removing his sutures too soon and reopening his wounds. He would wait this time until he was sure his wounds were finished healing. He had learned the hard way how rapidly one could get an infection in tropical climates from an open wound. He didn't need to learn that lesson twice because of impatience.

The convoy stopped just outside the city, and the Japanese let the prisoners out for a piss and a stretch. The benches in the back of the trucks were wooden without any padding. Each Japanese truck had a driver and a guard. The guards were not to prevent the prisoners from escaping but to prevent any problems with the bandits or looters that roamed the country. With the Japanese no longer responsible for the country, there was little motivation to prevent anything. They were understandably nervous about entering Hanoi, where the Vietnamese population was hostile and greatly outnumbered them.

Granier watched as one of the French soldiers wandered off to a nearby hillside. Granier followed him keeping out of sight. At the top of the hill, Granier could see the buildings in downtown Hanoi in the distance. Granier could see that the French soldier knew Hanoi and was looking for familiar landmarks to get his bearings. He was making little marks on the palm of his hand with a piece of charcoal.

The soldier returned to the trucks and had a hushed

conversation with a few of the commanders in the group. Granier watched. The French were definitely up to something, but he didn't know what and wondered it if was any of his business. For now, he would watch and wait to see how things unfolded. The men climbed back into the trucks, and the convoy drove off toward the city.

As the convoy entered the city, the French watched the passing buildings and streets until they saw what they were looking for. A signal was passed from truck to truck by letting a tin can holding a message attached to a long string dangle from the back of one truck until it passed underneath the next truck and out the back where it was retrieved, and the message read. The dust stirred up by each truck prevented the driver of the truck behind from seeing the string or the can. The process was repeated until all the passengers in the trucks knew when things were supposed to happen and what.

When the convoy drove over an iron bridge, the sound from the tires going from pavement to metal changed. That was the signal, and the French made their move. Two men from the back of each truck climbed on to the top of the truck cab. They clasped one of their hands to each other to prevent them from sliding off the roof. On cue, two more Frenchmen reached around from the back of the truck and pulled the door handle downward, opening the door. The men on top reached down, grabbed the two Japanese inside the cab and pulled them out the open doorway. The Japanese tumbled into the city streets; some smacked into benches or lampposts. Those that didn't suffer a collision were set upon by the pedestrians, more than happy to give them a kick in the gut or a smack on the head. The French soldiers on top slipped down into the cab and took control of the truck before it careened off the road. Within one minute, the entire convoy of French soldiers was free. The French had no intention of letting the Chinese ship take them back to France.

Granier was unsure what to do but decided he might as well go along for the ride. At least the French seemed like they knew what they wanted and how to get it. He had no way of contacting the Deer Team and wasn't so sure that he even wanted to. He couldn't help but feel that Dewey must have betrayed him by allowing the Viet Minh to do what they did to him. For the moment, he was better off with the French.

NINE

September 2, 1945

At the very center of Hanoi sat Bo Dinh Square – an open plaza surrounded by beautiful French buildings, including the palace of the French Governor-General of Indochina. Several hundred thousand Vietnamese, dressed in their best clothes, stood in the hot sun, waiting. They had seen flyers that Ho Chi Minh had promised to speak to all Vietnamese in the square that day. Many had made welcoming signs and banners that they held high.

Two black sedans drove into the square, flanked by a dozen Viet Minh soldiers on bicycles. Spitting Woman was the only female riding a bicycle. She had only learned how to ride the day before and was unsure of the two-wheeled contraption. After falling from it several times, she thought evil spirits haunted it. But Giap had ordered her to learn to ride the sinister machine, and she would do her duty.

After she had betrayed the American, Giap had grown to appreciate her loyalty. When they entered Hanoi and her services as a long-range scout were no longer needed, Giap decided to promote her to Ho's personal bodyguard. She was known and respected by all the Viet Minh as an excellent fighter. The promotion was well-received by all, and Ho was pleased. Now, she would use her body as a shield to protect Ho if required. Ho and Giap had little doubt she would sacrifice her life if needed. As the president's bodyguard, she was required to wear a new uniform and shoes. She didn't like the shoes. They didn't feel natural and gave her feet blisters. She was also given a Russian automatic pistol in place of her rifle. Firing and reloading the weapon efficiently took practice. Shells would often get stuck in the ejection port and keep the pistol from firing. The little gun pissed her off, and she threw it to the ground more than once. She missed her rifle, which she knew like the back of her hand and rarely jammed.

As the caravan slowly made its way to the wooden platform that had been constructed at the far end of the square, the crowd erupted in cheers and applause. People wept. Inside one of those cars was their nation's greatest hope. A man that was willing to sacrifice all for his people.

Nobody knew how the man that led the Viet Minh looked. He had changed his name, the way he dressed, and even the style of his hair dozens of times during his lifetime on the run from the French and the Japanese. He had traveled across the world to Russia, China, France, Great Britain, and the United States hiding, learning, living. He had become a communist and was a founder of the Indochinese Communist Party. But above all, he was a nationalist and longed to see freedom come to the Vietnamese people. He was sixty-five years old.

The two sedans rolled to a stop. The Viet Minh dismounted their bicycles and took up defensive positions, leading to the platform. The car doors were opened. Wearing freshly pressed suits, Ho and Giap stepped out along with Hoagland and Dewey, both wearing new khaki uniforms without insignia. Both Dewey and Hoagland were nervous about appearing in public after having served in a clandestine position for so long. But Ho had insisted they accompany him on the stand this historic day. Giap had personally guaranteed their safety. They had disagreements like any allies, but America was their friend, and they would do everything in their power to protect the warriors that had fought by their side.

They climbed the stairs and sat on the platform, shaded by an awning. It took almost ten minutes for the crowd to calm down to the point where an announcer could speak to them. A prominent Vietnamese civic leader introduced Ho. There was more applause when Ho stood and approached the microphone. A Vietnamese man held an umbrella above Ho to keep him cool from the heat of the day. Ho reached into his pocket and pulled out his speech, retyped to include Dewey's suggestions.

Ho began his historic speech with the words of Thomas Jefferson, "All men are created equal. They are endowed by their Creator with certain inalienable rights, among them are Life, Liberty, and the pursuit of Happiness. This immortal statement was made in the Declaration of Independence of the United States of America in 1776. In a broader sense, this means: All the peoples on the earth are equal from birth, all the peoples have a right to live, to be happy and free. The Declaration of the French Revolution made in 1791 on the Rights of Man and the Citizen also states: All men are born free and with equal rights, and must always remain free and have equal rights. Those are undeniable truths."

As Ho continued his speech, several miles away, the French soldiers pulled the convoy of trucks into a long alley and disembarked. They moved to the back door of an abandoned restaurant and formed a line to the first truck. Several men kicked in the back door and went inside the restaurant. Curious, Granier followed. There were two meat lockers in the kitchen. One had a lock on the door. A French soldier went to work picking the lock. Granier opened the second meat locker. The smell of rotten meat was overwhelming. Everyone complained until he shut the door. The French locksmith had tried several times and other soldiers, impatient, were now giving him advice. Granier walked over to a butcher's block and retrieved the butcher's steel – a rod used to hone knife blades for carving. He walked over to the locksmith, slid the steel rod into the lock's ring and gave it a swift wrench against the door. The lock broke open. The French soldiers cheered.

They entered. Granier followed, curious. The box was empty and smelled of rotten produce and eggs. A commander walked to the back wall. There was a crack in the wall which explained why it had not been in use when the restaurant was abandoned. He took a nail he had removed from one of the vegetable crates and slid it into the crack. He felt carefully until he found the spot he wanted, then lifted the nail. There was a thump, and the back of the wall seemed to move slightly. The commander pushed the wall, and it moved back into a hidden room.

Granier and the rest of the soldiers entered the dark room. Someone turned on a light overhead illuminating the interior. The room was filled with weapons and ammunition. In addition to hundreds of rifles and pistols, were nine Fusil-mitrailleur Modèle M29 machine guns, five British-made PIAT anti-tank weapons, three Brandt Mle 1935 60mm mortars, and an American-made M2 flame thrower. There were also six wooden crates filled with grenades, three satchel charges, and multiple stacks of wine bottles filled with gasoline – homemade Molotov cocktails. It was enough to equip a small army – a French army.

Granier moved up beside Laurent as if waiting for an explanation. Laurent gave him one, "When the Nazis surrendered, the provisional government run by French administrators in Vietnam saw the writing on the wall. They knew the Japanese could not let them remain in power now that Germany had fallen. Too much risk of them rejoining France and the Allies. We stored our best weapons in caches all over Hanoi. We knew we would need them again once the Japanese surrendered. It was just a matter of time."

"You will fight the Viet Minh?" said Granier.

"And anyone that stands in our way. We will take back

what is ours."

The soldiers removed the weapons and ammunition. They passed them like a bucket brigade to the trucks. They would sort through them later.

Something caught Granier's eye in the back of the room. A Fusil modèle FR-G2 sitting on a stand on a workbench as if someone had been adjusting it. The French-made FR-G2 was a highly modified MAS-36 rifle equipped with a match barrel with harmonic compensator and telescopic sight. Granier walked over and examined the weapon. It wasn't an M1 Garand, but it would do in a pinch. He checked to make sure it was properly assembled and fully operational. It was. The action was smooth like it had been well maintained. "Somebody loved you," he said to the rifle.

There were fifty rounds in a box sitting on the bench next to the rifle. The shells had been tweaked, the burrs sanded off, just like he would have done. This was a sniper's weapon. He almost hated to take it, wondering if the soldier who owned it might come back for it. He decided to borrow it until he found the owner or the owner found him.

With his new rifle in one hand and the box of shells in the other, Granier followed the last French soldier out of the hidden room and back to the trucks.

The back of the trucks were filled with weapons and ammunition. The men had to sit with their feet propped up. Granier climbed in an found a spot on a bench. He rested his rifle in his lap. He had no interest in letting it bang around with the other weapons. This gun was special. It was his.

Back in Bo Dinh Square, Ho's entire speech lasted less than ten minutes, less than one thousand words. But words that would generate two wars, cost millions of lives, and change the course of modern history. People watched in amazement as Ho ended his speech by declaring Vietnam's independence, "The whole Vietnamese people, animated by a common purpose, are determined to fight to the bitter end against any attempt by the French colonialists to reconquer their country. We are convinced that the Allied nations which at Tehran and San Francisco have acknowledged the principles of self-determination and equality of nations, will not refuse to acknowledge the independence of Vietnam. A people who have courageously opposed French domination for more than eight years, a people who have fought side by side with the Allies against the Fascists during these last years, such a people must be free and independent. For these reasons, we, members of the Provisional Government of the Democratic Republic of Vietnam, solemnly declare to the world that Vietnam has the right to be a free and independent country - and in fact is so already. The entire Vietnamese people are determined to mobilize all their physical and mental strength, to sacrifice their lives and property in order to safeguard their independence and liberty."

Concluding his remarks, Ho stood to receive the cheers and applause of the Vietnamese people. They chanted "Uncle" with a deafening roar. After several minutes, Ho was escorted back to the sedan that brought him. Giap was already inside waiting. "This is a great day. A historic day; the birth of our nation," said Ho as the sedan pulled away.

"Now we must hang on to it," said Giap.

"You seem concerned, my friend."

"We have news. Not good, I am afraid."

"Will it get any better by not telling me?"

"No. The French prisoners that were supposed to be interned by the Chinese Governor-General never arrived at their holding facility. It seems they jumped their Japanese guards and requisitioned the truck transporting them."

"Do we have any idea where they might be?"

"Someplace in Hanoi. We get reports, but by the time we check them out, they are gone."

"I see. So this is where the final struggle will begin. The French will attempt to retake Hanoi. We will crush them."

"Perhaps."

"You doubt we have the will of the people?"

"No. There is little question the people are on our side and are willing to fight. We vastly outnumber the French. But we are limited to the number of trained troops. To hold Hanoi, we must defend all of the public utilities, government buildings, transportation hubs, and all communication facilities, including the radio stations. Our resources will be stretched thin. If they are patient, the French will be able to consolidate their forces. They can take one facility at a time. They will dig in."

"And our people will still retake each facility they capture."

"And they will make us pay dearly each time we do. The French do not need to wipe out our forces to win. They just need to demoralize our troops and the militia. I have little doubt that we can put a million civilians in the streets of Hanoi. But we still lack proper weapons even for our trained troops, let alone a militia. Many will be fighting the French with knives, hoes, and spades. How long will our will to fight last once we start taking heavy casualties?"

"I see your point. But we cannot let them have a foothold. It will encourage the French government to send them reinforcements."

"I agree. But we need to be smart about deploying our best-trained troops."

"What do you suggest?"

"We need to focus our best troops on the most valuable assets. The ones we know the French will want to take over first. My best guess is that they will try to secure the radio, phone, and telegraph facilities first. They will attempt to cut off our communications so we cannot call for reinforcements or even talk to our people inside Hanoi. They will attempt to divide us. Once they have control over communications, they will go after the transportation hubs – the airport and train station. They'll put up roadblocks on the main streets and the highways. They will be careful not to stretch themselves too thin and only go after the main thoroughfares."

"Then what?"

"The power station and waterworks. They will shut off the lights and water."

"Why?"

"Our people have grown soft. They have become accustomed to the advantages of living in a city. Once the lights and power are cut, the city will become unsafe. The sewage system will not work, and disease will spread more easily. The street lamps will go out, and crime will rise. The people will begin to leave the city for the safety of the countryside. And that is exactly what the French want… to reduce our numbers."

"Then we must prevent them from accomplishing their purpose."

"Of course. I have already begun deploying our forces. We will only use the militia as a support force and to patrol the streets so we can find the French. And when we do, our troops will do most of the fighting. We shall not use our people as cannon fodder."

"While I appreciate your aspirations, we must do whatever is required to hold Hanoi, even if it means we must sacrifice some of our people to the French."

"I understand. Let's hope it does not come to that."

The Viet Minh were accustomed to fighting in the forests and countryside. They had rarely fought in a city and lacked the skills of urban warfare. Giap knew that his army must master the strategies required to fight in the streets of a city. He turned to the Americans for advice.

At first, Dewey was reluctant to help, because he knew that Giap would use the information to fight the French – one of America's allies. But he quickly realized that there was no way not to take a stand in the upcoming conflict. His last instructions from OSS HQ in China were to train the Viet Minh to the best of his ability. Dewey decided that giving Giap information on urban warfare was within his current orders. He knew his decision would be frowned upon, especially since the war with the Japanese was over, but he felt confident that he could support his position. There was a good chance that America would need allies in Southeast Asia and helping the Viet Minh would assure their support later when it was needed once again. He understood that both Ho and Giap were communists, but he found that they valued their relationship with the U.S. more their relationship with the Russians and the Chinese. Dewey felt it was in America's best interest to keep the relationship with the Vietnamese strong.

Dewey did his best to explain how to properly defend key positions within a city and the importance of not getting trapped by failing to defend or patrol properly. He instructed Giap on various strategies that the enemy might use to assault fixed defensive positions. He drew layouts that described correct placement of troops and weapons. He even showed him the proper way to fill and stack sandbags so they could withstand an explosion.

On receiving Dewey's instruction, Giap realized that his forces were far more lacking in training and experience than he had originally thought. Most of the fighting they had done in the cities were simple terrorist attacks on unsuspecting Frenchmen. But Giap knew there was a big difference between tossing a grenade into a crowded bar filled with French soldiers and holding a defensive position within a city against veteran fighters. In addition to many things, he needed more snipers on rooftops. He temporarily reassigned Spitting Woman back to her old unit as a sniper.

Like the other Viet Minh soldiers, Spitting Woman was not comfortable fighting in the city. It was all strange to her, and she didn't understand the simplest things, such as opening a window or climbing up a fire escape stairway on the outside of a building. She was often forced to work outside her comfort zone and constantly felt ill-at-ease. But she always obeyed and worked hard to master the new challenges.

It was almost noon when the French finished their reconnaissance of Hanoi's main radio station. From a rooftop overlooking the facility, two French scouts observed a company of Viet Minh troops taking up temporary firing positions in the station's doorways and windows as 300 militiamen and women filled sandbags and stacked them around the station in a defensive perimeter. "We should attack now before they complete their defenses," said one of the scouts.

"You keep watching. I'll go tell the commander," said a second scout.

Giap advised the Viet Minh commander defending the radio station that he should prepare to counter-attack the French once they started their assault. This would throw them off balance and reduce their troops' effectiveness. They would not expect a counter-attack from a band of guerillas. The commander was low on Viet Minh troops but had an overabundance of militia. He ordered that groups of one hundred militia station themselves inside the buildings surrounding the radio station where they would stay hidden until ordered to attack the French.

More French scouts were sent to explore the surrounding

buildings. They discovered the Vietnamese militia troops in several of the buildings with iron bars on the bottom floor windows. If the French attacked, the Vietnamese were well-positioned to fire down on the French troops from the windows on the higher floors while others could exit the ground floor and assault the French troops in the square. The scouts left quietly, unseen by the Vietnamese, and reported back to the French commander.

Inside a nearby warehouse, Laurent and the other French soldiers listened to the final assault instructions given by the French commander. Granier stood apart from the group and listened. His sniper rifle cradled in his lap. He was pondering what to do. As far as he knew, the Americans and Viet Minh were still allies. But he questioned giving his loyalty to his own country that so easily abandoned him to the Japanese. As for the Viet Minh, they had betrayed him and were now his enemy.

As the planning meeting broke up, Laurent walked over to Granier and said, "So, are you with us?"

"You will be killing the Viet Minh?"

"As many as we can find."

"Then, I am with you… for now."

"Alright," said Laurent, then pointed to the sniper rifle. "I assume you know how to use that thing?"

"I do."

"Then you will join me on the roof overlooking the radio facility. We will provide fire support once the assault begins."

"I didn't peg you as a sniper."

"Good. My disguise is working. I suggest you bring all the ammunition you have. It's going to be a bloody battle."

"I'm ready."

Hoagland and Dewey watched as more and more Vietnamese joined the militia and took up arms. Their numbers were growing rapidly by the hour. "They're going to get slaughtered, you know that?" said Hoagland.

"I don't know that, and neither do you. Giap believes their vast numbers will give them the edge they need to beat the French," said Dewey. "And frankly, I tend to agree with him. Eventually, the French will run out of bullets, and when they do, the tables could very well be turned in the Viet Minh's favor. But in any case... it won't be pretty."

"Pretty? This isn't some game, commander. The men we trained and fought beside are going to be killed."

"Don't be overly dramatic, Hoagland. It's war. Men will die on both sides."

"And we're just going to sit back and watch it happen?"

"Our instructions preclude us from being directly involved in combat with anyone but the Japanese. We can advise, but beyond that, we have to sit this one out."

"Look, the French must know they will eventually lose Indochina."

"I'm not so sure they do realize that. They've held on to it for almost two hundred years. It's never been easy, and this is not the first uprising they've had to deal with."

"Why are they here? What do they want?"

"Money, of course. A return on their investment. Especially now that they need to rebuild their homeland. France is broke. Indochina is their cash cow. They'll drain it for everything that it's worth."

"But surely a war will be more costly?"

"I have little doubt, especially if the French lose. But the politicians won't say that. For many, war is a profitable business."

"So, why don't we offer a compromise? Let the French keep their plantations and factories, but give the Vietnamese their freedom. The new Vietnamese government could guarantee French property rights."

"Communists guaranteeing property rights? I don't think the French are that stupid."

"Alright. So, maybe not forever, but just until France is rebuilt. Say… ten years."

"If the French are allowed to stay for another ten years, they'll never give up Indochina. Both Ho Chi Minh and Giap are smart enough to see that. Your ideas are just delaying a war that will happen anyway. Face it, Hoagland, we're warriors. Not diplomats."

"But we should at least try. America is the only honest broker. We have no dog in the fight. We could save tens of thousands of lives if we can avert war."

"Giap is not going to listen. He sees war as the only way to settle this argument."

"But Ho might listen. He's a reasonable man. He can be convinced if he believes it will benefit his people."

"Perhaps. I suppose I could try."

"With all due respect, Commander. I think Ho would respond better if I were the messenger. He listens to me."

"You did save his life," said Dewey, taking a long moment to consider. "Alright. You can try to broker a ceasefire with peace talks to follow. But be careful, Hoagland. Do not promise what you are not sure you can deliver."

"Of course."

The Viet Minh headquarters were located in an office building in downtown Hanoi. It was buzzing with activity as messengers came in and out with reports. The Viet Minh did not have enough radios to stay in contact with all their unit commanders, so messengers on bicycles were used. Although slower than radio, it was a surprisingly reliable method of communicating.

As sporadic fighting broke out, civilians cleared the streets. The French were indiscriminate in distinguishing between combatants and civilians. Everyone was a target. A hundred messengers became a second set of scouts traveling through the city that could report on enemy troop movements and skirmishes.

Hoagland approached the command headquarters. He was well known by the Viet Minh but less so by the militiamen that were now being used to support the Viet Minh. He was stopped at gunpoint by the guards in front of the building. One of the Viet Minh officers saw the American and scolded the two militia guards. It was difficult for most Vietnamese to tell the difference between a Frenchman and an American, especially if they were not familiar with the languages. The Viet Minh officer escorted Hoagland inside.

Hoagland was taken to Ho, talking with community leaders in a conference room. Ho stopped the meeting and asked for a few minutes alone with the American. The leaders left. "You and your men are safe, Good Doctor?" said Ho.

"Yes. Thank you," said Hoagland. "The guards you sent are doing an excellent job of protecting us."

"Good. Would you like some tea?"

"No, thank you. I've come to talk with you about the French. This conflict you are starting is unnecessary and counter-productive."

"We are not starting the conflict. We are merely protecting ourselves. It is the French that are attacking my people, not the other way around."

"I understand that, but only you can defuse the situation."

"And why would I want to do that?"

"To save lives."

"Why is Commander Dewey not here?"

"He… We both thought it would be better if you and I spoke first."

"Ah… politics then. So, where does America stand? Will they support us?"

"We have not been given orders one way or the other. For now, we are neutral."

"That is unfortunate. If there were ever a country that should understand our plight, it would be America."

"And I agree with you. But some things take time. Right now, our leaders are focused on the peace negotiations."

"You mean the Allied leaders are busy dividing up the world, don't you?"

"I don't know. I'm not a diplomat."

"And yet here you are proposing diplomatic solutions."

"The thought of good men dying... I had to do something."

"Of course. I would expect nothing less of you."

"What if we were able to get the French to call a ceasefire and negotiate?"

"I doubt the French would agree. They are determined to gain control of Hanoi. We cannot let that happen. We have them outnumbered one hundred to one. We will fight."

"And you may lose. You have no idea what a well-trained western army can do."

"I have some idea. After all, you Americans trained us."

"The training we gave you was to fight an enemy in the countryside, not a city. The French have been fighting in cities for centuries. They know the advantages of the territory far better than you do. They will use it against you to great effect."

"We will adapt as we always do. Westerners continue to underestimate our people and their determination. You have little faith in us. We defeated the Japanese; now, we will defeat the French."

"Perhaps, but at what cost?" said Hoagland. "Thousands will die on both sides."

"A small price to pay for freedom, don't you think?"

"Not if you could avoid it."

"Doctor, this battle is a long time coming. We knew it would happen. The French knew it would happen. It is inevitable."

"Are you saying that compromise is not possible?"

"Compromise is always possible if both sides are

reasonable. But that is not the current mindset of either side. We must settle our differences. I am afraid things are going to get much worse before they can get better."

"Would you allow me to at least try and find a path for peace?" said Hoagland.

Ho considered for a long moment. "If you can get the French to agree to a ceasefire, we will agree to negotiate in good faith. But I fear you are wasting your time."

"Thank you, Uncle," said Hoagland showing his respect.

"Of course, Good Doctor," said Ho. "I shall provide an escort."

"No, thank you. I believe I would have better luck with the French if I appear not to take sides."

"That could be very dangerous," said Ho. "The city is in chaos."

"I realize that, but it is our best chance at peace. I believe it is worth the risk."

"Then let me at least write a letter giving you and the other team members safe passage through the city."

"Thank you. That would be appreciated."

Ho got out a piece of paper and wrote in Vietnamese. He signed his name as Ho Chi Minh and handed it to Hoagland. Hoagland folded it and placed it in his shirt pocket. "Good luck, my friend," said Ho offering his hand.

"And to you, my friend," said Hoagland, shaking hands before leaving.

Hoagland returned to report to Dewey. Dewey was on the rooftop of the building, watching and listening to distant explosions and gunfire in the city. "I've got news, Commander. Ho has agreed to a ceasefire with the French if it can be arranged." Hoagland removed the letter from his pocket. "He gave us a signed letter that should help protect us as we move through the city to find the French commander."

"Well done, Hoagland. But I'm afraid it's too little too late," said Dewey, downtrodden, examining the letter from Ho, placing it in his shirt pocket.

"What do you mean?"

"Commander Patti radioed while you were gone. We've been given our marching orders."

"What?! Why?"

"He wants us out of the way when the shit hits the fan."

"We can't do that. We're on the verge of a breakthrough that could save lives, thousands of lives."

"It's done. A transport plane will pick us up first thing tomorrow morning."

"We're gonna just leave? Without saying anything?"

"What are we gonna say, Hoagland? Sorry, your country is on the wrong side of the world, and nobody gives a damn? That the French are more strategically important to America than the Vietnamese?"

"If we leave like this... If we just abandoned them, they'll never forgive us."

"Probably not, but we're soldiers. We did our duty and accomplished our mission. The rest is left to diplomats and historians. Pack your gear. We leave at first light."

Hoagland left, crestfallen.

Granier and Laurent pried open the back door to a tall apartment building. Each carried a rifle and backpack with ammunition. They entered cautiously and climbed the stairs leapfrogging – one providing cover while the other advanced up the stairs, then vice versa. After six flights of stairs, they came to the rooftop access door. It was locked. Laurent kicked it open and exited the stairwell. Granier followed.

There was a clothesline filled with well-worn underwear, white bedsheets, and a blanket drying in the sun. Granier pulled down the blanket, folded it, and rolled it up.

Careful not to give away their position, Granier and Laurent duck-walked, then crawled to the edge of the roof and looked over.

The apartment building on which they were located was not directly in front of the radio station. Instead, it was located a block away. It had a very good view of the front entrance and one of the sides of the radio station. More importantly, it was several stories higher, overlooking the rooftop of the radio station and all of the firing positions now being built around it. It was far enough away that they didn't need to worry too much about return fire from the Viet Minh troops below them. Laurent had done his homework in picking out the superior location and Granier was impressed. He liked working with experienced professionals.

Laurent smiled, pleased with himself. He knew a fellow sniper would appreciate how clever he had been in selecting this particular building.

Granier set the rolled-up blanket on the edge of the rooftop. When the time came, he would rest his rifle's stock on it, giving him a stable shooting platform. It wasn't fancy, but it would give him an extra fifty yards of accuracy. Granier wanted to survey the battlefield, but he didn't want to reveal his rifle. He removed the rifle's telescope and peered through it at the radio station.

Many of the Viet Minh defending the station were men he knew. He had fought with them side by side. He had defended them, and they had defended him; right up until they betrayed him. He wondered how they could turn on him. They had been his pack. He thought about the times they had eaten together and when they had played pranks on him. Now, they were just traitors… the enemy. It made him melancholy.

He thought about just getting up and walking away. Nothing was stopping him. He knew Laurent wouldn't do anything. But deep down, he felt the need for justice. He couldn't just let it go. The scales had to be balanced.

He picked out and prioritized his targets – the key firing positions. It didn't matter who occupied them. They were dead men in his mind. It was just a matter of timing – one moment alive, the next dead. The more he thought about it, the calmer he became like being prepared for a test in school. It was simple. He liked simple.

As Granier finished his shooting plan, Laurent watched the station and said, "Looks like we have company. Rooftop."

Granier shifted his telescope to the rooftop. He watched as three Viet Minh snipers exited the access doorway to the station's rooftop. He knew all three. He had picked them out and trained them personally. He fought his emotions, burying them deep. They were like all the others. They had taken the side against him when he was betrayed. They deserved no mercy. His justice would be even and swift. They each took up a firing position on the corners of the rooftop. They were in good positions to pick off any French soldiers assaulting the station from below. He would see that they never got the chance. They would be his first targets. He was resolved. The doubt gone, until…

The access door opened again, and another sniper stepped out on to the rooftop. Granier's heart sank on seeing Spitting Woman. She had a rolled-up blanket tucked under her arm. In the other arm, she carried her rifle. She walked to the back of the building, set her blanket on the edge, and laid down. An air vent obscured her legs, but her torso and head were in clear view. She was in range and uncovered. It would be an easy shot. "You gonna need some help?" said Laurent.

"No. I got 'em," said Granier.

"Good. I'll focus on the front and the left side. You do the rooftop and the right side. Deal?"

"Yeah. That's good."

Granier's mind was racing as he attempted to deal with his emotions. The assault would start at any moment. He had to be clear about what he was doing. Indecision would cost French lives. He owed them more than that. They were his new pack. He tried to calm himself. He thought about his list of priorities. Spitting Woman was at the back of the building. She would be fourth. *Fourth*, he thought. *That's all she is. A number on a list.* She had made her decision, and now he would make his. Fourth. A squeeze of the trigger and she would be gone forever.

Their relationship flashed through his mind like a film projector of captured moments – *the first time he saw her running across the field and killed the Japanese soldier that was going to kill him, the first time she spat on him, the time she saved him from a boobytrap, when he carried her on his back, then in his arms, as she laid in bed in the Chinese hospital begging him not to leave her, her smile when they jumped together from the plane and parachuted down into the forest, the first time they kissed and made love. Fourth. She was to be the fourth.*

In the square in front of the radio station, a Vietnamese milkman rolled a cart full of fifty-liter metal milk jugs. Seeing hundreds of Vietnamese militia and Viet Minh troops pointing their weapons at him, he abandoned his milk jugs and ran away, leaving the cart in the square.

The Viet Minh commander studied the cart. He didn't like it. He picked up a rifle, aimed, and fired a round into one of the metal cans. A stream of milk flowed from the bullet hole. The Viet Minh and militia laughed.

A French fighter, shouldering a PIAT anti-tank launcher, rose from his hiding place in the center of the milk jugs, aimed and fired. The rocket shot across the square and crashed into a Viet Minh machine gun position. The explosion blew open the sandbags protecting it and killed the entire gun crew. The French gunner ducked back down before the surprised Vietnamese could return fire.

The metal jugs protected him from small arms fire like a homemade tank. He reloaded and prepared to fire again.

Nearby, a French man carrying a wooden mallet and two wedges trotted up to the front door of the building in which the Vietnamese militia was hiding. He placed a wedge at the bottom of each of the front doors and gave them a whack with his mallet. His mission accomplished, he ran for cover down an alley.

Inside the building, the Vietnamese heard the two loud whacks at the front door. A militiaman tried to open the doors. They were stuck shut fast. There was a knock at the back door of the building. Two militiamen went to investigate with their rifles at the ready. One opened the back door and was gunned down by a spray of machine gun fire. The other militiaman returned fire out the open doorway, firing frantically at nothing. After a moment, a satchel charge with its fuse already lit flew through the doorway and skidded across the tile floor. The back door slammed shut. There was another whack from a wedge. The militiaman ran to the back door and tried to open it. It too was wedged shut. A militiaman in the center of the room yelled for his comrades to open the window shutters. He picked up the satchel charge and flung it toward the open window. The iron bars on the outside of the window blocked the satchel charges path, and it bounced back inside the room. The explosion killed everyone on the first floor and took out the supporting columns. The building collapsed in a heap of brick and wood crushing those to death on the upper floors.

Two more satchel charge explosions collapsed two more buildings nearby. In a matter of less than a minute, the French had killed one-third of the Vietnamese protecting the radio station. They knew urban warfare well.

The French soldier on the cart surrounded by milk jugs popped up again and fired another PIAT taking out another Viet Minh machine gun position. A Viet Minh sniper on the radio station rooftop shot him in the head. He fell against the milk jugs and toppled them into the square with a loud clatter. He was dead.

The French kicked open the back doors and charged into the remaining buildings surrounding the square. They took up firing positions at all the available windows on every floor and occupied the rooftops. They were now fighting the Viet Minh and militia on an equal footing, both firing from covered positions. The French set up their light machine guns on the higher floors and opened fire.

French mortar teams fired shells over buildings from alleys and back streets. Mortar shells rained down on the Vietnamese positions and the radio station rooftop. The explosions shattered the Vietnamese troops' morale. There was no safe place to hide anywhere. Just mayhem. They felt trapped in the city and longed for the forest where they knew how to fight and could easily retreat, if necessary.

A boat floated down the river next to the radio station. A French soldier with high-pressure tanks on his back rose up and unleashed a stream of fire from the nozzle of his flamethrower. The side of the radio station caught fire, and the blazing liquid rained down on the Viet Minh positions beside the building. Soldiers caught fire and ran for the river only to be met with more inferno from the flame thrower.

Spitting Woman shot the French soldier with the flamethrower. The tanks on his back ignited and exploded in a ball of flame, engulfing him. He tried to make it over the side of the boat but couldn't see where he was going. He fell into the bottom of the boat and died. The burning boat continued down the river.

The explosions below in the square brought Granier out of his thoughts. The assault was beginning. Laurent opened fire on the Viet Minh positions at street level, killing several soldiers.

Granier chambered a round and aimed at his first target. The moment when he first met the young Viet Minh soldier flashed into his mind. He drove the thought away, focusing on the task at hand. The soldier was opening fire at the French. Granier placed his crosshairs on the man's head and slowly squeezed. The rifle fired with a jerk. Granier realigned the telescope just in time to watch the soldier slump over his rifle, dead. He repeated the procedure on the second target, killing him. Then the third, dead.

He moved his sight to the fourth target. Spitting Woman had not noticed that her three comrades were dead. She was focused on her targets in the street below behind the station. She fired again and again, her empty cartridges flipping into the air. Granier knew that at that range, her aim would be deadly, and every second he waited was costing French lives. His pack was dying. He chambered another round in his rifle. He placed the crosshairs in the telescope's reticle over her head. He slowly squeezed the trigger, then... stopped.

The thought of her beautiful head exploding bothered him. She had children. He didn't want them to see that when her body was returned home. He moved the crosshairs to the left side of her back above her heart. The results would be the same. She would be dead. That's what he wanted. Justice. He again squeezed the trigger. And again he stopped. "Don't be such a pussy," he said to himself. "She's just a target."

But he knew that was a lie. She was far more than that. He released pressure on the trigger. He didn't know what to do. He thought about firing next to her to get her attention, but that might cause her to fire back, and he would have no choice but to kill her. That... or sacrifice his own life for hers. The idea was not abhorrent. His anguish would cease, and she would live.

Laurent looked over and saw that Granier was not firing. "Why the hell aren't you firing?" said Laurent, angry. "Our men are dying."

Granier didn't respond. Laurent looked at the rooftop and saw the woman shooting. "She has a rifle, and she is using it. Kill her and move on," said Laurent.

Still, Granier did nothing. Laurent aimed with his rifle. It was a bad angle, and his rifle lacked a telescope. With his hard sight, it was a long shot. He fired anyway. Granier heard the crack of his rifle and watched through his scope. *Oh, god, no,* he thought. The bullet bounced off the low wall on the edge of the roof. Spitting Woman immediately knew she was being targeted. The angle of the bullet meant that somebody was shooting from a nearby rooftop. She looked around.

Granier looked over as Laurent chambered another round and took aim. Granier swung his rifle around and hit Laurent in the head with the butt of his rifle at the same moment he fired. Laurent fell unconscious. Granier looked through his telescope at the station rooftop.

He found Spitting Woman. She had seen the flash of the second shot. It had missed her. Her rifle was pointed straight at him. He smiled. She was alive. She fired. The bullet ricocheted on the edge of the rooftop in front of where Granier was laying. He wondered if she had missed on purpose, then realized she had no way of knowing that it was him. It was too far to see his face. Like Laurent's, her rifle didn't have a telescope either. In a firefight between snipers, she was like a sitting duck. She was in his crosshairs. He could easily kill her before her next shot.

Instead, he stood up, leaving his rifle on the ground. His entire body was exposed. It would be an easy shot for her. He closed his eyes and thought of her as he did before. *Her eyes. Her skin. Her smile.* A long moment passed… and nothing happened. He opened his eyes and looked across the distance at her. *There was no way she could see my face,* he thought. *Why don't you shoot? I'm the enemy.*

But she didn't. Instead, she lowered her rifle.

He couldn't see her face, and he didn't want to scare her by looking through his telescope. He imagined that she knew it was him. That he was with the French. That he had betrayed her and the Viet Minh just like he had been accused. He was the enemy. And yet... she couldn't bring herself to kill him. He wondered what that meant. *Did she still love him? Was that even possible after everything that had happened? Could it all just be forgiven and they could go back to the way it was before?*

The French pressed their assault. Soldiers advanced in a staggered line, firing their weapons, keeping up a constant barrage, hammering the enemy.

Thirty Vietnamese militiamen and woman charged the advancing French line. They were armed with hoes and knives. Two Frenchmen using their light machine guns mowed them down before they could reach them.

When the French troops had closed enough distance, they threw dozens of grenades into the Viet Minh and militia positions around the radio station.

The stacks of sandbag became a deathtrap preventing the Vietnamese soldiers from fleeing when a grenade landed nearby. The grenade explosions torn into the soldiers, killing a dozen more. The Viet Minh and the militia had taken heavy losses and were pulling back, abandoning the radio station. There wasn't much time until the facility was overrun.

Granier could see that if Spitting Woman was to escape,

she had to go now. But she wasn't moving. Her eyes were fixed on him. He didn't want her to die. He wondered if she even realized the danger she was in. He thought she might not leave while she could still see him. He sighed, picked up his rifle and pack. He took one last look at her and turned away. He walked to the access doorway, opened the door, then... disappeared from the rooftop.

On the opposite rooftop, Spitting Woman stood, tears running down her cheeks. She picked up her pack and rifle. She took one final look at the opposite rooftop and left the radio station through the rooftop doorway just as the American had done.

She arrived at the bottom of the stairwell as the last of the Viet Minh pulled back from their firing positions. She followed them down a street and disappeared into the city. The Viet Minh had just lost their first battle with the French.

Within just a few days of World War Two ending, the First Indochina War had started.

Granier kept out of sight as best he could as he traveled through Hanoi. Technically, the Americans were not at war with either the Vietnamese or the French. But he knew the Vietnamese would only see the color of his skin and assume he was French, especially since he was armed.

He didn't have a plan. Things had just unfolded. He was alone without a pack. He wasn't frightened. He could defend himself if it came to it. But he lacked purpose, and it gave him an empty feeling.

He wondered if Laurent was okay. He had hated to hit him, but he didn't have much choice. He couldn't go back to the French, and he didn't want to anyway. To them, he had been just another rifle and was now a traitor.

The Viet Minh were still his enemies and would hunt

him if they learned of his whereabouts. Things had changed so fast. His options had narrowed. He knew he had to get out of the country. There were no trains and only a few roads to Laos or Cambodia. Both the French and the Viet Minh would be watching them for possible incursions. The Chinese were to the north. They were Allies with America and would probably welcome him. He thought about sneaking aboard a cargo ship. Hai Phong Harbor was a good distance from the city, and he would need to cross a lot of open land to get there. Not a good idea. He thought he might be able to bribe a taxi driver, but he would still need to contend with any roadblocks. He realized the odds of escaping by ship were slim. He considered finding a supply truck convoy heading north but then realized that with the war with the Japanese over, it was unlikely the Vietnamese would be shipping any supplies to the Chinese. It was more likely the Chinese would send supplies to the Vietnamese, who were starving.

He decided that Hanoi airport was his best chance at escape. He couldn't just steal a plane. He didn't know how to fly one. He would need a pilot. Feasibly a cargo plane heading north or maybe a smaller plane. He didn't care where the plane was going as long as it was leaving Indochina.

Gia Lam Airport was east of the Red River, and he was still on the west side. He would need to cross Paul-Doumer Bridge which almost assuredly would have checkpoints by either the French or the Viet Minh, depending on who controlled the structure at the time he wanted to cross. He could swim across, but the river was wide and the current strong. It would be risky. Bribing a boat pilot would not be too difficult, but he had no money. He might be able to trade if he could find something valuable. He would need to travel at night and stick to the shadows when possible so as not to be recognized as a foreigner.

Granier hid in an alley behind a laundry and watched. He waited until the owner was finished hanging out customers' clothes to dry on several clotheslines. When the owner of the laundry disappeared back inside, Granier went shopping. He snagged the largest set of dark pajamas he could find. They were still several sizes too small and barely made it over his well-developed muscles. They were a bad fit but would serve their purpose.

A street vendor rode by on a bicycle with two baskets filled with brooms on the back. Granier watched from an alley as the bicycle approached. He knew it was unlikely that the vendor would ever leave his bicycle unattended. He also knew that stealing that bike might mean the vendor and his family would lose their main means of financial support. It couldn't be helped. Traveling through Hanoi with a sniper rifle on his back was a sure way of being caught or killed. The brooms would hide his rifle. He needed that bicycle. He reached into his pocket and took out his grandfather's gold coin. He looked down at it. *I've shed blood for that coin,* he thought. *Screw it.* He put the coin back in his pocket, unslung his rifle, and chambered a round.

As the street vendor pedaled closer, Granier stepped out and leveled his rifle straight at the man. The man stopped. Granier motioned with his head that the man should leave. The man tried to turn his bike around. Granier reached out and grabbed the handlebars preventing him from riding off with the bike. The man's expression showed that he understood he was being robbed. He shouted at the foreigner, cursing him, drawing attention from others on the street. Granier stood his ground and motioned once again that the man should leave. The man wouldn't abandon his livelihood.

Granier thought about shooting him, but couldn't bring himself to do it. He liked that the man was putting up a fight. He had moxie. Granier pressed the barrel of the rifle against the man's chest right where his heart would be. Still, the man wouldn't give up the bike. People started to gather at a distance, watching, some shouting from across the street. Granier wasn't worried about the angry civilians. One or two bullets fired in the air would scare them off. But he was concerned that they might attract any Viet Minh or French troops that might be nearby. He had had enough of the argument. He reslung his rifle. The vendor's expression brightened, believing that the thief was giving up. He wasn't. Granier grabbed the man by his shirt, lifted him off the bike, and threw him to the ground. He mounted the bike. The man scrambled to his feet and grabbed the foreigner stealing his bike. Granier punched him in the nose, and he fell back to the ground. *A bloody nose is better than a bullet*, thought Granier, pedaling off down the street, people shouting at him as he rode past.

Once clear of the rabble, Granier pulled into an alley and stowed his rifle in the basket. He arranged the brooms to hide it. The brooms would serve a dual purpose, both hiding his gun and hiding him from anybody watching him from behind. His face was his biggest problem. He looked nothing like the Vietnamese. Passing a woman with a conical straw hat, he reached out and grabbed it off her head. She cursed him as he placed the hat on his head and rode off.

As the sun set on the horizon, he pedaled through Hanoi toward the Red River. His new disguise worked well. He was still bigger than most Vietnamese, but with his face hidden by the shadows of the hat, people didn't give the overly tall broom vendor too much thought.

It took Granier two hours to make it to the Paul-Doumer Bridge stretching over the Red River. As he suspected, there was a three-man Viet Minh checkpoint at the mouth of the bridge. He imagined there would be another checkpoint on the opposite bank. Even if he killed the Viet Minh on this end, he would surely face the Viet Minh stationed on the other end of the bridge when they heard the shots. Crossing the river by the bridge was very risky. On the bridge, places to hide or retreat would be greatly limited.

He decided to explore other options. He pedaled the bike upriver along the bank. There were plenty of boats tied up along the shore, but most were filled with families cooking their evening meal. Generations of Vietnamese fisherman and their families lived on their boats. It was cheaper than paying rent, especially in a big city like Hanoi, where the rents were beyond the means of most families.

He found a round basket boat flipped upside down on the shore, hidden in some tall reeds. He lifted it and found a paddle underneath. The one-man boat was made out of bamboo, and he wondered if he could fit the bicycle with the broom baskets. He flipped it over and decided that he and the bike would probably be too much weight for such a small boat. Its spherical structure made it less stable than flat bottom boats. He didn't like the idea of capsizing in the middle of the river. He could lose his rifle, which was far more important than the bike. He left the bike, slung his rifle on his back and dragged the boat to the river's edge. He stepped inside the boat and almost flipped it before sitting in the center which seemed to stabilize it.

He paddled out into the river's surprisingly strong current. The little boat moved quickly. He realized he had made a mistake cycling upriver. The bridge with its heavy pylons was quickly approaching. He maneuvered the boat to pass between two of the support pylons. There was a guard in the middle of the bridge, smoking a cigarette and watching the boat traffic around the bridge. Granier knew that his paddling skills would not pass muster with the guard or anybody else that knew anything about boats. He had no choice but to hope for the best. Granier kept his head down and tried not to look too obvious. He let the current do the work and tried to steer the boat rather than propel it. It worked. The guard was more interested in his cigarette than the little round boat passing directly beneath him.

Once past the bridge and out of sight of the Viet Minh guard, Granier paddled the boat to the far shore. Climbing out was just as tricky as climbing in. He stepped out on what he thought was the shore and sank deep in the mud. He almost fell into the water which would have meant his rifle would have gotten wet, but he was able to keep his balance. When he pulled his foot out of the mud hole he had created, he was missing his sandal. He was still several miles from the airfield and wasn't sure if he could make it barefoot. The Vietnamese had a bad habit of discarding broken bottles and open cans with sharp edges. It was dark, and he wouldn't be able to see the ground well. He longed for the forest where his biggest concern was a tripwire or a punji stick, things he knew to search for. He reached down into the water where he thought he had stepped. He found the hole in the mud, but it still took him several minutes to retrieve the sandal.

He pulled the boat to shore and flipped it over. Hopefully, in the morning, the owner would see it from the opposite bank and retrieve it. He climbed up the embankment and looked around to catch his bearings. The east side of the river was much darker and less populated than the west side. He could see the floodlights of what he thought was the airfield in the distance. He imagined the Vietnamese would keep the airfield well-lit at night to deter saboteurs. Since he no longer had the bicycle, he decided to head cross-country and aim straight for the bright lights. He would need to be careful of barbed wire fences, but he figured that would be safer than running into a French or Viet Minh patrol on the road.

As he walked through the darkness, he could hear gunfire and an occasional explosion from the city behind him. The Viet Minh and French were still going at it.

Hanoi was burning.

He wondered if Spitting Woman was okay. Knowing her, he was sure she would be part of the fighting. She was a furious warrior. He doubted he would ever find a woman like her again. He determined not to try. He was done with women or at least relationships with women. He would seek comfort when needed, but never allow his emotions to get involved. It would be easy. He just wouldn't lie and would never commit beyond the moment. Any woman that chose to spend time with him would quickly realize that he had no interest in her beyond sex. She would lose hope and discard him. That's what he wanted — no more attachments.

It took Granier most of the night to reach the airfield. When he arrived near the main gate, he saw two Viet Minh guards both armed with rifles. He unslung his sniper rifle and crawled onto a berm. He was well-hidden by the surrounding vegetation and mostly out of the glow from the airfield's floodlights. Taking them out wouldn't be a problem. His telescope made the job more difficult because they were so close. He considered removing it but decided against it since he did not know what he would encounter once he entered the airfield. He would kill both the soldiers within two seconds. He would sprint through the main gate and find cover near the edge of the airfield before anyone came to investigate the shots. Then it was just a matter of finding a plane that could carry him out of the country.

He considered waiting until dawn. The flash from his rifle's muzzle would be more difficult to see in the daylight. Besides, he was tired from traveling all night and thought he might be able to get a few minutes shuteye before what promised to be a long flight which might require him to stay awake, depending on the situation. He closed his eyes and immediately fell asleep.

Granier woke to the sound of a jeep engine. The sun was already up and in his eyes when he looked down the road. A jeep with five men wearing khaki was approaching the airfield. As the jeep passed, Granier couldn't believe his eyes. It was the Deer Team.

Santana was driving. Dewey sat in the passenger seat. Holding their weapons, Hoagland, Green, and Davis rode in the back.

The two guards shouted something in Vietnamese and raised their rifles.

Santana braked the jeep to a stop in front of the gate.

Granier used his telescope to see what was going on. He had mixed feelings about seeing his comrades. Part of him was angry that they had so easily abandoned him. Another part was glad to see so many familiar faces. He wanted to be part of the team again. The team protected him and gave him purpose. They were his pack. He wanted to believe they had a reason for doing what they did, but he wasn't sure he could ever fully trust them again.

The Viet Minh guards were waving their weapons, ordering the Americans to get out of the jeep. Dewey got out and ordered the other team members to stay put. He pulled the folded letter from his shirt pocket and opened it so the Viet Minh could look at it. "Ho Chi Minh," he said, pointing to the signature on the page.

The Viet Minh weren't interested in the document. The white faces and rifles were all they needed to see. They were outnumbered and frightened. Realizing that neither of the two Viet Minh soldiers understood a word of English, Dewey spoke to them in French, "Ho Chi Minh, your leader sign this document. It gives my team safe passage through Vietnam."

Hearing Dewey speak French, the eyes of the younger of the two Viet Minh grew wide with fear and anger. Dewey continued, "We are not French. We are Americans, friends of the Viet Minh. We fought with the Viet Minh against the Japanese."

Granier chambered a round and placed the telescope reticle over the head of the Viet Minh that seemed most threatening... just in case.

The younger of the two Viet Minh panicked and shot Dewey in the chest. Dewey fell to the ground with a shocked look on his face. "No!" screamed Hoagland jumping from the back of the jeep to tend to Dewey.

The other Viet Minh scolded his younger comrade for shooting.

Granier was shocked to see Dewey hit. It took him a moment to react. He fired and killed the Viet Minh that had shot Dewey.

Green leveled his BAR and fired a salvo of bullets into the second Viet Minh, ripping his body apart, killing him. Davis turned to see where the first shot had come from. Granier stood up, holding his rifle. "Buck?" said Davis, surprised.

Everyone in the jeep turned, shocked to see Granier. Granier walked toward the jeep, toward Hoagland tending to Dewey on the ground. Granier stood over Dewey as he gasped for breath, the Viet Minh bullet having punctured his lung and severed an artery. Hoagland was frantically trying to stop the bleeding, pressing down on the entry wound, his hand covered in Dewey's blood. Dewey looked up at Granier with a confused look and said, "Buck, you're alive?"

"Yeah," said Granier. "I made it."

"That's good. That's real good," said Dewey coughing up blood.

Dewey stopped breathing. Hoagland wouldn't stop trying to save him. He pounded on his chest to get his heart going again. He breathed air into Dewey's bloody mouth. There was no response. Lieutenant Colonel Paul Dewey was dead – the first American soldier to die in Vietnam.

"Doc, we gotta go," said Santana. "They'll be coming."

Hoagland realized Santana was right. "Will you help me?" he said to Granier.

Granier helped Hoagland lift Dewey's body into the back of the jeep. Hoagland climbed into the back of the jeep, leaving the passenger seat open for Granier. But Granier didn't climb in. He just stood there. "Quit fucking around, Buck. We gotta go," said Green. "The Viet Minh are gonna be pissed when they see we killed their guys.

"Get your ass in the jeep, Buck," said Santana.

"We've got a plane waiting," said Davis. "We're going home."

Home? thought Granier. Hoagland could see Granier was questioning what to do. That he didn't understand what had happened. "The Viet Minh told us you were dead. We took them at their word. That was a mistake. We would have gone back had we known you were alive," said Hoagland. "You need to get in the jeep, Buck. Everything will be okay. You'll see."

Granier took another moment before he decided to believe Hoagland and climbed into the jeep. He was part of the team again. It was what he wanted – to be part of a pack.

Santana drove onto the airfield. A C-47 with Chinese Air Force insignia was waiting near the end of the runway. McGoon stood next to the cargo door waving at them to hurry. The jeep pulled to a stop, and the Deer Team removed their commander's body. "Jesus. That's a crying shame," said McGoon watching the team load Dewey's corpse in through the plane's doorway. "I don't mean to be insensitive, but we're gonna need to strap him down. Don't want him rolling around. There's some rope by the door."

Granier was the last to climb up the ladder. He hesitated and looked back at the city of Hanoi. He could hear the gunfire and explosions in the distance. "I guess the Frenchies and the Viets are going to be slugging it out from here on. Glad it ain't no business of ours," said McGoon.

Granier didn't respond. McGoon looked at him, a little worried. "Are you alright?"

"Yeah. Just a little tired," said Granier.

"I bet. Traipsing around, living in the jungle like that."

"I wasn't so bad."

Granier climbed into the aircraft, followed by McGoon. The ladder was pulled in and the door shut.

A few minutes later, the C-47 lifted off the runway, banked to the left and headed for China. The American War in Vietnam was over... for now.

Dear Reader,

I hope you enjoyed *A War Too Far.*

If you wish to read in chronological order, the next novel in the series is *The War Before The War.* It's a novel based on true events about Congressman John F. Kennedy's fact-finding mission in Vietnam during the Indochina War. It's available as eBook and Paperback. Here is the link:

The War Before The War

Thank you for your consideration, and I hope to hear from you.

In gratitude,

David Lee Corley

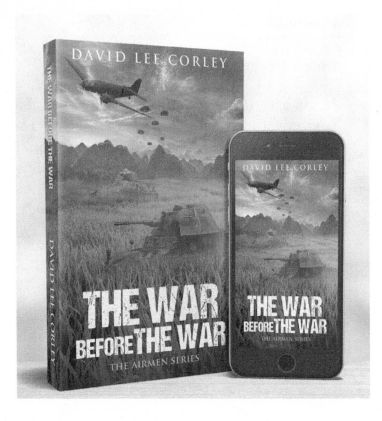

Author's Biography

Born in 1958, David grew up on a horse ranch in Northern California, breeding and training appaloosas. He has had all his toes broken at least once and survived numerous falls and kicks from ornery colts and fillies. David started writing professionally as a copywriter in his early 20's. At 32, he packed up his family and moved to Malibu, California, to live his dream of writing and directing motion pictures. He has four motion picture screenwriting credits and two directing credits. His movies have been viewed by over 50 million movie-goers worldwide and won a multitude of awards, including the Malibu, Palm Springs, and San Jose Film Festivals. In addition to his 23 screenplays, he has written nine novels. He developed his simplistic writing style after rereading his two favorite books, Ernest Hemingway's "The Old Man and The Sea" and Cormac McCarthy's "No Country For Old Men." An avid student of world culture, David lived as an expat in both Thailand and Mexico. At 56, he sold all his possessions and became a nomad for four years. He circumnavigated the globe three times and visited 56 countries. Known for his detailed descriptions, his stories often include actual experiences and characters from his journeys.

Made in the USA
Monee, IL
01 July 2020